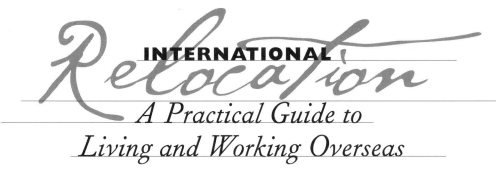

INTERNATIONAL Relocation

A Practical Guide to Living and Working Overseas

Marc Bond
with Rita Bond

AAPG Publications : TULSA

Association Editor: Neil F. Hurley

Publications Manager: Kenneth M. Wolgemuth

Managing Editor, Publications: Anne H. Thomas

Design and composition: Carl Brune

Editing: Hazel Rowena Mills

Typesetting: Patsy Dock

This and other AAPG publications are available from:

The AAPG Bookstore
P.O. Box 979
Tulsa, OK 74101-0979
Telephone: 1-918- 584-2555 or
    1-800-364-AAPG (USA)
Fax: 1-918-560-2652 or
    1-800- 898-2274 (USA)
www.aapg.org

Australian Mineral Foundation
AMF Bookshop
63 Conyngham Street
Glenside, South Australia 5065
Australia
Tel. +61-8-8379-0444
Fax +61-8-8379-4634
www.amf.com.au/amf

Geological Society Publishing House
Unit 7, Brassmill Enterprise Centre
Brassmill Lane, Bath, U.K.
BA1 3JN
Tel +44-1225-445046
Fax +44-1225-442836
www.geolsoc.org.uk

Affiliated East-West Press Private Ltd.
G-1/16 Ansari Road   Darya Ganj
New Delhi   110 002
India
Tel +91 11 3279113
Fax +91 11 3260538
e-mail: affiliat@nda.vsnl.com

This handbook is dedicated to Julia and Lauren, our daughters, who made our overseas journey all the more worth it. We thank them for their love and patience during all our hours working on this project. Their tolerance, particularly when we monopolized the computer, was much appreciated!

Table of Contents

Overview of expatriation, and the issues to anticipate
with an assignment

Step-by-step guide to moving from your home country
to an international location

What to do with the existing house, and how to find
a new home in the host country

Considerations and decisions relating to expatriate
children's education and social development

Documents needed for the transfer overseas, and
how to obtain them

Taxation in the home and host countries, and financial
issues to consider while overseas

Keeping healthy, and what to do when not, in the
new location

How to stay safe and secure in the host country

Culture shock and several effective adapting
techniques, with a special section on children

A look at adapting and settling into the new location, issues
you are likely to encounter, and how to react appropriately

Preface

You find yourself at home after an inspiring day at the office, discussing with your spouse the day's events at work. You have been offered, perhaps to your delight and excitement, a transfer with your company to an overseas assignment. As you are celebrating over a glass of Bordeaux from your wine cellar (which you will soon find that you most likely cannot take along), you discuss all the wondrous and exciting adventures a transfer will bring — immersion in a new culture, travel opportunities, job satisfaction, and an international education for your children.

Slowly, though, the ramifications begin to settle in. Perhaps not immediately, but soon, you will be faced with countless decisions and a reevaluation of your life and goals. If left to luck, your chances of having a satisfying experience living abroad is about one in seven (Kohls, 1996). The purpose of this handbook is to help you through this demanding but potentially exciting and enjoyable time. It is the authors' goal to help make the transition as smooth, enjoyable, and rewarding as possible. We hope this handbook will reduce your concerns, fears, and stresses to a minimum, enabling a smooth transition to your new assignment.

One of the first things you will find is that you have an insatiable appetite for information, soaking up all advice and data like a sponge. You will find that you cannot get enough of the above and that you are on your own during the relocation process. Do not despair. With some forethought and planning, this guide will help you through the often apparently treacherous paths to a successful transfer.

This handbook is arranged to give the reader a precursor of what to expect with the transfer and to be a handy reference guide to your move. It will give practical and informative guidance in understanding and adapting to the relocation. It is meant to be a user-friendly guide for relocating employees and families, with each chapter designed to address the specific issues you will encounter. In all instances, we will attempt not just to present the challenges and issues, but also to give practical suggestions and coping techniques.

The breadth of what needs to be accomplished in an international move is overwhelming. This handbook, therefore, will help you get control of your life during a demanding and emotional time. It will reveal new strategies and present practical suggestions to help improve your international assignment. Covering all aspects of an international relocation, this handbook will lead you through the complete process and offer step-by-step guidance. Checklists and work sheets are available to further aid your efforts.

If you are about to become an expatriate for the first time, this handbook will provide you with valuable information and coping techniques. For those repeating the experience, this handbook will reacquaint you with the practical and emotional issues you may have forgotten. In addition, you are probably at a different stage of your life cycle now and may have new concerns and goals.

Our aim in writing this handbook is to help transferring employees and their families anticipate, and therefore manage, the potential challenges resulting from the move. Concerns are always much smaller and more manageable if you know what to expect. Knowledge of potential issues and the related planning are two of the most important prevention measures.

This handbook is based on our experiences, many discussions and interviews with other expatriates and relocation experts, and considerable literature research. Much has been written on the subject of relocation, particularly as the tendency toward business globalization has increased. Yet most of the work is from the academic/research perspective, often aimed at the employer. Very little has been written from the employee's and family viewpoints, and we hope this handbook gives all expatriates and potential expatriates the tools to help master a successful relocation.

We, the authors, both have had direct experience in the relocating process, giving us a perspective on the trials, tribulations, and rewards of living overseas. Marc has extensive experience in managing international projects in a multicultural business environment. Rita brings a unique perspective to the book with her expertise in counseling and multicultural education.

We have lived and traveled extensively overseas, primarily in the Western world. Although our writings may have an American cultural bias and an orientation toward the experiences and issues involved in living in specific countries, most of what is involved in the relocation process will apply. Of course, there are some obvious exceptions, which we will also address.

Oddly enough, the difficulties and alienation felt in a Western culture can be similar to those in relocating to a more foreign location. Moving to a country where there are clearly major cultural differences (e.g., United States to India), you are prepared for culture shock. Yet moving to an apparently similar culture (e.g., United States to Great Britain), your first reactions are that the move should be fairly transparent. Surprisingly, the differences are great, and many of the similarities end at the common language!

The organization of the handbook is broken into three sections: home country before the move; the period of transition and arrival; and settling into the host country. Besides discussing the specific tasks, the handbook will also address some emotional issues you will be confronted with and their implications for your life. Individuals should come to their own solutions to these issues, but being aware of them will help greatly.

In our attempt to give an understanding of the challenges and issues you may encounter on a foreign assignment, you may feel overwhelmed and be tempted to forgo the experience. On the contrary, we suggest that the rewards are tremendous. For most people, an overseas assignment is truly enriching, rewarding, and a thoroughly enjoyable experience. Living in a foreign culture will give you and your family an outlook on life, an appreciation of another culture, and a way of life that you cannot experience as tourists. It is an experience like no other.

INTERNATIONAL Relocation

Acknowledgments

The authors would like to thank many people for their contributions and support. Without so much of it, we never would have been able to complete the handbook.

We would like to thank all our expatriate colleagues for their stories, ideas, help, inspiration, and participation in our research. Many individuals helped in adding ideas and material which greatly enhanced the handbook. To all of them, we are indebted. To others who added encouragement and support that kept us focused on our goal of writing a book for the international community, we express our gratitude.

Many individuals generously offered their assistance, which we would like to acknowledge. Their help, ideas, suggestions, and encouragement all made this handbook a reality.

Rob Sawyer's encouragement and advice turned the project into a superior product. He made us work harder on the handbook than we ever intended, but no harder than we should have. His contributions were many, but we particularly appreciate his assistance in developing the section on business and culture.

Todd Minnies reviewed the manuscript and offered many insightful improvements.

Ken Wolgemuth saw the potential of this manuscript and the need for it to be published. His guidance and advice made this handbook much clearer and brought the project together.

AAPG Publications turned this handbook into a well-designed volume. It looks so much better! Our gratitude goes to the staff.

Hazel Rowena Mills edited the manuscript and helped bring it to life. Her detailed editing and insightful comments gave clarity and coherence to the handbook.

We would like to thank BG International for giving us the opportunity to live and work overseas.

We and the AAPG are grateful to Eduardo A. Berenson for his insight into the value of this publication for AAPG membership.

Eduardo kindly introduced the idea to AAPG and encouraged us to work together to publish the book you now hold.

Finally, we would like to thank our mothers, one who exposed Marc to the wonders of international travel and culture, and one who encouraged Rita to explore the world.

Our apologies to those we have omitted.

Chapter 1 (at a glance)

Introduction

From this introduction you can ~

gain an overview of expatriation and the issues to expect with an overseas assignment.

understand the issues and costs relating to an international relocation.

determine successful assignments from those that "fail."

discover expatriate failure rates by country.

see the relationship among employer, employee, and family.

review the topics presented in this manual.

Some key points ~

❶ International relocation of employees is on the increase as companies attempt to acquire and develop business opportunities worldwide.

② Many assignments encounter challenges.

❸ All international relocations are unique.

④ International relocation is probably the only area of business in which the employer must consider the needs and satisfaction of not only the employee but also the family.

❺ There are six stages of the relocation process.

⑥ An understanding of the relocation process for the employee and family, accompanied by adequate preparation, is essential for a successful transfer.

❼ A primary ingredient of an international relocation is the support and commitment of everyone involved.

⑧ An expatriate assignment is an opportunity of a lifetime.

Chapter 1

INTRODUCTION

My experience of living, working, and traveling in western Europe truly brought home the effect and importance of culture. Throughout the 1990s, a dominant force on the Continent was the building of the European community. Two notions, economic and cultural, are at issue. As an outside observer, I saw how strong the latter was in forming a resistance to the European Union.

In the United States, there is a great deal of diversity, and even some animosity among various regions. Yet the roots, and therefore the bonds, are the same; they all relate to one another and identify themselves as Americans. Such is not true in Europe. The relationship is with the country (or even the region), and not with the Continent. Further, much hostility and negative stereotypes exist among the countries. The feelings run incredibly deep and are based on thousands of years of history. Even more divisive, animosity often exists within a country. For example, the Scots, Welsh, and Irish take major offense at being associated with the English, and there is even serious discussion of making the regions autonomous from Great Britain. When England played Germany in the World Cup, many fans from those regions had a difficult time choosing which side to support! In Italy, there is a very serious political force that wants to separate the country into two, North and South.

Repeatedly, I have talked with people who had strong opinions of the other European countries. Surprisingly, the stereotypes would be fairly consistent. The French are viewed as rude and arrogant, with a sense of superiority. The Germans and Austrians are considered very orderly, rigid, and self-righteous, strongly bound by rules. The

Swiss are considered very stiff and exacting, concerned only with money. The Italians are viewed as very chaotic, disorderly, impulsive, flamboyant, and corrupt. Spain is considered third world and a very "curious" country. Greece is considered to have beautiful beaches and to be a great place for a holiday, but is backward. The Scandinavian countries are viewed as very socialistic and expensive. The Irish are seen as disorganized. Finally, the British, who don't really see themselves as part of Europe anyway, are viewed as stiff, distant, and imperialistic.

In the United States, it is not acceptable to attribute people's behavior, good or bad, to their racial or ethnic origins. In Europe, however, Europeans apply these long-standing national stereotypes. Culture has an incredibly powerful influence on people. Arbitrary boundaries, whether they are national borders or business structures, cannot supplant the pull of a cultural orientation or easily unite people from different societies.

The past few years have witnessed major political, social, and economic changes that have remarkably changed the world. Along with expansion of global markets, these changes in the world are creating increased job mobility in the international arena. The increasing interdependence of world economics requires that companies become international to remain competitive.

International relocation of employees is on the increase as companies attempt to acquire and develop business opportunities worldwide. The use of expatriates to manage and operate these opportunities is crucial to the success of these organizations. For employees, international work experience is an opportunity to expand their skill base and to provide a vital foundation for future professionals and managers in the global marketplace.

Several characteristics of an expatriate employee and partner are necessary to help ensure a successful relocation.

Certainly, intelligence, self-confidence, self-motivation, creativity, and an appreciation of complex problems are all essential. These criteria fit most individuals who relocate overseas, yet relocations sometimes fail or often are a negative experience. Why?

According to recent surveys, 10% to 20% of U.S. expatriate assignments fail, i.e., the employee ends the assignment prematurely (Shannonhouse, 1996; Tan Powers, 1996; and Wall, 1996). The issue is further compounded by the additional expatriates who remain in a country to complete their assignment, yet they (or their family members) are unhappy. Therefore, the degree of "failed" assignments varies greatly, with a huge spectrum ranging from total failure to less than productive experiences. Nevertheless, if one considers "failed" assignment as not just those ending early but also those in which the expatriate or family member is very unhappy, the failure rate is surprisingly high.

The key point is that many assignments encounter difficulties. This is a major concern because the average cost of an international transfer is three to four times an executive's annual salary, potentially costing $1 million or more for a three-year assignment (Rehak, 1996; Wall, 1996).

An examination of a survey below (Table 1.1) by Windham International/NFTC (Shannonhouse, 1996) showing the countries and percentage of expatriate American assignments that fail (i.e., assignments cut short prematurely) reveals interesting results.

Table 1.1 Expatriate Failure Rates by Country

Country	Failure Rate	Country	Failure Rate
China	13%	France	3%
Russia	9%	Australia	3%
United Kingdom	7%	United Arab Emirates	3%
Hong Kong	7%	Italy	2%
India	5%	Netherlands	2%
Mexico	4%	Switzerland	2%
Indonesia	4%	Poland	2%
Belgium	4%	Germany	2%
Far East	3%	Saudi Arabia	2%

High failure rates in countries such as China and Russia, where the culture and lifestyle are completely different from those in the United States, are not surprising. Yet there are significant failure rates in countries in western Europe, where the lifestyle is not completely different from that in America. Further, a high percentage of assignment failures in the United Kingdom shows that, indeed, cultural differences, and not just language barriers, play a key role in an overseas assignment.

A major concern with many assignments is that the "total" individual is not considered. In the past, companies tended to send specialists in culture and language to foreign countries. Currently, as companies are expanding business overseas, they are sending a new breed of managers overseas (Kaufman, 1996). Usually, an employee is now chosen for an overseas assignment based on *technical expertise, management skills*, and *business knowledge*. Yet interpersonal skills such as flexibility and adaptability, for both the employee and family members, are just as essential for an assignment to be successful.

Phatak (1974) suggested that an ideal set of characteristics for an expatriate includes "the stamina of an Olympic swimmer, the mental agility of an Einstein, the conversational skill of a professor of languages, the detachment of a judge, the tact of a diplomat, and the perseverance of an Egyptian pyramid builder."

An expatriate must have a solid and positive belief in the transfer, an interest in and understanding of politics, a sense of cultural empathy, adaptability, and emotional stability. Flexibility, patience and, above all, a sense of humor are essential.

All international relocations are unique — different people with diverse situations move to different locations for different reasons. Each relocation is, therefore, a highly individualistic experience. Each is dependent on family circumstances, attitude of the expatriates, company relocation package, job, culture of new location, and length of assignment.

Because all families are different, the circumstances behind the decision of whether to accept an overseas assignment are diverse.

Some people have already decided that they want to be expatriates and have expressed that decision to the management in their companies. Others have never even considered the opportunity and are asked to move overseas with no prior consideration.

Whatever the situation, it is not a decision to take lightly. Even if this is not your first move overseas, you must consider all the reasons and ramifications.

Many motives and circumstances dictate whether to accept an overseas assignment. Some of the motives can include advancement of career, opportunity to experience new things, travel, ability to build a financial savings, chance to make a change, desire for "adventure and excitement," and the wish to help those less fortunate.

As with motives for being an expatriate, there are also possible circumstances that may suggest that a move overseas is not a good idea. Remember that all family members are at a different place in their lives, and what is advantageous for one may not be for another. For example, the experience of living overseas for a preadolescent may be positive, but for a teenager in the senior year of high school, such a move could be a challenge. It is important to assess the impact that a foreign assignment will have on each person in your family and on the family system as a whole (Kalb and Welch, 1992). If you decide to accept a transfer, be sure that you know what to expect and why you are deciding to go.

Although an overseas assignment is often good for the employee's career, it is not usually detrimental. Most employers understand the impact of an overseas posting on an individual and family and rarely force someone to move overseas. It would be extraordinary that a company would tell an employee, "Your paycheck is in India." The cost of a failed or unsuccessful assignment is too great. For many companies, an overseas posting may be necessary to achieve upper-management positions, but it is not a mandatory requirement for most positions.

Some issues you must consider that may influence your decision to go include:

- career implications of the new job
- medical requirements
- educational needs
- spouse or partner's career
- resistance by family member to the move
- needs of extended family
- specific personal or family problems
- marital status (i.e., divorced or separated)

The considerations above are examples of issues that require your attention and may lead you to decline an international assignment. Be honest with yourself in deciding if going overseas is a good idea for you and your family. Explore your motives for going, and understand why you made your particular decision.

In certain circumstances, turning down an international posting may be the appropriate option and can avoid a lot of pain and aggravation down the road. An unsuccessful assignment is an expensive venture for the company, employee, and family, both in financial and emotional terms. Yet there may be ways to work around any complications and make expatriation worthwhile. If your motivation to go overseas is quite strong, there are often creative alternatives to make the posting feasible and successful.

To help guide yourself through your decision, answer the questions listed below. Make sure you discuss your responses with your spouse and family. The decision to accept an overseas transfer should be a joint one.

- Do you want to take this assignment?
- Does living overseas fulfill your goals?
- What affect will this assignment have on all family members?
- Do the potential lifestyle changes of living overseas appeal to you?
- Are you easily adaptable to new and unfamiliar situations?
- Do you interact well with people from different cultures and values?
- Are you tolerant of foreign environments and living conditions?
- Are you open-minded?
- Do you like to travel?
- Do you cope well with uncertainty and ambiguity?
- Do you have a tolerance for frustration?
- Do you have a sense of humor?
- (for the employee) Will the assignment be good for your career?
- (for the spouse/partner) Will this be a positive change for you?
- (for the children) Will this be a positive change for you?

If you answered yes to all the questions, you are a good candidate for an expatriate assignment. If you answered no to some questions, you still may be successful. However, it is a good idea to explore your response and the reasons that you feel may make an overseas posting inappropriate for you.

The company and the employee may differ in thinking about who is responsible for the move.

Some companies may have a well-established relocation package, while others may consider a transfer the responsibility of the employee. Organizations often limit their assistance to the direct technical aspects of relocation (i.e., house search, rental payments, etc.), taking a limited view of relocation concerns. Some expatriates are sent overseas with little or no adequate preparation or support to help guide them through the emotional and practical transition from life at home to life abroad.

Public-sector expatriates (e.g., health-care, educational, and research professionals, for example) often will receive lower remuneration, which translates to fewer resources for housing, schooling, entertainment, and travel as compared with those in the private sector. Further, there is often less in-country support by the employer, which requires the expatriate to be more self-reliant and resourceful.

In particular, issues relating to spouse and children are often not considered to be the company's concern. Recent studies report that more than 50% of employers offer no support for the relocating spouse (Wraight, 1996). This is often not because the company does not care or feels that it is not important, but because it is reluctant to become involved in the employee's personal issues. Yet the family is perhaps the most important factor that determines the success or failure of a relocation. A survey by Windham International/FTC shows that family adjustment (42% of the cases) and lifestyle issues (24%) are the most common factors for overseas assignment failures (Shannonhouse, 1996).

Regardless of your company's policy, you and your family are the ones who will be affected. For that reason, you must take control of the transfer.

Relocation is probably the only area of business in which the employer considers the needs and satisfaction of not only the employee but also the family (Munton et al., 1993). Spouse, children, relatives, and friends all may suffer emotionally and financially because of the relocation. For example, the spouse may be giving up or postponing a career; children are uprooted from their schools and friends; relatives, particularly if elderly, can feel unhappy about the large distance and the inaccessibility of their children and grandchildren; the whole family can be unhappy and lonely with the loss of friendships and community support.

Unfortunately, although the family's emotional attitude can directly affect an employee's performance, many employers do not take the issue of an international relocation seriously. A common company philosophy is to have a standard "relocation package" which predominantly consists of financial assistance. Rent, cost-of-living adjustment, moving costs, and similar items are commonly paid by the company.

Yet the assistance does not address the losses and stresses experienced by the family. Further, although all relocations are unique and individual, the company's policy will often be "standard" and not allow for exceptions or differences. Expatriation is not just about "money" (Coyle and Shortland, 1992). Employees are becoming more concerned with quality of life and family needs, and are reluctant to relocate solely for career advancement or increased earnings.

The employee and spouse together should discuss the issues with the employer. Get the specifics of the relocation package and express concerns together. Discuss issues such as assignment length, house-hunting support, and interim housing, if needed, and availability of spousal career help. Do not direct anger at the employer for not "doing more," but rather work within the system to address your personal concerns. Be assertive and insist on your company's support. A failed transfer is expensive, both financially and emotionally, for the employee and family and for the employer.

Relocation Process

An international relocation is, in essence, a series of "minitraumas" all lumped together which create an overwhelming experience.

Issues that most people face over time are all confronted by the expatriate at once. Settling into a new country with a new culture and perhaps a different language brings added complexity.

There are, in essence, six stages of the relocation process:

- **decision:** the offer of a job
- **predeparture:** preparation for relocation
- **relocation:** the move itself
- **settling in:** initial adjustment
- **assignment:** the posting
- **repatriation:** repetition of the first five stages

Each stage not only has its own set of issues and challenges, but the reactions of all those involved will cause unique issues for a family.

You and your family will have many concerns and questions as you go through the relocation process. The major issues involved with the first stages of the relocation process include:

- premove preparation, including moving and dealing with your current home
- familiarization with the host country and cross-cultural preparation
- finding a new home
- selecting a school

The latter stages will involve:

- settling into your new environment
- day-to-day matters
- culture shock

The final stage, repatriation, will involve all the concerns you encountered in all the preceding stages, but to a lesser degree.

Preparation for the overseas assignment is crucial to the emotional and financial well-being of the employee and family (Coyle and Shortland, 1992). It is important that the family take action about the issues relating to an overseas transfer and the associated life overseas. These include concerns such as finding and obtaining suitable housing and schools in the new location, disposing of or renting out property in the home country, arranging for the packing and moving of personal belongings, dealing with complex financial matters, and learning about the language and culture of the host country.

Throughout the text, your home country is defined as the country/culture you feel the strongest affinity toward. The host country, on the other hand, is identified as the country you live in while you are on an expatriate assignment.

Yet as you are confronted with all these major decisions, often made with incomplete data, you may find yourself confused by conflicting emotions. Personalized incidents, which can include a brief encounter with the new culture or even talking with an expatriate, seem to carry more weight than they should in making decisions or forming opinions. Consider the following example, adapted from Cushner and Brislin (1996):

> You are looking for a house in your host country. You buy a guidebook put out by a group of expatriates to help newcomers. The developers of this guidebook sampled the opinions of 200 expatriates concerning good neighborhoods to live in. You happen to mention one of these neighborhoods to a person you have recently met who just returned from the host country. This friend says, "I know that area. A friend of ours lived there and didn't like it. They said that it was really sterile and there was nothing to do there." What do you think?

It is a strong and normal tendency to place a great deal of weight on personal opinion. In the above example, comments would probably be given with conviction and colorful gestures, as compared with the more objective and dry information presented in the guidebook. Yet closer analysis shows that you now have 201 "opinions," and the weight of the evidence is still strongly in favor of the neighborhoods recommended by the guidebook. Yet the vivid, personalized opinion is likely to carry a disproportionate impact.

This tendency to react to personal opinions is especially common among expatriates because they are exposed to many new events and must make many major decisions in a short time. Yet there is a significant danger that choices are made poorly. You should keep this point in mind and ask yourself if you are overreacting to vivid personal incidents. Consider if there is other information you might evaluate before making a decision.

Probably the most successful ingredient in an international relocation is the support and commitment of everyone involved. A positive attitude toward the relocation is crucial to its success for both employee and family (Coyle and Shortland, 1992). Moving overseas presents you and your family with a multitude of changes, and you should give considerable thought to whether this move is rewarding for the whole family.

You must examine what is important in your life and your family members' lives. Major questions relating to relocation involve long- and short-term goals, career, family life, children's education and emotional development, spousal situation, social life, relatives, and commitment to current location. It is hoped that you will have confronted many of these issues and discussed them long before you are offered a transfer, yet such an offer inevitably brings these concerns to the forefront.

It is easy, however, to lose sight of the wonderful opportunities afforded to all family members. Making friends all over the world, developing insights into different cultures, learning foreign languages, traveling, and becoming an "international" individual are only a few of the benefits for the expatriate.

As an expatriate living in another culture, you will be confronted with many attitudes and beliefs.

It is important, therefore, to have a good idea of what your own values are and what is important to you. You do not necessarily have to change your values, nor should you expect to. Rather, if you know yourself and what is important to you, you will be better able to handle differences.

For example, consider a female American executive going on a foreign assignment. Suppose this woman strongly believes in women's equality to men in the workforce, and it is a guiding principle in her business interactions. Yet if this belief is not held by the host country's culture, she might be highly offended and hindered in her effectiveness.

Before going on an overseas assignment, you need to consider four areas. Exercise 8 in Appendix B is designed to help you explore them.

- What is your ethnic heritage?
- What values are important to you?
- What are the cultural perspectives that define you?
- What attitudes and values offend you?

Your ethnic heritage plays an integral part in shaping your values and beliefs. For example, your religious orientation, nationality, and race all serve to give you a sense of who you are. You may differ from others of a similar background, but you will be guided by a certain set of principles which you gain from your family, culture, and other groups and ideas you have had contact with.

As you grow up, you begin to incorporate a set of values and beliefs into your self-concept. These lead to a set of behaviors and expectations of others that help govern your life.

Cultural perspectives (as defined in the business cultural model presented in Chapter 13) further reinforce your actions.

Certain behaviors or beliefs of others that conflict with yours may be difficult for you to deal with or accept, as in the example cited above.

Areas that you should specifically consider are your attitudes toward religion, politics, basic human rights, women's and children's rights, personal freedoms, the environment, and animal rights. You then need to think about what your reactions may be if you observe differences in the way a culture treats these issues. Attitudes toward family dynamics, marriage, making friends, crime, and punishment are other areas to consider. Remember that people may find different values more or less objectionable and more or less acceptable.

It is very important for an expatriate to be open-minded and able to consider alternate approaches and points of view. You need to accept that the values and beliefs of other cultures work for them, even if they are counter to your own.

Throughout this handbook, there will be discussion on the many facets of an international relocation.

You will gain not only an understanding of the process but also will learn many adapting techniques. An understanding of the relocation process for the employee and family is essential for a successful transfer. The more you understand the process and what to expect, the more your confidence will increase. Planning, action, and knowledge are all powerful tools in helping to reduce the difficulties and ensuring a successful relocation.

This handbook is organized to enable you to explore the many topics associated with the relocation process. It is recommended that you skim the entire handbook first to gain a general appreciation of the issues and to realize what is being covered. Read the summary page at the beginning of each chapter and look through related checklists and work sheets. Then as you encounter a specific issue, you can refer to the appropriate chapter in detail.

Chapter 2 describes the prepreparation period that marks the beginning of the international assignment. Many issues and details need to be attended to, and you may easily feel overwhelmed. At the conclusion of the chapter is a handy checklist to help you navigate through the many tasks.

Chapters 3 and 4 look at the continuation of the settling-in phase, in which you must be concerned with finding a place to live and an appropriate school for your children. Those two issues will be perhaps the most important tasks you will face initially.

Chapters 5 and 6 examine the more mundane issues of documentation and taxes, respectively. Although these issues may not appear to be critical, they must be addressed to prevent any mishaps.

Chapter 7 considers medical concerns and suggestions on appropriate measures.

Chapter 8 discusses security issues, to reduce any negative impacts resulting from your assignment. Most international locations are surprisingly safe, but you should be aware of some potential problems.

Chapter 9 explores the phases of culture shock and the many emotional challenges that accompany it. Suggestions on how to adapt and minimize the effects of culture shock are presented.

Chapters 10 and 11 present methods to improve your quality of life while on your assignment. Successfully dealing with everyday tasks and building a new social network are critical.

Chapter 12 presents suggestions for maintaining contact with your home country.

Chapter 13 examines the business issues resulting from an overseas assignment and why the cultural differences must be understood to make a successful working environment.

Chapter 14 touches on many issues that will affect certain expatriates, such as the accompanying spouse and dual-career families.

Chapter 15 discusses traveling and enjoying your time overseas.

Finally, Chapter 16 explores the often overlooked and neglected issue of repatriation. Returning home can be the most difficult part of international relocation. Advice on managing "reverse culture shock" should help to ease this final phase of your assignment.

It cannot be stressed enough. Living and working overseas are truly the opportunity of a lifetime.

It is an experience like no other, and the rewards and satisfaction gained are like nothing you could imagine. The chance to travel and experience another culture firsthand cannot be duplicated. You and your family will grow and expand horizons, becoming new and richer individuals. You will all certainly change from your experiences, by looking at the world and your life in a new way. It is also fun and exciting! The traveling, the daily living, and all associated experiences will give you lifelong memories. For the employee, it will expand horizons and increase skills like few other experiences.

As you read through the handbook, you may be tempted to think that living overseas is too difficult. Indeed, like any new experience, it can be challenging and frustrating. The purpose of this handbook is to make your assignment smoother. Proper planning and anticipation can ease the transition and maximize the success. Prior knowledge of potential challenges will help you to understand and deal with them more effectively. By reading this handbook, you will gain a sense of control of the assignment and your own life, and this will let you approach any challenge with greater ease.

When reading any of the ideas and suggestions presented in the following chapters, please keep this in mind: For most expatriates, the experience of living and working overseas outweighs the trials and tribulations by a huge order of magnitude. This cannot be stressed enough. Also remember that each individual's tolerance is different. Although one person may find something to be difficult, another may see no obstacles.

So even though many of the topics addressed throughout the handbook may be presented as challenges and give you the impression that an expatriate experience is a negative one, remember that for most people, the overall experience is very positive and wonderful. Because this handbook is a guide, challenges and concerns of international relocation are presented, rather than only positive aspects. Visualize this handbook as a guide to successfully navigate the challenges, leaving you and your family to get the most out of your assignment.

Chapter 2 (at a glance)

Preparation

In this chapter you will find ~

a step-by-step guide for moving from your home country to an international location.

sources to learn about your new country.

the steps needed to get ready for the move.

the importance of a valued inventory and how to prepare one.

what to bring and not to bring in the overseas shipment, and how to organize the packing.

how to prepare for the actual moving days.

the steps to prepare your children for the moving process.

the expenses involved when moving to an international location.

Some key points ~

❶ The most important feature of a successful move is planning and organization.

② Although there is a great deal of preparation to be done, you must also remember to deal with the emotional issues that all family members confront when moving overseas.

Chapter 2

PREPARATION

As I look back to those weeks before moving overseas, it seems like a total blur. I remember piles of boxes, a continual chaotic mess, and lists upon lists of things to do. It was an experience to get through rather than something to enjoy — sort of like studying for a major exam!

It was incredibly easy to get lost in the tasks and not appreciate the momentous occasion the move actually represented. We were excited about going overseas and looking forward to the experiences. Yet we were also very sad to be leaving our family and friends.

One memory that truly stands out was when the movers had loaded the last box onto the van. As they closed up the van and drove off, I had the sense of all our belongings except the clothes on our backs disappearing into the sunset. I walked over to our neighbor's house to get my children (then aged two and six). We all went into our house for a final check. My children stood inside the house, their mouths agape, and then broke into tears. Their home, which represented fun and security to them, now stood as an empty shell with only memories. It was at that moment that I truly understood what a major undertaking we were about to embark on.

Preparing to pick up and move an entire household to another country can be a daunting prospect. It is usually a very hectic period in which there is much work to be done in a short amount of time. One of the most important features of a successful move is to be organized. It makes things easier and gives you more of a feeling of control. Thorough planning makes the whole process less stressful and hectic. Do not try to do everything at once. No move is perfect, but you can reduce the difficulties by being prepared and spreading out the chores over time.

The reaction of the whole family, especially the spouse, can make or break the assignment. It is therefore crucial, for an overseas assignment to be successful, to put your effort during the preparation stage into resolving concerns and conflicts. The pre-move period is critical in establishing a positive attitude toward the relocation for both the employee and spouse.

One can get caught up in the physical preparation of the move, with little time left for the mental and emotional preparation. Although there is a great deal of preparation to be done, you must also remember to deal with the emotional issues that all family members confront when moving overseas. Communication among all family members is essential, and it is important to have an open discussion of the concerns. Family counseling can be a very effective tool in focusing on the opportunities, challenges, and difficulties.

Prepreparation

At times, your life may seem to be governed by an unending series of lists.

This will be a hectic time. Tasks seem to pile up at an impossible rate, and you may find it difficult to keep your senses of proportion, priority, and humor. Try to proceed one step at a time, being careful to set aside some time each day for yourself and your family.

One of the first steps in emotionally preparing for the move is to learn more about your host country's history and culture, and to gain further insight into the relocation process.

Besides the obvious result of helping you to understand the host country, this new knowledge will also give you the background for managing your life in your new environment. There are many sources to obtain information about the host country (see Checklist 1, Appendix A). They can include:

- embassy or consulate of the country. Some larger embassies have libraries that you can access.
- local library

- bookstore
- country briefing document (e.g., from U.S. government, Craighead's International Executive Travel and Relocation Service, etc.)
- university. Seek out foreign student adviser, history or social science department, library.
- current or past expatriates from your assigned country whom you can write or call with questions. Most people are quite willing to share their overseas experiences with others. Do not take their opinions and views as definitely applicable to your situation. Remember that all relocations are unique.

Briefing and information should cover data (i.e., climate, language, local inhabitants, communications, politics, cultural differences, religion, laws, lifestyle, and living conditions). Books, tourist information, magazines, daily newspapers, country and city maps, guidebooks, public-transport maps, and restaurant guides are all good sources of information. An organized orientation and briefing seminar can also be an excellent introduction to the country. Make sure that you include your children.

An unfortunate practicality of the business world is that often you and your family initially may be given only an indication of the chance of an overseas transfer. You may be aware of the *possibility,* but it is not until the actual *confirmation* that you can begin to physically and emotionally prepare for the move. Occasionally this lag will leave little time for preparation. You can use this time, however, to learn about the country and its culture.

Moving Companies

As you begin the relocation process, you will be overwhelmed with the amount of work and projects that you will be facing.

Issues such as selling your home, packing your belongings, completing various house projects and repairs, schooling, etc., will all come to the forefront. Do not try to do it all at once. Instead, break down the tasks into manageable parts and develop a strategy and schedule to complete them.

The first task you will face is to put your household in order, including selling your house (if applicable) and packing your belongings. Usually your company will have a reliable and established firm that it contracts with for the shipping arrangements. Try to gather any information about the company's reputation and proficiency from your personnel department and past expatriates. Evaluate performance records of previous moves, service reputation, insurance claim procedure, previous complaints, and the quality of the company office and storage facilities. Make sure you are satisfied with the preparations. If you are required to seek your own arrangements, it is imperative that the moving company has *experience in overseas shipping.* Packing and shipping for an overseas move require a specialized expertise that is very different from a standard domestic one.

Moving companies like what they call "good customers." A good customer is one who sets the moving date and stays out of the way, letting the company "do its job." This would involve the movers coming in, packing and unpacking your belongings, and leaving as quickly as possible. *You should avoid being this type of customer.* Remember that the movers are dealing with all of your worldly possessions! You must be very assertive about the move and make sure the moving company meets all your requirements. For instance, the movers should completely unpack all the boxes and then remove them.

Make sure you have a clear understanding from your company on procedures and allowances regarding shipping your belongings — how they will be transported, how much you can bring, insurance coverage, storage, and payment.

Each company has different shipping arrangements and allowances. If you are allowed an air-freight shipment, definitely take advantage of this benefit. Although it will add another step in sorting your belongings, the benefits will strongly outweigh the extra work. Air shipments will normally be much safer from damage or theft.

Anything of value that you are concerned about, particularly irreplaceable items such as valuable books, family photographs, paintings, etc., should be sent by air shipment. You may want to consider not taking anything precious or irreplaceable with you (i.e., keepsakes, family heirlooms, special photographs, collectibles, or expensive art and antiques). As with any move, you run the risk of having such items lost, stolen, or damaged. Put those items in a climate-controlled storage facility or leave them with a friend or relative. Consider having valuable items appraised.

The second benefit of air shipment is that it is usually much faster. Sea shipments can take as long as three months to arrive, another month to clear customs, and an additional month to be delivered. Yet sometimes the whole process could take only three weeks! This uncertainty can be greatly alleviated by using air shipment. Therefore, include things in the air shipment that you will want right away, to help make the initial transition smoother. For instance, children's toys and books, cooking utensils, linens, and basic tools will all make your life easier when you move into your new house. In addition, including anything that will help make your accommodation feel more like home will also be appreciated.

Make sure you have adequate insurance coverage (i.e., full replacement), and consider purchasing additional insurance to cover "specialized" items that exceed the minimum. Furthermore, leave all the packing to the moving company. Anything that is not packed by the company will be labeled "PBO" (packed by owner). For insurance purposes, the moving company will *not* be liable for any breakage or damage to PBO items.

If you are storing any of your belongings in your home country, approach your evaluation of the storing company as you did with the moving company — make sure it is a *reliable* and *established* firm. Consider visiting the storage facilities to satisfy yourself about the arrangements. Make sure you have adequate insurance coverage. Some storage companies have a special climate-controlled place where you can store items that require more protection, such as photographs, paintings, collectibles, valuable books, and antiques. Take advantage of this benefit.

One of the first things you will be required to do is to prepare a valued inventory *of everything you own, including full replacement values.*

The moving company will insist on this inventory, and it is truly a benefit to you to be as complete and accurate as possible. Do not underestimate this task, which is very time-consuming but invaluable. It will protect you from any loss or damage to your property.

You will need to compile this inventory by providing a detailed, room-by-room record of all your possessions and their *replacement values.* For insurance and replacement purposes, it is imperative that you note not what the item is currently worth but what it would cost to replace it. Often, this is a subjective process, particularly for keepsakes. To protect yourself, always estimate on the high side. Increase the values by as much as 50%, particularly if the replacement cost is significantly higher in the host country. If any of your possessions are particularly valuable or irreplaceable, you should document them with photographs. Finally, while on your assignment, regularly update your inventory. This will make your repatriation easier. Do not forget to allow for inflation when estimating replacement values.

The valued inventory must be completed *before* moving day. Trying to assign values to items as they are being packed, wrapped, or loaded will not be possible. By being very thorough, you can also get a better idea of which items you want to bring with you, store, or discard.

Write down the serial numbers of all appropriate items (e.g., electronic equipment, cameras, etc.). Videotape or photograph all your belongings as a complement to the written record.

To be prepared for packing, know exactly what is being shipped and how it is being transported (i.e., air, ocean, and storage), before the move.

After the packing commences is not the time to make these decisions. The packing period is very chaotic, and you will find it hard to make any major or detailed decisions then. Decisions made in advance will be more rational and will help your move go smoothly.

If you have multiple shipments (air, ocean, storage), it will help to separate and label things as much as possible. Prepare separate valued inventories. For instance, small air shipments should be consolidated in one room. Ocean/air and storage shipments will be packed on separate days, in almost every case.

Allow plenty of time to sort out your possessions, particularly those in "storage" areas (i.e., attic, garage, garden shed) that contain an odd assortment of collectibles. These places take the longest to sort and clear out. Another advantage of presorting items that are not in daily use is that they can be stored or discarded. Furthermore, these items would be best to be packed together so they can be unpacked at leisure in your new house.

Be extra careful when lifting or carrying heavy weights. Now is not the time to injure yourself.

It is essential to label boxes and cases. The packers will label each box, but you may want to be more rigorous and involved in the process. You may think you will remember or easily figure out what each box contains, but you will not! Arriving at your new location with several dozen boxes piled on top of one another and trying to remember what they contain are exasperating.

You may devise your own system of labeling, according to room or type of contents or some combination. Choose whatever method works for you, and let the packers know your system. One method that works particularly well is to code each room by a letter. Have the movers mark each box with the appropriate letter. You can post the room letter on the room door for the movers' reference. When you get to your new home, post the room letter on each door. Then when the movers unload, they will know exactly where to put the boxes. This will save a great deal of confusion and hassle and will reduce language barriers.

Containers that are to be emptied immediately should be noted. By preplanning, you will know which rooms in your new house the boxes are to be placed in and which boxes to unpack first.

It is advisable to separate items in cupboards or closets into groups for storage and shipment before the movers arrive. For instance, items to be packed for shipment can be taken out of cupboards and closets to avoid the possibility of their ending up at the wrong destination.

It is a good idea to prepare a "survival kit" (so labeled for inclusion in the air shipment and immediate unpacking) that contains the essential items you will want on your arrival

(see Checklist 5, Appendix A). These could include:

- set of dishes
- glasses and mugs
- utensils
- frying pan
- cooking pot
- teakettle
- can opener
- knife, scissors
- linens (including sheets, blankets, and pillows)
- towels (cloth and paper)
- toilet paper
- soap
- first-aid kit
- toolbox
- tape measure
- flashlight
- cellophane and heavy-duty tape
- large plastic trash bags
- address book
- stationery supplies (paper, pens, pencils, markers, stamps, envelopes)

You will need to set aside personal items that you will want to hand-carry with you on the airplane (see Checklist 6, Appendix A). These can include valuable items and documents, such as valuable jewelry, personal papers and documents (i.e., birth and marriage certificates, will, passports, work permits, etc.), insurance policies, extra passport photos and copies of passports, traveler's checks (keep receipts of numbers separately), valued inventories, address book, and any irreplaceable keepsakes.

What to bring and what to store?

This can be an agonizing part of the move. It is very difficult to know what you will want and need. The children's possessions are relatively straightforward because you will most likely bring everything. Your new accommodation's dimensions will dictate what house items you will bring. Certainly you will bring much less if you are moving into a furnished place. Keep in mind that one overseas assignment can stretch into two or three; try to look beyond the immediate future as you consider what to bring.

The best rule of thumb is that the lighter you travel, the better off you will be. When considering an item to bring, ask yourself these questions to determine if it is appropriate to take with you:

- Do we really need this to live comfortably?
- Will this fit or operate properly in our new home?
- Is this really essential?

Most likely, when you get right down to it, you can do with a lot less.

More often than not, you will probably have less storage space in your new place, so you will not want to bring everything. Probably the best advice is to bring what will make you feel "at home" and what you will use regularly. Whatever you do, you will find that you will have shipped something you never will use and will have left something in storage that you wish you had with you.

It is difficult to compile a general list of what to bring (see Checklist 4, Appendix A). This varies considerably from individual to individual, and it also depends on what your situation will be overseas (for instance, are you renting a house or apartment; is the property furnished or unfurnished; does it have a garden?). Some things to consider, though, are:

- Clothing: Do research on climactic conditions in your new country (i.e., seasonal temperatures, humidity). If you are going from one extreme to another, consider leaving some of your clothing items behind. If you have any special needs (i.e., special shirts, sizing, etc.), purchase those items before you leave.
- Equipment for games, sports, and celebrations of your home country. Include sporting equipment and holiday decorations and ornaments.

- Eyeglasses, contact lenses, and related prescriptions.
- Kitchen goods: measuring cups and spoons, cake and pie pans, favorite nonperishable food items, cookbooks, and recipes.
- Linens and bedding: towels, mattress covers, permanent-press sheets, blankets, and table place mats. This is particularly important if you are taking your own bed because sizes differ from country to country.
- Medicines: prescription drugs, cold medicines, and vitamins (particularly for the children).
- Household items: a limited supply of your favorite toiletries, such as shampoo, cosmetics, and other personal-care products, can be helpful to ease the transition.
- Phone book from your former city: This can be useful for tying up loose ends or for future correspondence.
- Materials for hobbies, arts and crafts: Also include basic hand tools and gardening equipment.
- Children's things: Do not compromise on children's toys and clothes and baby items. Remember that children grow up quickly, and things that you may not think they need, such as books and games, will soon be appreciated.
- Mementos: It is often the treasured mementos that give a home personality, so these should be included. Examples include favorite paintings, photographs, and family keepsakes.

There are many items that you do not want to take, which include lightbulbs, electrical appliances (unless accompanied by a transformer), TV and VCR (unless the format is compatible or you are using them in tandem for videos only), and an abundance of furniture, if you are moving into a furnished accommodation. With regard to television and video equipment, the format varies from country to country. For example, North America and Japan use the NTSC system, whereas much of Europe and the Far East use a form of PAL. Check your owner's manual for details.

It is not a good idea to take anything that is especially valuable or irreplaceable.

Be aware of the customs laws in the destination country. There are many goods that are either prohibited or restricted. Some examples include controlled drugs, firearms, pornography, videos, gambling items, meat and poultry, plants and vegetables, live animals, body parts of protected animals, certain food items, alcohol, tobacco, and certain valuables. Surcharges on wine, spirits, and tobacco are high and will often exceed the purchase price. All goods not properly declared are subject to forfeiture and additional charges. Depending on the country, some items are not allowed. The moving company also has certain restrictions. Any flammables, combustibles, explosives, and corrosives (e.g., paints, thinners, oils, varnishes, motor fuels and oils, aerosol cans, and candles) cannot be transported. Frozen food and open food containers will also not be transported. Discuss any questions or concerns with your moving company's representative and the local immigration department.

Moving is always an excellent opportunity to "spring clean."

Be ruthless in discarding and parting with items, and consider a garage sale. You will be amazed at the amount of "junk" you have collected during the years. If you plan to have a garage sale, there are a few things you should consider.

Timing: Saturday is the best day; Sunday tends to be much slower. Consider a multiple-family sale. This will increase the items for sale and enable you to share the workload.

Advertisement: Proper advertising is an important aspect of a garage sale. Post signs at busy intersections and near your street. Place notices on bulletin boards in grocery stores, shops, etc. Finally, consider placing an advertisement in the local newspaper.

Salable items: The more popular items that people buy at garage sales include jewelry, furniture, lamps, tools, appliances, books, CDs and records, games, puzzles, toys, sports equipment, jackets, and children's clothes. Adults' clothing does not sell well.

Pricing items: Price your items for sale. Remember that the primary purpose of the garage sale is to get rid of stuff and reduce the amount to be stored or moved, which in itself is a cost savings. Making money is a distant second priority. The value of your items has no bearing on what it would cost to buy them in a store. Remember that for some people, garage-sale shopping is a hobby, and they are looking for bargains. Do not get caught up in quibbling over a dime!

Tips for the day: Be ready for early-bird shoppers. Remember to have lots of change for the garage sale. Mark each item with a colored dot that equates to a particular price. Have the price guide prominently displayed. Near the end of the day, reduce the prices. Finally, arrange for a charitable organization to come to your house the next day to pick up whatever you were unable to sell.

During the premove time, you will also need to accomplish all the tasks involved in leaving a place.

Assign responsibilities and target dates, and review progress at regular family meetings. Set up a file for collecting important papers and receipts in connection with your move.

Notify all your insurance agents of the move. Current coverage should be maintained until the move. If you will be renting out your house, you will need to convert your coverage to the appropriate policy.

Notify your bank, charge, and utility companies of the move and change of address (see Checklist 9, Appendix A). If closing an account, request that any outstanding balance be sent to you. Give the incoming occupants of your home your new address with a request to forward mail. Bring along extra change-of-address cards for those you forgot to notify (see Checklist 8, Appendix A).

Before leaving, obtain the toll telephone numbers of any organizations you may wish to contact. Many companies publish only their toll-free numbers, but this can be an expensive option when overseas. Just call the toll-free number before leaving and ask for the toll number.

Review Checklist 3, Appendix A, for an extensive listing of moving tips.

Moving Day

Moving day is, in essence, the climax of all the past weeks' preparations and worries.

The importance of your preplanning and organizing will become evident. Although things may go wrong or you may forget some last-minute details, your preparations will make the day go considerably smoother.

You must be present during all phases of your move. The packers and movers will have questions, and you need to be available. Furthermore, the movers will not be liable for missing items if you do not supervise. Do not plan any other activities, errands, or appointments for moving days. It is not necessary, though, for both spouses to be present. It is not advisable to have children and pets present. Arrange for them to be looked after during this period (plan an activity for them, have a friend watch them, etc.). It can be very traumatic for children to see all their belongings "disappear" into boxes.

You will probably find that the day begins very hectically for you as you involve yourself in last-minute tasks. This will diminish during the day, and you will most likely find yourself with not much to do. You may even feel that you are in the way of the movers. Use this time to collect your thoughts and relax.

The packing of your belongings will take the movers one to two days. The packing crew may be a different one than the actual movers. They will probably first pack all your belongings that you will be taking with you, followed by items that you will store. *Make sure all the things you are bringing with you, such as clothes, jewelry, and important documents, are safely out of sight of the movers.*

When the packers arrive, show the supervisor around your complete house, including garage, attic, and garden shed. Go through each room individually, explaining what goes in which shipment. Show them what is not to be moved (i.e., what stays in the house). Have labels on each item not to be packed. Your preorganizing and labeling will aid them greatly and will help to ensure that you end up with what you want. Explain to them the labeling system you have adopted and which items are to stay with the house. Usually they will supply carpet protectors, but if not, make sure you can provide them with something. Try to establish a professional and friendly working relationship with all the packers, in particular the supervisor. Offering all of them a cup of coffee immediately will help to foster this attitude.

At this stage, leave the crew to do the job and keep out of the way, but remain nearby to answer questions. Occasionally, investigate the progress and add any additional instructions. At the end of the packing process, do not forget to tip the packers if you feel it is appropriate.

While the packers are working, begin various tasks that you have saved for these days. This would include:

- final washing of clothes
- disconnection of washer and dryer
- disconnection of refrigerator and freezer, and giving away food
- removal of curtains, yard items, smoke alarms, fire extinguishers, hoses, hooks and nails in walls, etc.
- watering of plants
- complete packing of items to take with you
- disposal of all flammables and combustibles
- cleaning out the car and removing any items to be packed

The night before the actual move, have a good night's rest, and start the day with a substantial breakfast, because lunch probably will not happen when most needed. Try to get the help of a neighbor for supplying needed snacks and lunch, and moral support during the move. If not, have the telephone number of a local takeout.

Wear comfortable, loose-fitting clothes and shoes. The season and climate will further dictate your choice. It is a good idea to have large pockets in your clothes to stuff with odds and ends during moving.

Your first tasks of the day will be to tackle the last-minute jobs, such as stripping beds, washing stray dishes, and the final clearing up. Prepare any snacks or beverages at this time. The movers will appreciate offers of coffee and cool drinks (nonalcoholic) during the day.

After the movers have completed removing the contents of each room, check to see that everything truly has been taken. Make sure to check all cabinets, shelves, closets, and drawers. When everything has been packed and loaded into the moving van, inspect the entire house, including the garage, inside and out for any overlooked items. Do not forget to take your telephone!

Before the removal men leave, check the inventory and destination contract and the driver's bill of lading. It is a good idea to get the driver's name and van number for future reference. If you feel it is appropriate, tip the movers.

When leaving your house, make sure to turn the heating and air-conditioner system to an appropriate level. Close and lock all windows and doors. Make sure that the keys are left with the new owner or renter. Arrange for a professional cleaning service to do the final cleaning after you and the movers have left. It is well worth the money spent.

You've made it! Now is the time to treat yourself to a nice meal or room service at your hotel.

En Route

Going to your host country can be a time of excitement and anticipation.

It is best for the family to travel together as a unit, rather than the employee going on ahead to work. This will add to the sense of the relocation being a shared experience. Book your tickets and seats well in advance to avoid any problems. (Travel tip: Contrary to popular belief, bulkhead seats are not more convenient. They lack space for carry-on luggage and do not have a foldout table for games, coloring, eating, or working.).

Travel by air is fun for the children, and this probably will be their first trip overseas. They will most likely enjoy the amenities on the flight, such as movies and headphones, but it is a good idea to bring along their favorite snuggly bear or blanket. You may want to consider ordering a special child's meal in advance. Do not forget gum or hard candy to help minimize air pressure during takeoff and landing. Have snacks and games for the inevitable delays in airports. Remember that you will also have to cope with the effects of jet lag on your children as well as yourself.

Preorder a taxi or limousine to pick you up at the airport on arrival. Make sure that the trunk is large enough to accommodate your excess baggage!

It is highly recommended that you take a few days for yourselves before rushing over to your new life, even if you have to be in the host country quickly. Plan some time to relax and be together. Rather than a trip that includes major sightseeing and experiences that heighten your senses, consider a short holiday in which the main attraction is relaxation, such as a beach resort. Such a trip can be truly remarkable because you may find it very stress free and relaxed. The tension and challenges of the move are behind you, and the future is unknown and temporarily out of your control.

It is rare that your new home will be ready for you to move in on your arrival. Therefore, you should arrange to stay in a hotel or the equivalent. Depending on how long it will be until you move into your permanent housing, you may want to consider different options. If it will be only a few days before moving into your new house, you will most likely want to consider staying in a hotel. You can either choose a hotel near your home or in the major city if you are living in the suburbs or country. The latter have the romance of enabling you to ease the transition by exploring the city as a "tourist." This is a highly suggested option because it can begin your overseas assignment on a very positive note.

The whole family will appreciate being "pampered" and enjoying the sights. One major issue of the hotel option is that many foreign hotels are not geared for children, and finding appropriate accommodation for the family can be difficult. If you look for a hotel with a family-size room, consider the American chains (e.g., Hilton, Marriott, Holiday Inn, etc.)

If your temporary accommodation is going to be long term (i.e., more than one week), it will be best to stay in a more permanent place, such as house, apartment, or residence hotel. The extra room and kitchen facilities will be much appreciated and will ease the transition.

Moving In

Moving into your new home can be very exciting, yet also very stressful.

Some keys to a successful move are to stabilize the family life as quickly as possible, arrange for a quick arrival of some of your personal belongings and furniture, and reintroduce a normal family schedule (i.e., regular mealtimes, leisure activities, and bedtime schedule).

As with the initial move, you will need to be present for the unloading. If possible, you should go to the new house well before the movers arrive to peacefully explore your new accommodation and get a general idea of where to place things when they arrive. Have a good idea of how you want the furniture and any other heavy pieces arranged. Prepare a diagram before the movers arrive of where you want the furniture placed. The unloading process is very fast paced, and you will need to make decisions rapidly, with little time to think. Also clean any cupboards, shelves, or closets before you fill them.

It is a good idea to have at least two adults present, one to check items off the inventory as they are unloaded and one to direct movers in the proper placement of boxes and furniture in the home. It is your responsibility to make sure all the inventoried items have been delivered. Remember that there will most likely be language and cultural barriers (i.e., foreign language, work ethic, amount of breaks, etc.). If the language is different, it is a good idea for you to have learned some key phrases and words to direct where you want furniture and boxes placed. Establish a professional and friendly working relationship. Do not forget to offer the movers tea or coffee during the day.

Based on your labeling system (i.e., by color or room), prelabel each corresponding room on the door for immediate identification. Also prepare a diagram showing the rooms and labels that you can display for the unloaders. The movers can then immediately put the boxes where indicated. If your new house has any storage place, try to place there the boxes that contain items you don't use every day so they can be unpacked over time.

If you are moving into a furnished accommodation and wish to rearrange the pieces, have the movers do this before unloading the van. There will be more room to maneuver, and this will enable any of your pieces to be placed directly where you want them.

You will find that the boxes will accumulate quickly. One area that fills rapidly with several boxes will be the kitchen. If possible, have a mover help you unpack these. The unpacking of most all other rooms will flow relatively smoothly, but the kitchen, which has a huge inventory complete with many breakables, will prove to be a demanding task. Having an extra person to help will be of great assistance. Second, a great many waste boxes and wrapping paper will accumulate, and this will enable the movers to remove them that day.

Other items to unpack while the movers are still there are wardrobe cartons. They can be unpacked quickly and they take up a great deal of space, so their early removal is helpful. Make sure the movers will return later to remove the remainder of the boxes you have unpacked. Otherwise, you must find out how you can dispose of them. It is a good idea, though, to keep a few boxes (which you can break down for more convenient storage) for future use.

Unpack your "survival kit" and make up the beds. You will find yourself exhausted at the end of the day and will welcome an inviting bed. If you continue to unpack, do only the essentials.

When the movers are ready to leave, double-check the van to see that it is truly empty. Have the movers help with any final moving of furniture or boxes. They should reassemble anything that they took apart for the move. Finally, have them remove any packing materials. You can arrange for the moving company to come later in the week to take away the remainder of the boxes. If you feel it is appropriate, tip the unloaders. You will have to sign a document noting that the job is complete. If you have any comments, write them down on the receipt. For your protection in any later insurance claims, notate, along with your signature, that the shipment is "subject to final inspection."

At this stage, try to stop the unpacking process. You will already have done a great deal, and you deserve a break. Although the inclination will be to continue unpacking, it is not worth exhausting yourselves. Treat yourself to a nice meal, or at least get some take-away.

It will take another couple of days to unpack most of your items. It is best to tackle one room at a time, beginning with the areas that are most used. Given that you may have a limited stay in the country, you should try to be completely moved in as soon as possible. Try to be completely unpacked and settled in only a few weeks. You will want to reduce the length of the settling-in process. If you spend a disproportionate amount of time and energy getting settled, you may feel cheated if your assignment is prematurely cut short.

As you unpack, try to make a mental note of where you place things. One issue of moving is trying to find something later and not remembering where you placed it. You may not even remember if you brought it with you or left it in storage! Check every box and piece of packing paper very carefully so as not to discard any of your items. Try to get your house in a livable and homey condition as soon as possible, including placing mementos and hanging pictures. This will make the transition easier.

Some things you should be prepared for as you unpack include discarded packing materials and empty boxes, piles of books unloaded but not on shelves, desks and tables completely covered with items and boxes, paintings stacked against the wall, and dirt and debris all over. In other words, expect chaos and disorganization! Approach the whole process with a positive attitude, and things will go much smoother.

As you unpack, record anything that is broken, damaged, or lost. Keep the list current, and after you have completely unpacked, contact your moving or insurance agent. Most moving companies have a specified period in which you must submit your claim (i.e., one to two months). They will send you a claim form to complete and perhaps will send a representative to your house to inspect the damages. Most moving organizations are very professional, and you may be surprised at how low the claim is. In any case, do not agree to a final settlement until you are completely satisfied.

Family outings are a good idea in the first weeks. Seek out interesting and exciting places to visit. Consider a few overnight trips. This will enable you to explore your new surroundings and give you a break from the physical and emotional stresses associated with moving. Use this period to enjoy the first phase of your assignment and to strengthen your positive attitude toward the transfer.

Children and the Move

Most children also find moving to a new house a chaotic and stressful period.

They should be as informed as soon as possible after the decision to move abroad has been made. Older children should be encouraged to look forward to the move and to feel involved in the process. Even if the children are very young, talk to them well in advance about what is to happen. They will not fully understand what it is all about and all the ramifications, but you will be laying the groundwork for a major change that will be occurring. Do not treat the transfer as a mysterious event by concealing the move and changes from them. The children should be incorporated into the move and involved in planning and organizing, when appropriate. For instance, let them sort their own toys and belongings. Perhaps they will have some contributions for the garage sale!

It is important to let the children help choose the things they would like to take with them. By shipping their favorite items, you will help bridge the gap from the old environment to the new. Do not use the move as an opportunity to discard children's belongings that *you* think should be left behind. They are going through an emotionally difficult time as well as you, and they need to exert some control in their lives and have the security that comes with belongings. Be sensitive to their needs and feelings.

If you have time, videotape any TV shows, movies, or specials your children may enjoy.

On the day of the move, it is a very good idea to leave the children with relatives or a neighboring family with children. When the house is empty, try to avoid bringing the children back to see it because the experience can be traumatic for them, particularly for the younger ones.

Let your children hand-carry special "treasures" with them in a small bag or backpack.

When you get to your new home, arrange for sufficient time

before the movers arrive for your children to find their way around, explore their new surroundings, and enjoy the excitement of discovery. Make it a priority to arrange their bedrooms to be as familiar as possible. Prepare their beds and put out their favorite stuffed animals, toys, pictures, etc. They may feel insecure in the new and strange surroundings, so anything that can be done to alleviate this will help. Although watching their belongings being packed away in a box can be traumatic for young children, they will be delighted when they unpack their familiar possessions.

After arriving in the new area, look for children in the neighborhood of similar age for yours to play with. Your children will miss their former friends and will need new ones quickly to ease the transition. On the positive side, children of all nationalities gravitate to one another and enjoy playing. If you can time your arrival to coincide with the beginning of school, children will have a familiar routine. This will help them adapt and meet new friends.

Most relocations occur during the summer, which enables your children to get over jet lag, enjoy the initial excitement, and begin to settle in before starting to school (Northern Hemisphere only — a summertime transfer to a country in the Southern Hemisphere will coincide with the middle of the school year). Be advised, though, that most often, nationals and expatriates go on holiday during that period. This can result in bored children and exasperated parents. You can look into summer camp, going on a holiday, or seeing the sights in your host country.

See Chapters 4, 9, and 16 for additional information on children's issues.

Moving pets can pose significant challenges, yet they have an important role in the family.

The primary consideration should be the best interests of the animal. Consider the overall health and age of your pet, whether pets are acceptable in the culture, and if proper care will be manageable in your new environment. Appraise the environment (i.e., climate, local conditions, diseases threatening animals, the host country's attitude toward pets, etc.).

If you are planning to ship pets, you must look into the country's regulations. Different countries have different rules regarding shots and quarantine. For example, some countries require a strict quarantine period, such as six months; others do not even allow bringing in any animals. In almost all cases, special inoculations will be required. Make sure all shots are in order and that you have the appropriate documentation (e.g., type, date, and the name of the veterinarian who administered the shots). You may need to update shots during your assignment to ensure that the animal can return home.

The actual moving of your pet should be discussed with your moving representative and veterinarian. They can advise you on the best procedure to transport your pet, the type of kennel, required vaccinations, diet details, necessary import documents and permits needed, and possible quarantine periods. Before moving, you will also need to contact custom officials for any regulations regarding bringing animals into the country.

Certainly, it is best to leave your pet with a relative or neighbor or at a kennel during the packing and moving phase. The presence of many strangers, coupled with all the activity, will cause a very stressful and disruptive time for your pet. Consider leaving the pet with a trusted person or kennel worker who can then send it after you have arrived and settled. This will allow you to meet the pet on arrival. Horror stories of pets being left on the open pavement at the airport in the blazing hot sun are real.

If your pet must be quarantined for a long time, look for a government-approved kennel that you are happy with which is located in a convenient place near home or office and has suitable visiting hours.

If you are considering shipping your car, you must carefully evaluate all the risks and costs.

Some countries do not allow the importation of vehicles. Others impose regulations and require modifications (e.g., emission control, fog lights). Shipping costs and import duties can be significant and may outweigh the savings of not having to purchase a new automobile. Most companies' relocation packages will not cover the shipping of a car. In addition, the length of shipping time can be long and erratic.

The servicing and availability of parts may be a significant problem, particularly for "foreign" cars. If you are considering shipping your car, you should contact the manufacturer to determine the feasibility. Also be aware of any special considerations, such as "improper" placement of the steering column (as in Great Britain).

Buying a car overseas and shipping it back home after completion of your assignment may be an option to consider. As an example, Volvo will deliver the car to your home and pay for return shipping costs. Individual car manufacturers can provide details.

Electrical Appliances

Electric current in almost all countries is 220–250 volts, 50 H$_{\chi}$, as compared with that used in the United States, which is 110–120 volts, 60 H$_{\chi}$.

This difference can create much confusion in trying to decide which appliances to bring with you. An appliance meant to run on 110 volts will be severely damaged if connected to a 220 outlet. You essentially have three options on how to approach this dilemma (i.e., in considering a move from the United States; going to the United States, the reverse applies).

- Take your 110-volt appliances with you and use them with transformers to step down the higher voltage to the required level.
- Purchase, in America, 220- to 250-volt appliances in stores specializing in multivoltage electronic appliances.
- Purchase appliances in your new country.

In practice, all three have their drawbacks, and you will most likely end up doing a combination.

The main disadvantages of using transformers are that your electrical goods may work less efficiently and wear out more quickly; obtaining spare parts for appliances can be difficult; and the transformers themselves are inconvenient, cumbersome, and expensive. If an appliance is used daily or works with a 60-Hz motor, a transformer will shorten the equipment's life span.

When you use a transformer, it must correspond in size (i.e., wattage) to at least the electrical item connected; you can usually find the wattage information on the appliance. Note that some appliances are expressed in the units of ampere; 240 watts = 1 ampere.

After you have decided which appliances you want to bring, you will need to match them with the appropriate transformer. Try to determine the approximate placement of all your electrical items so as to purchase the optimum number of transformers and therefore minimize the inconvenience factor. Never connect to an appliance requiring a greater wattage than its capacity. The following table will give you a rough guide to help you figure out the approximate size of transformer you will need. Check the wattage on your appliance to be sure (see Checklist 10, Appendix A).

Transformer Size	Appliance
100 watts	electric blanket, small radio, heating pad, handheld vacuum, answering machine, battery charger
250 watts	stereo, blender, sewing machine, small fan, television, VCR, coffee grinder
500 watts	refrigerator, power tools, computer
1,000 watts	coffeemaker, vacuum cleaner, food processor, toaster, small space heater, waffle iron
2,000 watts	iron, electric frying pan, toaster oven, hair dryer
3,000 watts	electric kettle, dishwasher, washing machine, dryer, air conditioner

The greater the wattage the appliance has, the larger the transformer you will need. Bigger-capacity transformers also imply larger size and weight! However, you can purchase a small large-capacity transformer. It heats up quickly and can be used for only a few minutes at a time, but it is excellent for small kitchen appliances (e.g., blender, mixer, coffeemaker).

Your stereo amplifier and receiver will work on a transformer. Tape decks and record and CD players that are relatively new (i.e., post-1985) will all be 50/60 Hz internally convertible and therefore should not be a concern. If in doubt on any electrical items, consult the manufacturer and talk with the service department. Lamps are easy to convert; simply change the plug to fit the electrical socket and use a 240-volt bulb, for example.

Because electrical wall sockets are different throughout the world, you must purchase an adequate supply of the appropriate electrical adapter plugs. These adapters slip over the plugs of your appliances. To avoid inconvenience in your host country, purchase them before leaving your home country.

Some items, such as television, VCR, electric clock, microwave, and vacuum cleaner, cannot be adapted and will not work. Appliances are always on offer for sale by returning expatriates, so you can often purchase used appliances at a reasonable price. Where the format is different, though, you can use your own TV and VCR in tandem (on a transformer) to watch *videos only*. Consider purchasing a multisystem television and VCR.

Expenses

A great many expenses are involved when moving, particularly to an overseas posting.

There are many major expenses and incidentals that add up over time. Many of these expenses are incurred after your arrival at the new location.

Most of the major expenses are covered by your employer during a company relocation. However, it is a good idea to be familiar with all costs and to plan accordingly. Make sure you understand beforehand what your employer will pay for and what it will not. Many moving expenses are tax deductible; it is a good idea to consult your tax adviser. To help cover the incidental expenses, try to budget and establish a contingency fund to meet the added costs. Keep receipts for all costs incurred that relate to your move, no matter how trivial.

Some of the expenses that you may face include:

- home sale (i.e., closing costs, commissions, repairs, and improvements)
- rental of home (i.e., commission, managing fees, repairs, and improvements)

- removal (i.e., packing, transporting, and storage)
- temporarily living in both home country and new location (i.e., meal and lodging expenses)
- transportation to new location for whole family
- services (i.e., disconnection and installation charges)
- house hunting in new location (i.e., travel and subsistence, fees, meals and lodging, time off work)
- incidentals (i.e., thank-you presents, postage, meals out, tips, telephone calls, and currency-exchange commissions
- purchase of additional items that are duplicates of current items you own (i.e., appliances and electronics with different voltage)
- documents (i.e., work permit, passports, driver's license)
- legal and accounting fees

The first step of an overseas assignment, after deciding to go, is to prepare for the move.

You are faced with a myriad of decisions and tasks. Dealing with the practicalities of the relocation process is not particularly enjoyable. Yet with proper planning and organization, you can make the process run smoothly, and it will launch you into the exciting experiences of a successful expatriate assignment. It is also a time when you are preparing yourself not only physically but also emotionally to become an expatriate. During this time, you may experience excitement and anticipation of your new adventure.

Chapter 3 (at a glance)

Housing

This chapter can help you decide ~

what to do with your existing house and how to find a new home in your host country.

whether to sell or lease your current house, and the important steps to take.

how to search for a suitable home in your host country.

the best way to prepare for the house-hunting trip.

what to look for when viewing homes, and how to set priorities.

Some key points ~

❶ The decision to buy or lease your current house will depend on a multitude of factors.

② Usually it is not a good idea to purchase a property in the host country during your assignment.

❸ Finding a new home before moving is preferable to looking for a house after you move.

④ Make sure your house-hunting trip is well planned and highly structured.

❺ Before embarking on your search for accommodation, prepare a list of what is important to you.

⑥ Rentals in foreign countries can be complex, and it is a good idea to have the help of a qualified local lawyer.

❼ After you have chosen a property and organized the rental contract, arrange for the utilities and phone to be connected on your arrival.

Chapter 3

HOUSING

We have been on the expatriate trail for many years, moving several times. At one point, we lived in six houses in five years. Needless to say, we became very good at moving out of our old house and into the new. We got it down to one week from unpacking all the boxes to getting the pictures onto the walls! One of the many downsides, though, is that we never knew where anything was. We spent many hours looking for something, only to say, "I remember where it was in our previous place...."

House-hunting trips were always a major adventure, to say the least. I vividly remember flying to the United Kingdom and being driven to houses all over the Thames valley, with not a clue where I was. I had a map and could see where I was in relationship to the surrounding cities, but none of it made any sense. I was just trying to get used to driving on the "wrong" side of the road!

We always had an idealized view of an international house. Excitement soon gave way to frustration, exhaustion, and disillusionment. Time after time, our little fantasy would be shattered when we saw substandard houses. Not only did we need to get used to the smaller sizes and lack of space, compared with what we were used to back in America, but given our budget, there was little to choose from. Looking for furnished accommodations made it even harder. Our taste was not extravagant, but it is amazing to see the tacky and rundown furniture people leave in rental houses.

After a while, all of the houses we visited blended into one another, and it was difficult to visualize them. Surprisingly, with all the complexities and compromises, we always seemed to do rather well. Each house we found had something unique associated with it, such as having a *charming characteristic or being in a lovely location, that made our overseas experience all the more enjoyable.*

You will have two prime considerations when you transfer — what to do with your existing home and finding a new place.

If you own your home, you must decide whether to sell or lease.

This decision will depend on a multitude of factors, including the company's relocation package, cost, current housing market, tax implications, and plans to return. A good accountant can advise you of the best course of action.

If you are involved in a company transfer, you may be offered a relocation package that could include the company purchase of your house and all related expenses. Often, the offer price is less than the fair market value, and you could attain a higher selling price on the open market. On the other hand, most relocations allow you a minimum of time to sell your house, and the sale of a home involves considerable time and energy, both of which are in short supply.

If you are selling your house, definitely consider using a real estate agent. The commission involved is significant, but the reduced hassles and pressures more than offset the cost. You will also need to have your house ready for immediate sale, which includes getting any necessary repairs done and making the house presentable. A good agent will be of significant help in pointing out what needs to be done and even organizing the work. As with all facets of your transfer, delegation of tasks is essential.

If you decide not to sell your house, you will then need to rent the property. If your assignment is short term or you will be returning often, you may wish to keep your home available for your own use. You would then want a friend or relative to act as a "house sitter." Financial arrangements will vary depending on your circumstances, and they can include accommodation in return for looking after your property.

In either case, you will need to find suitable tenants. As with the sale of your home, an agent can be an invaluable aid in finding and screening tenants. You also will need to have someone man-

age the property while you are overseas. This will include the collecting of rent, preparing the lease contract, taking care of problems and repairs, and finding new tenants at the expiration of the
lease. It is extremely difficult to be a long-distance landlord, and a
good manager is essential. It is also a good idea to have a repair
person available to take care of minor problems that arise during
your absence.

If your current home is a rental property, you must notify your
landlord immediately of your intention to vacate.

The Internal Revenue Service has special regulations for overseas individuals concerning their houses. These are covered in
Chapter 7, which deals with taxation issues. Other countries may
have other regulations.

Most companies will assist in paying for rental property in the destination country.

Further, they may discourage you from purchasing a house and
often will give only financial assistance for renting. Given the legal
complexities and your unfamiliarity (i.e., culture, location, customs, laws, taxation, etc.), it is not a good idea in most cases to
purchase a property in the host country during your assignment.
The need for mobility and, most likely, the short duration of your
stay require renting. Purchasing a house, though, could be a good
option if your assignment is very long term.

Some countries may have a relocation service that specializes
primarily in finding rental accommodations. It is strongly encouraged that you take advantage of this service. You could probably get
your company to pay for it, particularly if it does not have its own
staff to handle this matter. Some companies will have preselected
"expatriate areas" or even existing expatriate housing. You may
wish to consider taking over your predecessor's accommodation.

There are essentially two ways of looking for a home. The first
is to take a house-hunting trip ahead of the start of your assignment. The second is to embark on the assignment, stay in a hotel or
furnished residence apartment, and look for a house. A house-
hunting trip is hectic and exhausting, but it enables you to minimize the length of time you must spend in temporary accommodation. More importantly, it allows you to settle in much more quick-

ly. If your family includes young children, this may be particularly important. On the other hand, if you look for a place to live after you arrive, you will be more familiar with where you want to live and what to look for.

House-hunting trips, sometimes known as familiarization trips, are usually very short (i.e., five days) and confusing. Make sure such a trip is well planned and highly structured. Most likely, all you will know is where your place of employment is on the map, but you will have no idea of distances, neighborhoods, shopping availability, traffic patterns, and schools. The more knowledge and information you have before you leave for the trip, the more you will gain from it. This is a very demanding job, but as much as possible, try to focus on selected areas before you start.

Someone who is more familiar with the area can direct you to locations that are more suitable to your needs. If possible, contact colleagues who are or have been living in your new location to get their thoughts and impressions.

A typical structure of a house-hunting trip includes:

Day 1: arrival and general orientation
Day 2: school visit and evaluation
Days 3/4: house hunting
Day 5: finalization of school and house selection

All house-hunting trips are exhausting, and your emotions will run the gamut from euphoria to despondency and back! Yet in the end, it all usually works out. If you are heading home with no resolutions (i.e., there was nothing available in the housing market or no space for your child in the school), it is not a disaster or failure. You now have a much better idea of what your options are and will be better equipped to find what you need. The housing market changes continually, with new places made available, and the turnover is very high in international schools.

Before embarking on your search for accommodation, prepare a list of what is important to you (location, commute time, number of rooms, etc.). You will most likely not find the "perfect" place, but preplanning will enable you to know what is crucial for you to obtain. It is a good idea to make up a short spreadsheet of your needs for analyzing houses that you visit. This will prove invaluable when memory starts to blur after the thirtieth viewing. Write down as a list of rows, line by line, all the factors you can think of that are significant (see Checklist 11, Appendix A). These could include:

- situation and location of the house or apartment
- physical environment and noise level
- neighborhood
- proximity to local schools, shopping, public transport, major highways, etc.
- commute time
- general layout
- number of bedrooms
- number and quality of bathrooms
- quality and size of kitchen
- type of heating and cooling
- structural state
- furnished or unfurnished
- decorations and furnishings
- garden
- household help (i.e., gardener, security, maids)
- garage
- drive and roadway
- storage space
- access to and type of neighbors
- when available
- rental cost and what is included in price
- conditions of the lease (i.e., length, opt-out clause, pets)
- any special things you want or do not want in a house
- your overall impression

Leave room for additional points that occur to you as you go along. Create columns to the right of these headings and a heading at the top representing the address of the houses you will view. As you view a house, you can tick off "yes" or "no," number of bedrooms, condition, etc. Draw the floor plan on the back of each spreadsheet. You will then have a reminder of each property viewed, with comparative merits.

Get family members to list all the positive and negative attributes they want in a house, and ascribe a ranking (weighting) system (see Checklist 12, Appendix A). This will help you focus on the most critical factors that are important to you and your family. Always remember that no matter how quantified your evaluation is, an objective approach cannot encompass your feelings and the many intangible issues. You must "live" with your final decision, so even if a house comes out on top with your weighting system, it just might not "feel" right. Trust your instincts.

If possible, consider including the children in the house-hunting, or preview, trip. This can forestall innumerable questions and lessen their anxiety. The downside, though, of taking your children along is that it will slow the process and make it more difficult. Usually, it is not a good idea to take younger children along on your house-hunting trip. Still, it is important to include them in the selection process. Involve your children in discussing the potential house, and incorporate their wishes into your search. Take photographs or videos of the new home, neighborhood, and school to show them. Bring things back, such as postcards and souvenirs. This will help them to focus on the transfer.

Always take a pen, notebook, and measuring tape with you. Also have a map of the area so you can annotate the location of the property. It is also important to look at the local area and environment, including shops, schools, and amenities.

While you are looking for housing, you will learn that there are no rules about the condition and appearance of houses or apartments. Some will be in excellent condition, and others may need serious work. Some owners may be willing to do some repairs and upgrading.

"Unfurnished" property can mean different things from country to country. Sometimes, such as in the United States, it implies that a complete kitchen is present, but no furniture. Carpets and drapery also tend to be included. On the other end of the spectrum, in Italy, for example, unfurnished accommodation can imply no carpets, drapes, wardrobes, and furniture, with only pipes sticking out of the walls in the kitchen! You are expected to install your own kitchen. Semifurnished accommodations also have a range of possibilities, usually including the kitchen, carpets, drapes, and possibly some furniture.

As you look at the house, try to concentrate on the layout of each floor and each room, with careful consideration of your needs and wants. Do not be too picky. No one house will provide all that you want. It is up to you to decide what points are most important and relevant and what you are willing to forgo. Remember that you are not buying the property. Do not be influenced or misled by the furnishings or decorations, particularly if it is being rented unfurnished. On the other hand, if it is to be rented furnished, you will have little latitude to change things, so you must be able to "live" with the furnishings.

Rentals in foreign countries can be complex, and it is a good idea to have the help of a qualified local lawyer or agent. There are many intricacies and differences, not to mention language and cultural variations, which you should let professionals manage. Also be aware that large monetary advances often will be required. Try to get any repairs or redecorating completed *before* paying the rent and moving in. Document the condition of the house and furnishings with the owner or agent, as you will most likely be held responsible for any damages not itemized.

Before signing the contract, make sure you have completely read it and are happy with the terms. For instance, often the landlord will insert a "break clause" enabling him to cancel the lease after six months, although the lease term is one year. Make sure you have the complete address and phone number of the property, and a contact for the landlord or managing agent. Organize for a time to pick up all the keys and to be shown how to operate the utilities (e.g., gas furnace, gas and electric meters, water shutoffs, etc.).

After you have chosen a property and organized the rental contract, arrange for the utilities and phone to be connected on your arrival. Again, a qualified agent can be very helpful. Be aware that red tape and inefficiency can delay and frustrate you. You may have to take care of things in person, pay in cash, and bring along certain documents. There may be additional confusion because of language barriers and different ways of doing business. Keeping a relaxed attitude will help you get through it!

Deciding what to do with your existing house and finding a new home overseas are very important.

As with the moving phase, proper planning is essential. You will have many decisions to make and probably will feel that making the "right" one is crucial. Actually, there are probably no truly right answers, and you will make compromises. If possible, it is a good idea to enlist the help of professionals (i.e., a real estate agent in your home country and a relocation specialist in the host country). Their assistance, experience, and advice can be invaluable.

Chapter 4 (at a glance)
Children's Issues and Education

This chapter will help you to know~

the considerations and decisions relating to your children's education and social development.

the effects moving has on children.

how to provide a quality and secure education for your children.

ways to evaluate and choose an appropriate school.

what changes and development issues affect your children.

Some key points ~

❶ Expatriate children need supportive parents who provide the time and effort to help them adapt to their new environment.

② Providing an education for their children is an immediate concern for parents.

❸ There are no fixed rules to deciding on the best educational option and specific school.

④ Your primary task will be to bridge the gap between your children's current stable environment and having them settled into their new home.

❺ Throughout the relocation process, it is essential to keep communication lines open at all times and to listen to what your children are saying.

⑥ Your children will become international citizens and will develop a sensitivity to other cultures and people because of their experience overseas.

Chapter 4

CHILDREN'S ISSUES AND EDUCATION

First, let me say this: As a mother, I love school uniforms. No arguments over what to wear in the morning, no peer pressure to have the latest in trendy fashion . . . in a word, wonderful! But my initial experience was a little different!

We had just moved to the U.K. and decided to enroll our daughter in the local school, where all schools require uniforms. I admit I was a little anxious about the idea, worried that my children would lose their individuality and that their lives would become terribly regimented. However, I was determined to have an open mind as I began visiting schools. We settled on a small school with a relatively short uniform list (I couldn't quite face the one with the regulation navy blue underwear!), although I was a little bit worried about the "brown sensible shoes." My girls had worn only sneakers or party shoes, and I really didn't know how things would work out.

So on a lovely late summer morning the six-year-old, the two-year-old, and I set off for Windsor to the uniform section of the local department store. "A quick bit of shopping and then we can catch the changing of the guard at Windsor Castle," I told the girls. I must admit I was intrigued with the novelty of shopping across the street from a famous tourist attraction.

We started at the top of the list, and for the next two hours worked our way through it. The sales staff must have thought I was from the moon as I tried to figure out everything we needed to buy. Yet they were very patient, and even expressed sympathy when I questioned why the green sweater was a different (i.e., clashing) shade of green from the blazer and beret. "What the school ordered," they shrugged. We staggered out of the store weighted down with several large shopping bags, just in time to see the last of the Windsor palace guards disappearing around the corner.

Next, I spent several hours sewing name tags in everything. When it came to the socks, though, I resorted to marking initials with a felt pen. The first day of school arrived and I managed to assemble all the required pieces of the ensemble (including the beret), and off our daughter went to school.

Two years later, our younger daughter enrolled at the same school, and I felt like a pro. I knew the mother in charge of the secondhand uniforms, my kids loved the summer dresses (which, in my opinion, looked like a doughnut-shop waitress's uniform from the 1950s!), and the school had broken tradition (aghast) and decided that "black sensible shoes" were also appropriate!

For many parents considering relocation, a fundamental worry is the possible effect on their children. Educational and social development, ability to establish new friendships, and the disruption of their children's current stable environment are some of the concerns faced by every parent. Children have a profound influence on the outcome of an expatriate assignment. They can generate a high level of anxiety and stress for the family, and at the extreme, their unhappiness can result in poor adjustment, anger, and resentment.

Research suggests that it is often the older, adolescent children who are more likely to experience difficulties (Munton et al., 1993). Therefore, for many families, it may be easier to transfer when their children are younger. Yet the effects of a move on children are very individual and cannot be generalized. The reactions of the children are dependent on many factors, such as age, timing, emotional makeup, and maturity. Just as a move may bring dormant issues to the surface in the adults' relationship, families may find specific emotional concerns raised in their children. These can be addressed through discussion or perhaps counseling.

Most importantly, expatriate children need supportive parents who provide the time and effort to help them adapt to their new environment.

It is important to know the effects relocation have on children. They have similar fears and anxieties as their parents and can feel helpless in a situation that they have no control over. Children, particularly younger ones, tend not to verbalize their concerns, but rather express them in mood swings, tantrums, withdrawal, defensiveness, or rebellion. It is therefore critical to communicate with your children throughout the process and to be sensitive to their concerns and moods.

All children should be included in the relocation process to their level of ability, and they should be encouraged to express their feelings and fears. Parents need to be alert to potential problems and behavioral changes. Their primary task is to provide an environment in which their children can feel safe and secure, and to consider their needs so they can handle all the changes.

The effects of relocation on children primarily fall into three classes: educational development, social welfare and adjustment, and friendships.

To children, the loss of friends is probably their greatest concern and worry. The age of the child is a critical factor. For example, adolescents find it difficult to break into what are often close-knit groups. Other children can be insensitive, and at this age, "being different" can be a liability rather than a novelty. Younger children, on the other hand, are often more flexible in forming new friendships. They may, however, react more strongly to small changes of routine, in a seemingly unpredictable manner.

Providing a quality and secure education for their children is one of the most immediate concerns for parents.

Schooling is typically a difficult and emotional consideration for parents and children, and an overseas move can make it all the more intense. The critical point to tell yourself is that in most situations, children are considerably more resilient and adaptable than their parents. Further, an overseas move can be considered an adventure for them. It will indeed enrich their lives and expand their horizons. Most likely, the children's primary concern will be if they will have new friends and if they will "fit in."

When evaluating a school, you must allow for your children's individual educational requirements, abilities, and interest. You must look not only at their current needs, but also consider the future and how the school fits into their total education (Roman, 1992).

Your first decision will be to decide if you will send your child to an international school, particularly one tied to your own nationality, to a church-affiliated or missionary school, or to a local national school. This local option is usually possible only if your native language is the same as that of your destination country (e.g., United States–Great Britain transfer) or if your child is very young. If you decide on a local school, you will also need to consider either public or private school. Other educational options include boarding school or home schooling.

In some situations, the children's needs will take precedence, and either you will decide against transferring altogether or will seek other alternatives. For example, if your child has only one year left of secondary school, some alternatives could include one parent remaining behind in the home country with the child, leaving the child with relatives or close friends, or sending your child to boarding school.

To help in the school-selection process, you should have full and current records of your children's academic profiles. Records that help chart a child's social, emotional, and academic growth are a valuable tool for teachers, counselors, educational advisers, and parents (Drake, 1997). Because it is much easier to obtain copies of transcripts in your home country, compile them *before* leaving for your overseas assignment.

Prepare a file for each child, which will include:

- all transcripts from previous years
- standardized test scores (e.g., Iowa, NFER)
- preparation test scores (e.g., PSAT)
- specialized reports (e.g., dyslexia)
- prospectus from most recent school
- list of textbooks and literature from most recent year

- recommendations from principals, guidance counselors, and teachers
- representative sample of the child's work

There are no fixed rules for deciding on the best option and a specific school.

It depends on your children, their ages, their dispositions, proximity to home, and cost. If possible, try to talk with other expatriate parents to get their experiences and opinions. Contact the local educational authority and host-country embassy for available information on schools. You can write directly to the schools for information and to arrange a visit. Do *not* commit your children to a school until you have visited it.

Begin your search immediately, because most schools have quotas and can fill up quickly. It is important to apply for places well ahead of arrival, if possible. To obtain information on international schools available in the host country, contact your embassy in the country. **The International Schools Services, Inc.,** and the **European Council of International Schools** publish a directory of overseas schools (see Resource 1, Appendix C). **The Association of Christian Schools International** provides details on Christian schools around the world. For local schools, contact the embassy and the local educational authority of the host country to learn about the country's educational system and available schools. Finally, there are school-placement agencies that (for a fee) can present an array of options for each child based on individual family and child needs, availability, cost, and location.

When you have compiled a list of potential schools, contact them immediately, asking each for a prospectus and details of the school. It is important to consider your home search along with your school search. Living near the school has the advantage of shortening your children's commute and may increase the likelihood of their having friends nearby. International schools, however, drawing students from a wide area, provide bus service from various parts of a city. When you visit a school, the officials can tell you approximately how long the journey will be and how much it will cost.

Another excellent source of information on schools is the parents. If possible, try to get the name of current expatriates who have children of similar age in schools you are considering. Contact any expatriates you may know through your company or in other companies in the related industry, call the school for names, and call the head of the school parents' association for potential contacts. Often, the parents can give you valuable insight and advice about the school and how appropriate it may be for your own children. Remember, though, that all parents have strong opinions about education, and you must evaluate their advice on how it relates to your own situation.

One issue that is critical in your decision is what curriculum you want for your child. Most international schools use an American or British curriculum and style of instruction, and that can be an appropriate option for English-speaking children or expatriates who anticipate being posted to more than one international location. Major international cities often have schools using other national curriculums (e.g., Japanese, Italian, Spanish, French, German, Arabic, and Hebrew). The governments of some countries, such as Germany and France, even operate schools for their expatriates in certain countries. Note that the educational philosophies of these schools can be quite different than you may be accustomed to. Instruction will also be in the national language. Some companies, particularly in remote locations, establish schools for their expatriate families. Expatriate groups also organize after-school or weekend instruction in their own languages and cultures, as a supplement to the international or local school curricula.

The international baccalaureate (IB) is a comprehensive system of courses and exams which focuses on the development of high-quality liberal-arts education (see Resource 1, Appendix C). This program is offered in schools around the world. An international baccalaureate diploma is recognized for university admission throughout the world. The IB diploma course is offered in the last two years of secondary school, with a curriculum that challenges academically talented and highly motivated students.

Most international schools are fully accredited. Often, however, they do not have programs that are specifically targeted to the gifted child, aside from the international baccalaureate. In addition, they usually do not have resources for helping children with learning disabilities. If your child is in either situation, you will need to take the initiative to find support.

Local schools can be appropriate options for younger children, who are not as entrenched in a particular curriculum. It is an excellent way for them to learn the local language, which they often pick up quickly. At that age, being different can be an asset, and often the national children will accept and befriend them quickly. They will make local friends and will provide the opportunity for you to meet their parents and become part of the community.

This contrasts with adolescent children, for whom conformity with peers is important and social circles have developed. There are greater differences academically at the secondary level, and it is more difficult to move between them. By attending a local school, children may be at a different level when they return to the home country's school system. It can be very hard for a teenager to make new friends, and therefore an international school can minimize this difficulty. Most of the student body in an international school is in a similar transitional situation. Most international schools are aware of the challenges children face when moving overseas and provide activities to incorporate new students into the student body.

Boarding school and home study are options, particularly for expatriates who are going to a hardship location or where no educational opportunities are available (particularly secondary school). When parents plan to be continually on the "expatriate trail" and would like their child to have continuity in education and social life, boarding school can be a viable option.

Finding a preschool or play group is usually accomplished best when you arrive in the host country and have settled into your home. The best source for finding an appropriate preschool is other parents.

When you have narrowed your possibilities to a few schools, it is essential that you visit them. Interview the head of the school and the teachers, and critically view the surroundings. If it is possible to visit while the school is in session, all the better. You not only must evaluate academic qualifications but also must decide if the environment is friendly, warm, and safe.

You will undoubtedly have your own concerns and questions

when evaluating a school (see Checklist 13, Appendix A). Some issues you may want to consider include:

- accreditation
- academic standards
- academic test results
- mean SAT scores or equivalent
- percentage of students from high school applying to and being accepted by universities (and which universities)
- curricula, particularly language and math
- grouping of students
- availability of elective subjects
- diversity of programs, including music, art, drama, foreign language, and computer training
- honors program
- opportunities for exceptional students to pursue gifted programs and advanced study
- special-education availability
- standardized testing program
- counselor on staff
- student support services
- college preparation assistance
- provisions for new students
- sports programs and facilities
- extracurricular activities
- school history
- atmosphere of the school
- enthusiasm and attitude of teachers, staff, and students
- overall philosophy, values, and policies of the school
- dress code
- disciplinary procedures and current problem areas
- size of classes
- student-teacher ratio
- teacher credentials
- parental involvement
- building construction
- size and quality of library
- tuition
- transportation arrangements and fees

- your children's personal needs (e.g., academically gifted, special musical or athletic abilities, learning disabilities)

It is important to involve your children in choosing a school. It may be appropriate to have older children accompany you on your visits and take a more active role in choosing a school. They will have different concerns than you, and it will be important to consider them. Whereas your concerns may focus on academics and curriculum, they are more interested in their teachers, friends, after-school activities, and lunch.

After you have settled on a choice, you must register your children with the school. Most likely, that will involve some paperwork and paying a small deposit. Send a copy of your child's transcript. Contact the school principal and ask for children in your child's class to send letters, clippings, pictures, school newspaper, yearbook, etc., to your child. This will give your child an idea of the new school and the types of activities available, and make the transition all the more tangible.

During your visit to the school, observe the other children — the kind of clothing and shoes they wear, their hairstyles, the backpacks they carry, etc. Find out it there is a dress code. When you get home, pass this information along to your child in a rather casual conversation. This can help to ease some of your child's anxiety about "fitting in."

When you arrive in the host country with your family, try to settle the children immediately. Adjustment to a new school is always a challenge, and it is compounded by being overseas. You must be very active and involved in the school life, continually monitoring your children to see that they are receiving the proper academic and social development.

In addition, there are many ways to become actively involved in their school. These can include:

- attending parent-teacher conferences
- serving on the school board
- becoming active in the PTA or equivalent
- serving on special committees related to the school
- becoming a tutor or teacher aide
- becoming a room parent

- acting as a field-trip and social chaperone
- working in the library
- organizing after-school activities, clubs, and holiday programs
- raising money for extracurricular activities, special equipment, or other support services
- providing the school with unique expertise

Go to school with your children for registration and orientation. Talk with the principal and counselor. Try to meet the teachers and other tutors who will teach your children. Discuss with the teacher and school authorities any special needs your children may have. You should help the teachers and administrators understand the transition your child will go through. Ask about extracurricular activities your children enjoy (e.g., sports, music, drama, etc.), and find out how to get your children involved. Strongly encourage them to sign up for one or two activities so that new peer relationships can be fostered. Take your children to their classrooms and explore other parts of the school together. Knowing their way around and being familiar with their new environment will boost children's confidence on the first day of school (Piet-Pelon and Hornby, 1992).

Most likely, their biggest concern will be how they will be perceived by other children and whether they will make new friends. School is your children's primary source for making new friends. The majority of children are most concerned about fitting in and whether they will be accepted and liked.

Try to find other families that will have children in your children's classes, and introduce your children to them *before* the start of school. Friends, neighbors, and school officials can be a contact. Your children may resent your interference, but knowing a familiar face, having an acquaintance to show them around during the first days, and just having someone to eat lunch with are very important.

If necessary, take your children to school for the first few weeks and stay until they feel comfortable. This will also be a good opportunity for you to meet other parents. Attend school functions to get acquainted with staff and other parents, particularly in the first months.

As time progresses, be supportive, but let your children find their own friends, based on their values, interests, and the activities they enjoy. Encourage your children to invite new acquaintances to your home when you are there. Try to trust your children's instincts in selecting friends. Quietly monitor their progress, though. Sometimes the first kids to approach a new child are from the "bad" group.

Remember that the many changes and adjustments are hard for children, so patience and understanding are essential.

Social Development

Children go through an enormous period of change, growth, and development, and an expatriate assignment has a profound influence on them.

They will face many of the same challenges and concerns as adults.

What are the primary concerns and feelings children have when moving? Ervin (1995) interviewed several hundred children from kindergarten through college who have moved. Samples of their responses may help to put into perspective their feelings from both before and after their moves. Perhaps the most enlightening is that 82% of teenagers polled, who had recently moved, said that although they were scared and resentful at first, moving ended up being a very positive experience.

Initial Feelings

"The biggest thing you worry about is making new friends and being accepted."

"I worried about what school would be like."

"I was mad because I liked where I lived and I had good friends."

"Let yourself be sad, but don't dwell on the negative feelings."

"I was afraid that I would lose track of my friends."

"It was hardest telling my best friend."

About their Parents

"My parents spent a lot of time talking to me *before* and after the move; it helped a lot."

"Parents cannot push too much; they have to give you time to adjust and find friends."

"It really bothered me that my life was being influenced so much by someone else's decision; I felt out of control."

Thoughts on How to Make Friends

"Be yourself."

"Get involved in extracurricular activities."

"Try to meet someone *before* the first day of school."

"Don't always talk about your old school, friends, etc. The new kids get sick of hearing about it."

"It is not the end of the world."

Your primary task will be to bridge the gap between your children's current stable environment and having them settled into their new home. Whatever you can do to reduce the trauma in a move is advisable. Children can deal with a move if they are dealt with honestly. A move always brings a certain amount of anxiety for a family.

It is essential that the children are involved in the whole relocation process — from making the decision to move to preparing for the move to finding a new school and home to adjusting to life overseas. It is important that your children feel that their opinions are valued and that they have some control over the change in environment. The degree of help and explanation will depend, of course, on their ages. Children need to know why they are going, yet the details and sophistication of the explanation will be based on their ages. They will have many questions and concerns, and you will need to help them through the process. Speak only about the move, and encourage lots of questions about their concerns.

It is important that children be given as much notice of the move as possible because they need time to understand the ramifications. It is essential that they hear the news from you rather than someone else; make sure that you tell your children *before* you start discussing your plans with other people. Be honest and up front with your children about the reasons for the move and what the ramifications are for the whole family. You should respect your children's feelings, and allow them the opportunity to tell their friends in their own time. Once situated in the new city, bring your family to visit your office. This will make the reason for the move more tangible for them.

You must consider what the children will lose and what they will gain by the move *from both your perspective and theirs.* For instance, gaining international exposure and sensitivity is certainly a benefit for your children, but they will not appreciate or realize the value until they are older. Their concerns are much more immediate, and such a concept will not be a significant motivator for them. Rather, their immediate lives (i.e., school, friends, etc.) will be the most significant concern.

Parents have to be prepared for the gamut of emotions, from joy to sorrow, from anger to enthusiasm. Although sometimes difficult, it is wise to let your children vent their feelings. It is also a good idea to share your own feelings, concerns, and ambivalence. Even if you are enthusiastic about the transfer, you are bound to have questions and doubts. After a few weeks, the reality of the move will have sunk in, and you can then more openly and calmly discuss the practicalities of the move. Continue to reassure your children that they are not alone.

Throughout the relocation process, it is essential to keep the communication lines open at all times and to *listen* to what your children are saying. You must be willing to listen to the frustrations and complaints your children are expressing. Watch for signs of adjustment problems, such as changes in daily attitudes, habits, attire, and mood. Make time to spend with your children, especially during the beginning phases of the assignment. Set aside time each day during the relocation to spend time with your children. An occasional family "open forum," around the dinner table, for instance, is a good idea, so everyone can share problems and feelings. Frequent meetings through all stages of the move go a long way toward getting family members to work together. Ask open-ended questions (i.e., "How are you feeling?") as compared with those that will elicit only a "yes" or "no" response (i.e., "Did you have a good day at school?"). Children need to be able to share what they are experiencing and feeling.

If your work permits, try to spend more time at home during this period. Do not expect too much too quickly; it will take time for your children to adjust. Allow them a certain amount of quiet time, with no commitments or demands. Remember, roots grow slowly. Be patient.

You must be very aware of and sensitive to your children's concerns. This can often be difficult, since you are going through a very stressful and active period as well. You should try to be positive about the move and your new environment. Children will pick up parents' attitudes and feelings and make them their own. If you are worried or very stressed, your children will most likely be so as well. It is important not to be continually wrapped up in the relocation process by always discussing the move, being frantic, and having your whole life revolve around the move. Children will pick up on your emotions. Remember to have fun and to take some time off from the whole process. Maintaining a normal routine, such as meals, church, and sport activities, and scheduling time to be together go a long way toward relieving stress before and after the move.

It is important that your children gain an understanding of the host country and culture before moving. Find out where the country is on a map, look up some interesting geographic and cultural facts, and learn about the different people, customs, dress, and food. Your local library, museum, and bookstore can provide a wealth of information. Travel agents and tourist offices can provide colorful brochures. Perhaps your child has already expressed a particular interest in countries or cultures that you can exploit. You also should teach your children the social customs of the host country, particularly the appropriate behavior and dress, so they will be better able to fit into their new environment.

Alert your children's teachers to your move and try to get them to talk about the host country in a history or geography lesson. You can help by supplying them with books, currency, postcards, and pictures. Be careful, though, to gear the information to the child's age group. This will help to serve two purposes. First, it will help your children learn about the new culture. More important, they will become more involved with the decision to move and will look forward to it with excitement. When children see that their friends and teachers are excited about the move, they too will become more positive. It is surprising how the little things make such a difference in a child's attitude.

Children like routine and stability in their lives, and you must ensure this in your lifestyle. Try to keep the family schedule as normal as possible. Stress comes with change, but maintaining a structure will help give your children the extra security needed in their new surroundings. When you live overseas, it is necessary to manage the lives of your children more actively than you may be currently, whatever their ages. You need to not only help them get settled in school, but also help them seek out friends and activities. These may be available through school, organizations, or clubs. Sports, music, drama, dance, scouting, and local cultural activities are usually available. Expatriate or local parents can be very helpful.

It is also important not to reject or neglect your home country. Help your children to retain positive feelings about their home country. You must keep your own culture, customs, and traditions alive in your family. Many customs and holidays you take for granted may not be present in your new culture. For instance, Christmas is certainly not an event in Muslim countries. Thanksgiving and Fourth of July are truly American holidays, with no presence in other countries. You will often need to be creative, but it is important to celebrate and keep alive your family traditions. It is important for your children to have roots, to know their own culture, and to be proud of it. When they return home, they must know their own customs and traditions to successfully adapt and be comfortable.

Leaving friends behind is usually cited by children as the worst part of the move (Ervin, 1995). Encourage your children to stay in touch with family and friends in their home country. Help your children assemble a list of addresses and phone numbers of close friends so they can keep in touch. Put your new address on 3 x 5 cards so your children can give them to their friends. Because you will want to telephone friends back home, allow your children to do the same. You will find that letting them talk with their friends will make the transition much easier. Young children do not have a good understanding of the concept of saying good-bye to friends, often feeling that they will never see them again when they leave. For families that are continual expatriates, moving from assignment to assignment, this can be a significant challenge. Although your children may make friends easily, living in a transient community and always saying good-bye can take their toll.

You should bring along educational materials, reference books, and reading books. These can be hard to obtain in many foreign countries. Also remember that your children will be growing and maturing during your assignment, so you will need to plan ahead. For example, addition will turn into multiplication and picture books will turn into novels. Bring along some workbooks on your home country's history and geography.

Resources for your children's special interests, activities, and hobbies may not be available, so try to bring any related materials or supplies. Also help them to develop new interests related to the host country's traditions or opportunities. This is important because it will help them connect with the local culture. They also may have more time than they did at home, partly because they will probably not be watching as much television!

Boy and Girl Scouts are active throughout most of the world. If you have Scouts in the family, take uniforms and other items they will need. For information on scouting activities abroad, contact your scouting association in your home country and international schools in your host country. They may also be able to enroll in local Scout groups.

For families with girls, it is important to know that there are often few positive role models for them in many foreign countries (Piet-Pelon and Hornby, 1992). Many cultures are very traditional, putting women in the more conventional roles, often even subservient. There is less exposure to women doing different things, particularly career oriented. It is therefore important for both the mother and father to create a positive and enriching environment for their daughters.

Your children will become international citizens and will develop a sensitivity to other cultures and people because of their experiences overseas. They will probably learn a foreign language and will have firsthand exposure to history and geography. The experiences, the travels, and the opportunities are all some of the exciting advantages that will enrich their lives as children and later as adults. Your challenge is to provide a secure and loving environment to help them realize these benefits.

Your children's education and social development are a major concern for all parents.

As an expatriate, you are faced with new challenges, and you may be uncertain of the best choices. Careful research and investigation can greatly narrow your search for quality education. For the most part, educational opportunities in the international community are very good.

This is also a stressful time for your children, and your love, support, and attention are essential to help them adjust successfully. You must be aware of and sensitive to your children's concerns. Yet also remember that in most situations, they are quite resilient and adaptive and will thrive in their new environment.

For related information on children and various phases of the relocation process, please see separate headings in related chapters. For information on moving with children, refer to the section on children and the move in Chapter 2. For additional discussion on culture shock, see the section on children and culture shock in Chapter 9. To learn more about children and repatriation, refer to the section on children in Chapter 16. There is an excellent list of references specifically directed for children and moving in Kalb and Welch (1992).

Chapter 5 (at a glance)
Documents

In this chapter you will learn ~

what documents are needed when you transfer overseas, and how to obtain them.

the key documents you should obtain.

what documents you should bring with you.

Some key points ~

❶ The documentation requirements vary from country to country.

② There are four primary documents you need.

❸ You should call the embassy of the country you are going to and find out what documents are needed for your spouse and children.

④ Make sure you are aware of all expiration dates.

❺ When traveling to your overseas posting, hand-carry all original documents. In your host country, keep them in a safe place.

Chapter 5

DOCUMENTS

I am sure the same thing happens to expatriates who come to the States to work, but the bureaucracy one confronts with the immigration officials is a nightmare. I had heard many horror stories.

Unfortunately, I made the mistake of leaving all the paperwork with my Employee Relations Department. Thinking everything was under control, literally the day before we were leaving for our overseas assignment, I wondered what documentation my wife and children needed. I called the consulate to find out that they too needed documentation from the embassy! A last-minute scramble saved us from a disaster. They would have been sent back home on the next available flight. Certainly not a good way to begin an assignment!

So off we head on our flight, thinking that we had dodged that bullet. On arrival, complete with major jet lag, two cranky children, and eight suitcases, we got stuck in mud. The immigration officials took hours writing up the paperwork. Finally, when we thought it was all over and we could get out of the airport, they said that they needed to give us all a physical. What?! We had just completed extensive medical examinations before leaving, and they want some airport doctor to check us out. You must be kidding? Well, they did a few pokes and prods and checked our vital signs. In the midst of all the excitement, our two-year-old daughter managed to fall off the examination table. She refused to let the doctor touch her, and her loud wails convinced the officials that we were all OK. At that point, they hustled us out of the airport.

So now we can all put our energies into settling into our new environment. Well, not quite. We then had a seven-day grace period in which we had to register with the local police. We could envision another bureaucratic nightmare.

A few days later, we trudged off to the local station. Their attitude was one of nonchalance. They would look for any avenue to not complete our application. It seemed that the official just wanted us to leave. In other words, if he could decide that we did not have the necessary paperwork, he would not have to do anything. We would leave, and then it would be another person's problem.) Fortunately, we were prepared and had everything in triplicate that we needed and more.

So we sat for several hours as they scribbled on papers and stapled photographs on everything. We finally left with a document that looked like it came out of something created fifty years ago.

One of the first things you will need to do in preparing for your move is to secure the necessary travel documents and complete the paperwork that is required to live and work in your host country. On your transfer overseas, you will need several documents. Your company may facilitate obtaining these, but it is best if you are on top of the matter. Often, things can slip through the cracks. The following situation is a true incident that provides a warning. One couple finally arrived at their overseas posting only to have the spouse turned away at customs because she did not have the necessary associated work permit, although her husband's documents were all in order. The company had supplied the work permit for the employee, but did nothing for the spouse.

The documentation requirements will vary from country to country. You must therefore find out what necessary documentation you and your family need to enter and work in the country, and how you must go about obtaining it.

All countries have different requirements, but most likely, the four primary documents that will be needed are a valid passport, visa, work permit, and residence permit for all members in the family.

For example, the U.S. government has streamlined the acquisition of a passport, and in major cities, it is possible to receive one in only a few days. To obtain a passport, you will need an original birth certificate (or an old passport), passport photo, and the necessary application and fee. In the United States and EU countries, for example, adult passports are valid for ten years and a child's for five years.

Your transferring company should take care of the visa and work permit for the employee. When inquiring about visas, make sure you specify that you are relocating to the country to live and work there, and not just to travel. There will be certain restrictions on the work permit, such as applying only to a specified employer and job. The work permit will be valid for a certain time and often can be renewed. You may also need to get authorizations to import household belongings, cars, and pets. Consult with your moving company.

An employed spouse who will also work abroad will need a separate work permit and should not be designated as a dependent on the work permit or other documentation of the person being relocated. The spouse needs individual documentation for most countries.

You should call the embassy of the country you are going to and find out what documents are needed for the spouse and children. Most likely, it will require for each a valid passport, visa, and residence permit, which can be obtained by supplying the passports and letter of intent from your employer. You will also need a passport photo.

When you arrive, some countries require you and your family to register with local authorities and obtain a residence permit. This must usually be done quite soon after entering the country. Find out what documents you must bring along with you and what costs may be involved. Usually, payment can be made only with cash. It is also a good idea to register with your embassy or consulate.

Make sure that you are aware of all the expiration dates of your documents (e.g., passport, work permit, visas, driver's license, etc.), and do not let them expire before renewing.

Other documents you need include marriage certificates, birth certificates of all family members, driver's license, and Social Security (or equivalent) numbers. It is a good idea to make multiple copies of all these documents, as well as the passports and work permits, and keep them separate from the originals. This will help in replacing the originals if they are ever lost or stolen. Passports can be renewed or replaced in the foreign country by going to your embassy. When actually moving, keep the originals with you rather than packing them.

Below is a comprehensive list of documents that are important to bring with you when you transfer overseas

(see Checklist 7, Appendix A). Remember that you should always hand-carry these documents rather than packing them in the air/sea shipment.

Passports

Each family member needs a passport, including children. Make copies and keep them separately. It is also a good idea to bring some spare passport photographs, because American passport photos are of a unique size. Also get several small photographs from photo booths (less expensive than passport photos), because they will be handy for the multitude of documents you will need in the host country. This will save you much time and aggravation!

Work permit and visa

Have your valid work permits and associated documents for *all* family members on entering the host country. You will not be allowed into the country without them. Include a copy of the offer letter or other related document from your company, outlining your new posting overseas.

Immunization records

These records are required and must be adequate for the specific country.

Will

Make sure you have an updated will covering all your needs and wishes for your spouse, children, and estate. Leave a copy with your lawyer back home and the location of the will with a family member or friend. You may also want to consider drawing up a power of attorney and leaving it with a responsible relative or friend. This will let you have someone who can legally act on your behalf while you are overseas.

Insurance policies

Make sure you and your family are fully covered by medical and accident insurance during transit and your international assignment period. Your insurance should adequately cover yourself, your family, and your belongings, both overseas and in storage.

Obtain a letter of reference from your auto insurance detailing your driving record. This can be helpful in getting adequate coverage in the host country and can be a potential reference when you repatriate. In some countries, there are companies that offer road insurance, similar to AAA in the United States. If you currently have such coverage, you can put your membership on hold by contacting your insurance agent. This will enable your status to remain active so that you will not incur joining fees on your return.

If you are renting out your house, contact your insurance agent to change the policy to reflect the change from owner occupied to tenants. You will not need contents insurance if you are leaving the house unfurnished.

Marriage license and birth certificates

Take both originals and copies for all family members.

Special papers

When appropriate, bring along any certificates for naturalized individuals, adoption papers, and divorce and child-custody papers.

Traveler's checks and cash

Have an adequate amount of traveler's checks and cash, in both U.S. and foreign currency, available as easy access for emergency funds and for travels back home.

Driver's license

Look into the rules governing driver's licenses in the host country. Every country has its own laws, and they can differ markedly. Some countries allow driving with a foreign license for a limited period, after which they require a national license. This would necessitate passing a local test. These tests can often be very difficult, involving both written (in the local language) and practical demonstration. Taking driving instruction is well advised in these cases. Some countries require an international driving license, which can be obtained in your home country before you leave. Other countries have an agreement with some countries regarding the exchange of driving permits and only require a local translation into the host country's language.

No matter which license you use, it is a good idea to familiarize yourself with the different "rules of the road." Make sure your current license is valid and renew it before transferring, if it will expire shortly. Change the address on your license to ensure that you can renew it during your overseas posting, if necessary.

Joint checking and savings accounts

Make sure your checking and savings accounts are active and have sufficient reserve funds for easy access. See Chapter 7 for more details.

Tax forms and papers

Take all relevant past income-tax forms, papers, and supporting documents to assist in future tax-return filings.

School records

Obtain all current records and related information that will enable teachers to become familiar with your children's academic levels.

Medical records

Obtain copies of all family medical records (i.e., doctor, pediatrician, dentist, optical, etc.), X rays, and any current prescriptions you may have. Take along extra medical insurance forms and documentation describing your benefits.

Housing records

Bring lease or rental agreement for both home and host-country houses, and corresponding insurance records.

Valued inventory

The inventories of your personal luggage, air freight, and household shipments are the key records of your belongings. If you are shipping your car, bring the necessary ownership and insurance records.

Having the proper documents before leaving your home country is essential to ensure a hassle-free entry.

Documentation requirements vary from country to country, and you must make sure you know what they are. A valid passport, visa, work permit, and residence permit are required. There are also other personal documents that you will want to have with you. It is a good idea to make photocopies of all your important documents and keep them separate from the originals.

Chapter 6 (at a glance)

Taxation and Finances

In this chapter you will find ~

the aspects of taxation in your home and host countries, and the financial issues to consider while overseas.

ways of transferring money overseas.

how to manage your bank accounts and money.

home and host-country taxes, and the rules that apply when living overseas.

ways to manage your investments while overseas.

Some key points ~

❶ Financial matters can be broken down into three main categories: day-to-day finances, taxes, and investments.

② It is imperative that you make sure your personal affairs are in order before you leave your home country.

❸ Opening a local bank account is a priority.

④ There are many ways of transferring money from your bank account in your home country to your foreign account, and all are surprisingly easy.

❺ A United States citizen is required to file federal income tax and pay any taxes on worldwide income.

⑥ To help you build your savings and prepare for repatriation, careful financial planning is essential.

Chapter 6

TAXATION AND FINANCES

Starting one's home finances is always an adventure in a foreign country. I knew that one of the first objectives was to open a bank account, so I set this as one of my first priorities when moving to Rome. I had the name of a bank manager who spoke English and specialized in international accounts. I set up an appointment with him during the week of my house-hunting trip.

The morning of the visit, my wife and I were cordially and enthusiastically greeted by the manager. We were led upstairs to a most elegant conference room. Coffee was served, and the atmosphere was very open. Also attending the meeting was a very distinguished gentleman. He spoke no English and did not seem to be a part of the meeting, yet there was clearly an air of importance surrounding him.

During the meeting, they continually seemed to sidetrack to discuss my company. My intention was solely to open an individual checking account. It soon became apparent that the grand treatment we were receiving was related to the bank's wanting my company's business! Nevertheless, we successfully opened our personal account and negotiated a 10% interest rate.

As the weeks progressed, the memories of the wonderful treatment we had received began to fade with the reality of living in the country. Italy is predominantly a cash economy, so checks are rarely used. Never does one send a check through the mail, and bill paying is usually done at the post office. This means standing in a long line for an hour in a building with no ventilation. And even when I do write a check, I am at a total loss. Try writing out a check in Italian for 1,856,347 lire (a little over $1,000).

The country does have the modern convenience of the

debit card, but it does not always function. I remember one day shopping in the local supermarket, going to the checkout with a full trolley of groceries. I was greeted by a handwritten sign saying that the computer was not functioning, so the store would not be accepting credit cards. I had to then park my basket, go outside, and find the closest automatic teller to withdraw cash. The first two machines I encountered were either broken or out of cash. Thirty minutes later, after finally having gotten my cash, I returned to pay for my groceries. I noticed that the sign had been taken down, and the store was now accepting debit cards! Aghh! On a good day, it would be an inconvenience and minor irritation. I could almost laugh it off. On a bad day, it would be a disaster, and I probably would be ready to take the first plane back to America.

Oh, yes, at the end of the year, when I got my final bank statement, I found the interest my account was earning was 2%, and the bank charges were exorbitantly large.

When moving to a foreign country, expatriates are concerned about financial circumstances as well as housing, education, and social opportunities. Taxation, bank accounts, credit, and pension and Social Security entitlements are financial issues that you are faced with currently, but they are more complex for an expatriate.

Financial matters can be broken down into three main categories: day-to-day finances, taxes, and investments. They are all very complicated, and you are urged to consult your financial and tax adviser for professional advice. The intention of this chapter is to alert you to some of these issues. It is not intended to be a comprehensive discussion or to take the place of advice from a qualified specialist.

It is imperative that you make sure your personal affairs are in order before you leave your home country. Make sure that you have a will and that it is up to date. You should have an executor and guardian for your children in the unlikely event of an accident.

Day-to-day Finances

Most likely, you will be paid in your home country's currency as an expatriate, so you will need to be concerned about transferring money from that currency to the host country.

Even if your salary is paid in local currency, you may still find it necessary to transfer money from your home-country account. A major concern as an expatriate is that you may have enough cash, but it is in the wrong currency and in the wrong country!

At one point, I was being paid in dollars, my bills were in Italian lire, and my company reimbursement was in British sterling!

Balancing your expenses with your income can sometimes be very confusing. Fortunately, modern banking provides many solutions.

Many countries operate as a cash economy. The use of credit cards or checks may be very difficult or even impossible. You may have to pay for everything from groceries to electric bills in cash, and find little use for your checkbook or credit card.

When you arrive in the host country, you should open a local bank account. This is best done before you arrive permanently, and it should be one of your three priorities on your exploratory trip, after finding an appropriate school and house. Bring along a letter of reference from your current bank (it is helpful if it can be translated into the local language), along with necessary documents of identification. To find a bank, contact your embassy, current expatriates in the country, estate agents, or local expatriate clubs. Your company may also have an established relationship with a local bank. Often, there are local banks that specialize in expatriate accounts.

There are many ways of transferring money from your home-country account to your foreign account, and all are surprisingly easy.

Each has its associated advantages and drawbacks, in terms of time, ease of use, availability, and charges incurred.

Unfortunately, in all transfers, there will be commissions and exchange-rate losses. The charges invoked on any transaction can be substantial, and it is important to be aware of them. Exchange-rate losses can be significant as well, but harder to manage. Because you will need your money on a daily/monthly basis, it is difficult and inadvisable to try to "time" the currency market. You can, however, try to obtain the best exchange rate (i.e., commercial) for any of your transactions.

One of the best things you can do is to establish a relationship with your bank managers in *both* your home and host countries. They can be immensely helpful in dealing with the complexities of international banking.

Some options to transfer money include:

Check exchange

You can write a personal check from your checking account and deposit it in your local foreign bank account. You should arrange to receive the current exchange rate, subtracting only for a modest commission and service charge. The benefit of this approach is that usually the charges will be minimal and only one-sided (i.e., charged only by the foreign bank account). Sometimes the bank will allow you to request whether you want the current exchange rate of the date of the check or when the check clears.

Sometimes the bank will credit your account immediately, but some banks will wait for the check to clear before crediting your account. This transfer can take as long as a month and can pose difficulties if you need cash immediately. Another drawback to this approach is that you must go to your foreign branch bank to present your check, which may be inconvenient. This method is best if either your bank will credit your account immediately or you do not need your money for some time.

Wire transfer

This method involves cabling money from one bank account to the other, similar to the check exchange. It is fairly convenient and requires only a phone call to your home-country bank. The transfer and account crediting are "immediate." This method, however, will incur more charges because your home-country bank will also charge commissions. The wire-transfer method is best if you need your money immediately.

Cash advances

This approach involves obtaining cash advances with your current bank credit card. This approach is probably the most convenient and immediate because you can use many bank teller machines available in foreign countries. The downside to this approach is that the charges are significant. You will incur service and finance charges, and an exchange rate below the commercial rate (see below). This method is good if you need cash quickly or are on holiday.

If you have a debit card, you can use it to withdraw foreign currency from an automatic-teller cash machine. Usually you will incur only a small bank charge, and the exchange rate will be the prevailing rate. This is also an excellent way to obtain foreign currency while you are on holiday.

Credit-card purchases

Rather than a transfer of money, you can use your home-country credit card to make purchases for your everyday use. More and more retailers are accepting credit cards, even for purchase of groceries. Credit cards are also good as far as convenience and safety are concerned. The exchange rate offered by your credit-card company incorporates a commission into the exchange rate (approximately 1–2%).

If you use this approach to transfer money regularly, you are advised to set up an automatic monthly payment of your credit card from your home-country checking account. This will avoid any finance charges incurred by late payment of your bill. The time delays between receiving your monthly statement and paying your bill can be longer than the period allowed by your bank. This method is a good supplement to the actual transferring of money.

Because you are dealing in two currencies, it is important to maintain an appropriate balance in your accounts.

If you can afford it, you should try to have a financial cushion in both your home and host-country bank accounts to avoid any unexpected surprises. To maximize your investment return, try to have checking and saving accounts tied together. For instance, some accounts, given the appropriate balance, can be arranged so that your money remains in the savings account, earning a higher interest. It will automatically be transferred to your checking account as needed to pay charges.

It is also a good idea to have home-country traveler's checks with you (remember to write down the numbers and keep them in a secure place). These will come in handy for holidays, return trips to the States, and emergencies. Have some of your own currency in cash for immediate use when you return home for visits or business. U.S. dollars and EU currency (the euro will be available January 1, 2001) are also good to have for emergencies because they are commonly accepted in many countries.

Exercises 13 through 16 in Appendix B will help you put your financial position in order.

Taxation

Taxes are an ever-present concern in our lives. All countries have different tax laws and regulations.

Some countries, such as the United States and Italy, tax an individual on worldwide income, but others, such as the U.K., do not. Given the complexities of U.S. tax laws, a brief discussion of tax issues in this country is given below. Nevertheless, whatever your home country is, you are encouraged to become familiar with the appropriate regulations and to consult with a tax adviser.

As would be expected for an expatriate, there are several additional complications in filing tax forms. Through your working years, you have most likely developed an understanding of the U.S. tax system (!) and become familiar with completing the forms and filing your own tax forms. Taxation issues associated with an international assignment are an incredible nightmare, complete with forms and rules you never even knew existed (see Checklist 14, Appendix A). Consultation with a qualified tax specialist and subsequent tax preparation during your assignment should be a mandatory benefit of any expatriate package. If not possible, it would still be money well spent to hire a specialist yourself. Nevertheless, you should be familiar with the tax code as it applies to U.S. expatriates.

The following paragraphs are an attempt to give a brief overview and to acquaint you with some tax issues and implications you will face while overseas. They are not intended to be a replacement for proper tax advice, and you are again strongly encouraged to seek professional guidance. It is also important to realize that tax laws are continually being revised, and changes to the system will most likely occur in the future. Some information included in this section, therefore, could likely be revised by the IRS.

Introduction

All U.S. citizens who work overseas must file U.S. income-tax returns, even if they can exclude all of their earned incomes.

A good starting point to familiarize yourself with the tax issues is to consult Publication 54: *A Guide for U.S. Citizens and Resident Aliens Abroad.* This can be obtained free of charge from the IRS. This publication discusses the special rules for U.S. citizens who work abroad. You can also call the IRS hot line or visit the IRS Internet home page (see Resource 1, Appendix C).

Make sure you bring all pertinent tax data and documentation with you, including past tax returns. While you are moving, keep records of your moving expenses and home sale. Even if you have a professional tax adviser fill out your returns, you must supply all the information.

General rules and conditions

One of the first things you should do regarding taxes is to notify the IRS of your address change. Obtain and submit Form 8822: "Change of Address" to the IRS before moving overseas.

If you must pay tax on your foreign income to a foreign country that has a tax treaty with the United States, you will be entitled to certain benefits under this treaty. These include, but are not limited to, special status for teachers and students, exemption from income tax on certain income, and tax-credit provisions. See Publication 54 for the list of countries that have tax treaties or conventions with the United States.

Your income-tax returns are due on April 15. Even if you do not have a U.S. tax to pay, you must file a return. If both your tax home and your abode are outside the United States, an automatic extension is granted to June 15 for *filing* the return. Further, you can file Form 4868: "Application for Automatic Extension of Time to File U.S. Individual Income Tax Return" before April 15 to give a further automatic extension to August 15. It is a good idea to attach a note to your tax form that says "taxpayer abroad" so the IRS employee who gets your return after April 15 does not penalize you for filing late. All taxes and penalties, though, are due on April 15. Interest will be charged on the return from April 15. There is no free lunch!

While overseas, if you can claim certain income exclusions, you should file your return with the **Internal Revenue Service (IRS) Philadelphia Service Center.** In some foreign countries, you can file your return at the U.S. embassy.

As a United States citizen, you are required to file your federal income tax and pay any taxes on your worldwide income, regardless of where you live or where the income is paid.

As mentioned earlier, the United States has tax treaties with many countries that will offset the potential for double taxation. You will be required to pay foreign taxes to your host country. Different tax-year periods, tax on worldwide income versus income only locally sourced, and tax rates are only some complications involved. Again, you will need to consult a tax professional who specializes in the host-country tax system. The U.S. federal tax rate is lower than many countries, so most of the tax paid will be to the foreign country.

The tax policy is designed to ensure that a taxpayer is not subject to both foreign tax and U.S. tax on the same dollar of income. The foreign-tax credit alleviates this double taxation. In essence, this credit is a dollar-for-dollar tax credit which reduces the U.S. tax.

Tax equalization is one important concept you must explore with your employer to learn if this is a benefit included in your expatriate package. If part of your relocation package includes the payment of foreign taxes, your company will equalize your taxes. The general objective of most expatriate packages is that the employee should be no better or worse off (in terms of the tax liability on base salary) because of the foreign assignment. This policy is designed to protect an expatriate from any adverse tax consequences resulting from a foreign assignment.

Under a typical tax-equalization policy, the employer guarantees to the expatriate employee that he or she will pay the same amount of tax while on foreign assignment as the employee would have paid in the home country (Relocation Tax Service, 1998). The underlying theory of tax equalization is that the expatriate assignment should be tax neutral (i.e., there should be no tax benefit or detriment) to the employee.

The basic mechanics of the tax-equalization policy is that during the year, a hypothetical tax is deducted from your monthly salary. In return, the company will pay all the actual U.S. and foreign income taxes you owe during the foreign assignment. At the end of the tax year, after the tax return is prepared, a tax-equalization calculation is prepared, comparing the tax you would have paid if you had resided in your home country and the total hypothetical tax you paid out during the year. The difference is the amount owed to or from you. You will owe any taxes related to other income, such as capital gains and dividend payments. If your company has a tax-equalization policy, you should work with your company to obtain specific details.

Sometimes you may have to pay an estimated tax for the year. The requirements for determining if you must pay the tax are the same as for a taxpayer in the United States. Payments can be made on a quarterly basis. See Publication 505: *Tax Withholding and Estimated Tax* for more information. Again, consult your tax specialist.

Another tax that you may be exposed to is the alternative minimum tax. The purpose is to ensure that high-income taxpayers pay a minimum amount of tax on their economic incomes. Publication 909: *Alternative Minimum Tax for Individuals* and the related Form 6251: "Alternative Minimum Tax — Individuals" have more details.

One important issue that you must consider is the location of your tax home.
If you meet the necessary requirements, you will qualify for the foreign earned-income exclusion or deduction.

Your tax home is defined by the IRS as the general area of your main place of business or employment, no matter where you maintain your family home. Further, the location of your tax home often depends on whether your assignment is temporary or indefinite. A temporary assignment entitles you to deduct your expenses away from the United States (i.e., travel, meals, and lodging) but not to qualify for the foreign earned-income exclusion.

An assignment is considered indefinite if your employment in the foreign country is longer than one year. This may entitle you to claim the exclusion but not to deduct related expenses. An indefinite assignment will in essence qualify you for the "bona fide residence test." This is a fancy term coined by the IRS declaring that the location of your tax home is in a foreign country, that you intend to remain there indefinitely or for a prolonged period, and that you intend to make your home in that country.

The second determination you must make is how long you are working in the foreign country. To qualify, you must be physically present in the foreign country for 330 days. The qualifying days do not have to be consecutive. This is known as the "physical-presence test." This test is concerned only with how long you stay in a foreign country or countries. It does not depend on the kind of residence you establish, your intentions about returning, or the nature and purpose of your stay abroad. However, your intentions regarding the nature and purpose of your stay abroad are relevant in determining whether you meet the tax-home test.

Note that to meet the requirements of both tests, you must live in or be present in a foreign country. This is different from your "domicile," which is your permanent home and the place to which you always return or intend to return. As always, there are certain exceptions to the test. Consult Publication 54 or your tax specialist.

There are three main income exclusions that you may claim if your tax home is in a foreign country and you meet the bona fide residence test or the physical-presence test:

- foreign earned-income exclusion (currently as much as $72,000 per year)
- foreign housing exclusion (or deduction)
- expenses relating to overseas assignment (i.e., moving expenses — deduction; foreign income taxes — credit or deduction)

There are many provisions resulting to the application of these credits and deductions. Note also that the only income that qualifies for the income exclusions is income from the performance of services abroad. Investment income, including income from foreign investments, is not earned income.

Forms 1116: "Foreign Tax Credit," 2555: "Foreign Earned Income," and 3903-F: "Foreign Moving Expenses" are all related to these income exclusions and deductions.

A major tax consideration that you will be confronted with when transferring overseas is what to do with the home you own.

Your decision will be based on both financial and emotional reasons. Questions you need to ask include: Do I intend to return to my house after the assignment? Can I afford to rent my property? Am I prepared to be a long-distance landlord?

There are two major issues to consider when either selling or renting your home in the United States. Consult Publication 523: *Tax Information on Selling Your Home* for more information. For any principal residence sold, there is a capital-gains exemption of $500,000 (if married, filing jointly) as long as the taxpayer or spouse has used the house as a main residence for at least two of the five years prior to sale. The exemption is reduced if this condition is not met. You will still be required to complete Form 2119: "Sale of Your Home" if you sell your house.

Normally, you cannot postpone tax on the gain of a rental property, even if it was once used as your home. Yet in the view of the IRS, you have *not* changed your home to a rental property if you *temporarily* rent out your old home before selling it as a matter of convenience or for another nonbusiness purpose. Unfortunately, the law is significantly vague when dealing with this issue for people transferring overseas, and it is therefore not a straightforward issue.

If you have placed your home on the real estate market *before* you transfer overseas, are unsuccessful in selling it, and subsequently rent out the property, your home should be considered by the IRS to be your principal home. This should qualify for suspending the tax on your gain. The income, expenses, and related home depreciation will be considered as they would be for a normal rental property for tax purposes. Given the ambiguity of the law, you are strongly advised to consult a tax adviser.

While you are on a foreign assignment, you may need to refer to certain tax documents.

You should take the following documents with you:

- copies of federal and state tax returns for the prior three years
- copies of Social Security cards
- records of the cost basis of your home, investments, and other assets
- closing statements from the sale of your house
- records of all outstanding loans

During the assignment, you will want to make sure that you keep accurate records of all relocation expenses and expenses related to your foreign housing costs, and have all supporting receipts.

Social Security and Medicare taxes

In general, U.S. Social Security and Medicare taxes apply to payments of wages for services performed as an employee. The

United States, however, has reached agreements with several foreign countries to coordinate Social Security coverage and taxation. Under these agreements, dual coverage and dual contributions (i.e., taxes) for the same work are eliminated. The agreements generally make sure that Social Security taxes are paid to only one country. More information can be obtained from the United States Social Security Administration and Publication 54. You can also request from the SSA the form "Request for Earnings and Benefit Estimate Statement." The SSA can be reached by mail, telephone, or the Internet (see Resource 1, Appendix C). After you return this completed form, the government will send you a statement outlining your Social Security benefits at retirement.

Foreign accounts

All U.S. citizens must file annual reports with the U.S. Treasury Department if they hold or have an interest in foreign accounts if the aggregate value of these accounts exceeds $10,000. If you qualify, you must file Form TD F 90-22.1 by June 30 of the following year.

Investments

One benefit of living overseas is better access to global markets, particularly those in the area of your posting. International investing is increasing dramatically, and you will now have a good opportunity to tap into these markets.

Depending on the relocation package offered by your employer, you can probably save additional money. The goal of your assignment and related acceptance should not be based *solely* on the ability to "save money." It can certainly be a side benefit, but most packages will not be large enough to offset the challenges if that is the only reason for going. Your daily living costs will be higher, and on repatriation, you will incur costs that you would not ordinary have all at once (see Chapter 16).

To help you build your savings and prepare for repatriation, careful financial planning is essential. You may want to take this opportunity to consult a financial planner who specializes in advising expatriates if you do not feel comfortable in managing your funds. **The International Association of Financial Planning** can assist you in finding a professional financial planner (see Resource 1, Appendix C).

Although you will have access to financial news, investment management can be more inconvenient from overseas. Perhaps one benefit is that you will have the tendency to purchase investments for the long term and therefore not get caught up in making hasty decisions based on short-term situations.

You may feel it is appropriate to hire a professional to take care of and manage your finances. There are also several discount brokerage firms at which you can deposit your funds and make investments over the telephone. Many of them have Internet sites and allow you to make trades electronically.

The financial issues related to an overseas assignment can be considerable.

Often, financial and tax advisers can greatly simplify your financial situation. It is important to actively manage your cash and investments. You will need to balance your home and host-country cash flows. Taxation, in almost all countries, is a complex matter. Although you should consult a qualified tax adviser, it is beneficial for you to understand the issues.

Chapter 7 (at a glance)
Medical Concerns

In this chapter you will discover~

how to keep healthy in your host country, and what to do when you are not.

medical-coverage options when you are overseas.

Some key points ~

❶ Quality, difference in treatment methods, basic health standards, cost, and language problems are all medical issues the expatriate must confront.

② On your arrival in your host country, you will need to learn the local medical system and find a suitable family physician.

Chapter 7

MEDICAL CONCERNS

National health. I had heard many horror stories throughout the years and was skeptical of a large and bureaucratic government institution. But heck, it is worth a try. Surprisingly, our family has had quite good luck using the system. The doctors and staff seemed quite competent and well trained. The doctor's office seemed like one back home. The care we received was very good. And it was free!

So with this new experience, I went to have an elective operation on my eye. The whole idea of operating on my eye did not appeal to me in the first place, and I was a bit nervous about using the national health system. Anyway, I had myself put on a waiting list for the operation. Three months later, I received the scheduled date for my operation — smack-dab on my birthday! Ah, national health!

On the scheduled day, I entered the hospital at noon as requested, two hours before the operation. It was supposed to be a day surgery. Fortunately, I had brought a novel, and I sat and sat and sat. Of course, I was not to eat or drink anything before the operation. There was not much to the waiting room, and only a few of the normal hospital waiting-room magazines. Finally, after about three hours, the surgeon (whom I had never met before) called me for a preoperative examination. He could not find an empty room, so he took his keys out and opened a door. It was to a library. He sat me down on a couch, surrounded by books and clutter. He did a quick check and then left. I went back to my uncomfortable waiting room.

I sat and sat and sat. Fortunately, my novel was a Tom Clancy (i.e., several hundred pages long). At this point, I began to feel very unsure about the whole ordeal. I thought long and hard about just walking out and forget-

ting the whole thing. I didn't like the idea of an eye operation anyway, and I certainly was very uncomfortable, to
say the least, with my surroundings.

But I didn't give it up. At about 5 P.M., a nurse took me
to my room and told me to put on the hospital gown. The
room was an interesting sight, right out of a 1950s movie
set, except the TV was a color one. Vinyl floors, hospital
beds, no decor. You first walked past the women's room,
and then next door is the men's. Eight people sharing a
room, no privacy. Given the nature of my operation (i.e.,
eye), all the people were in the prime of their lives —
average age probably about seventy. I certainly spiked
that average. It was not a pretty sight. I changed, watched
someone's teeth fall out, and stuck my head in my novel.

After six hours of waiting, they came for me. I was
about to get dressed and sneak out. They wheeled me into
the operating room, and the next thing I remember, I was
waking up with seven old men looking at me.

Well, the operation was indeed a success. And since it
was a late hour, they said I could spend the night if I wanted. The gentle snoring of the men and my own grogginess
convinced me to stay.

The next morning, after the surgeon and my eye doctor
came to check on me (pronouncing a successful operation), I got dressed and waved good-bye to my colleagues.
I went to the front desk to check out, and asked what I
needed to pay. Get this. I had walked in the day before,
had not signed any papers or registered or shown any
insurance documents or shown any "if you die here, we
are not responsible" forms. This morning the lady looked
at me as if I were from outer space. "Sign something, pay
something? Why?" I was free to leave. I had not paid one
pence for anything.

Postscript: Perhaps my surroundings were not the Ritz,
but the care, the professionalism, and the operating room
were all first-rate. And that is all that truly matters. And
heck, I even had a color TV!

No matter what your destination is, traveling abroad poses risks to your family's health. Quality, difference in treatment methods, basic health standards, cost, and language problems are all medical issues the expatriate must confront. You are used to having your own doctors and a familiarity with the medical professionals, procedures, and system. These differences can heighten the anxiety of expatriates when dealing with medical issues overseas.

Health issues and the availability of quality medical care are concerns that are paramount to expatriates, particularly those moving to "developing" countries.

Your company's expatriate package will often determine the level of your apprehension.

If your company maintains health insurance for you and your family, you will always have access to high-quality medical care overseas. You can probably tap into local private care, and if a serious condition arises, you will be able to immediately return to your home country for treatment. As an expatriate, you also can control your living conditions to enable you to maintain a relatively healthy family environment, even in difficult conditions.

On your arrival in your host country, you will need to learn the local medical system and find a suitable family physician. Do not wait until you need a doctor! Medical systems vary from country to country, but many have some form of national health insurance for the whole population. The quality and service of the system vary considerably. Some countries have an excellent health system that you will want to use. In others, you will want to avoid the national health system and use private care. Talk to other expatriates and local professionals to help learn the best approach for your family and to get references for quality doctors. Many foreign communities have well-trained physicians who speak English and are familiar with the U.S. style of health care.

A physical examination for each family member before you depart on your assignment is often company policy and is highly recommended. It should include physical, dental, and eye examinations. Obtain a copy of your medical records and the appropriate addresses and telephone numbers so you can contact your current doctors if necessary.

If you have any special medications or dietary needs, check the availability in the host country. Unless you can definitely obtain the medicines or an equivalent, take an extra supply and provide for a method to obtain refills. You will need to check the local regulations, though, for transporting medicines. An accompanying letter from your doctor describing the medicines can be helpful. Local pharmacists are often highly trained and can help you to obtain equivalent medications (sometimes even without a prescription from a doctor).

Determine your coverage before you go overseas. Many insurance policies cover you and your family overseas. Do not worry too much about insurance when seeking medical care abroad. Most foreign hospitals do not require you to fill out insurance forms before caring for you. Get the treatment first, and get a detailed bill when you leave to file your insurance claim.

Below are some tips to maintaining a healthy and secure life in an overseas posting

(see Checklist 15, Appendix A):

Common health problems and diseases

Become aware of the common health problems and diseases that exist in the host country. Familiarize yourself with their causes and symptoms, and know the appropriate precautions. In some "developing" countries, health-care considerations are much greater, and you will have to investigate options available and precautions needed. Talk with other expatriates, your personal physician, your embassy or consulate, and medical authorities. If you are posted to a country in the tropics (e.g., Africa, Southeast Asia, South America, or Central America), you will want to take particular care.

Immunizations

Make sure your routine immunizations and specifically recommended inoculations for the area are all up-to-date for the whole family. A routine medical examination for each family member is advisable. Note that some vaccinations must be given over a period of time. **The International Traveler's Hotline at the Centers for Disease Control** (see Resource 1, Appendix C) can provide you with current information on required immunizations, diseases, and epidemics in foreign countries. All your medical and immunization records should be brought with you and filed in a convenient location. Retain your current doctors' addresses and telephone numbers. Consider giving your medical specialists written permission before you leave to forward all your medical records to your new doctor.

Blood type

Be sure to know each family member's blood type.

Medical insurance

Confirm that you have sufficient medical insurance coverage for your time overseas. Find out what the local procedures are for medical payment. All countries have different formats. For example, if you are posted to an EU country, you may be entitled to free coverage under its national health program if you meet certain requirements. In other countries such as the United States, you will be obliged to pay for your medical services and reclaim the money from your insurance coverage.

Consult your employer to understand the coverage and procedure for claiming expenses. If you need insurance forms, make sure you take a large quantity with you. Get the phone number of your insurance company's customer service.

Physicians

Seek out appropriate physicians and pediatricians as soon as possible after arriving in the host country, *before* you need them. Local expatriates and nationals can be a good source of recommendations of quality doctors and medical care. You can call the **International Association for Medical Assistance to Travelers** (see Resource 1, Appendix C) to obtain a listing of English-speaking physicians in foreign countries. Prepare a list of telephone numbers of your local doctor and emergency facilities. Familiarize yourself with the location of the nearest hospital and emergency center.

Local medical procedures

Become familiar with the local medical procedures and the system. Each country has a different medical style and service, and you need to know the differences and what is important to you. Identify any special health needs of family members, and find out whether they will be adequately supported in the host culture and environment.

Emergency procedures

Learn and practice your own emergency procedures. Find out how to call the local emergency resources (e.g., police, fire, and ambulance), and post the phone numbers in a readily accessible place. Know where the nearest hospital and emergency room are located, and practice getting to them. If the language is a problem, prepare a list of necessary words and phrases. Often, your local embassy or consulate can assist in contacting medical professionals. There are also private organizations that assist people living overseas with telephone advice, referrals, and full-scale international evacuations through a worldwide network of medical personnel.

If the area is subject to natural disasters (e.g., earthquakes, floods, hurricanes, or tornadoes), familiarize yourself with the necessary safety precautions and emergency procedures. Be prepared.

Home medical care

Prepare an adequate home medical kit. Include basic medicines and medical supplies. Include any special cold medicines for your children. You may be able to purchase them locally, but others may not be available or are different from what you are used to back home. With any medicines that you do purchase beforehand, make sure you are aware of the expiration dates. This kit will ensure that you are prepared as you begin your assignment. You will then have time to replenish your supply with local varieties or on trips to your home country.

Know the generic or chemical name for any of your medications. Some may have different names, but a doctor can always look them up. For example, acetaminophen (e.g., Tylenol brand) goes by *paracetemol* in Europe. Note that prescription drugs in one country may be obtained over the counter in another, and vice versa. Prescription medications can be mistakenly viewed as illicit drugs, so they must be labeled in a manner that is acceptable to the customs officials of the host country. In many countries, pharmacies remain open beyond normal hours or even all night.

Have your prescription for glasses and contact lenses. Take an extra pair of glasses and/or contact lenses. Also take enough contact solution to last until you can find a suitable replacement product.

Emergency travel kit

Prepare an emergency travel kit that includes all the appropriate supplies and medicines. Many of these kits can be purchased already assembled, but they are much more expensive than creating your own. By putting together your own, you can stylize your kit to your own needs. Your current doctor can advise you on additional supplies to include.

The kit should contain at least: topical antibiotic, various sized bandages, sterile dressing and tape, eye pad, disinfectant, antiseptic wipes, scissors, tweezers, safety pins, sunscreen lotion, thermometer, and lotion for sunburn and bites. Medication to include are: aspirin (and acetaminophen, if you have children), tablets for indigestion, medicine for diarrhea, medicine for motion sickness, medicine for malaria (if appropriate), and tablets for water purification (if appropriate).

Health-care manual

Purchase a good manual on health care that covers home diagnosis and suggested treatments. You should not use such a manual as a substitute for quality medical care, but rather for gaining an understanding of symptoms and possible causes when they occur. If you have children, you will also want to have appropriate books on child care, including medical, emotional, and developmental issues. If you are considering starting a family while overseas, purchase books on pregnancy and newborns.

Healthy home environment

Make sure you maintain a healthy environment in your house, particularly when living in a "developing" country. Be aware that issues of safety and construction are not always up to modern standards.

Safety and accident prevention

Make sure you are familiar with common safety and accident-prevention methods. You may want to take a first-aid course before leaving your home country. Make sure you have smoke detectors and fire extinguishers installed. Check to see if they are available to purchase in the host country, and if not, take them with you. One note of caution: Most countries run equipment on a current of 220–240 volts, which can be significantly more dangerous than the U.S. standard of 110 volts. You must guard against the danger of electric shock.

Food and water safety

Be aware of the need for and appropriate practices for maintaining healthy water and food supplies. For example, in some countries, the water supply may be contaminated, which requires boiling and filtering of water. Where appropriate, avoid vegetables that may have been washed in contaminated water; peel your fruit; make sure meat, fish, and poultry have been well cooked; and avoid street-vendor food. In some locations, vegetables and fruit must be soaked five to ten minutes in a disinfectant solution before they are eaten.

Healthy body

Maintain a healthy body. Rest, a proper and balanced diet, and exercise are all essential to staying healthy. Do not forget your emotional well-being. Your new assignment will bring about many new stresses, and it is easy to ignore the basic rules of good health.

Household help

If you have household helpers, take an active interest in their health and hygiene, because they will directly affect those of your families. Before employing household aides, send them for a comprehensive physical examination at your own expense. If they become ill during employment, medical care should be provided promptly and under your supervision. Insist that they abide by your health standards for cleanliness and food care. To encourage healthy practices, supply your employees with suitable articles such as soap, toothbrush, and clean clothes, if needed.

Maintaining a healthy environment is possible when you live overseas, but it may require you to take an active role.

Quality care is available in most locations. It is important, though, that you become familiar with the local medical and emergency systems. Make sure to have up-to-date information on local health conditions and hazards.

Chapter 8 (at a glance)

Security

In this chapter you will discern ~

how to keep safe and secure in your new location.

the common unlawful incidents in
foreign countries — how to protect yourself.

how to reduce your exposure to terrorist activities.

Some key points ~

❶ Compared with the United States, most countries do not
have many violent incidents involved in everyday life.

② The main problem a foreigner faces in confronting
common crime is lack of knowledge.

❸ Careful planning and precautions should reduce any
encounter with terrorist activities.

④ Review your security practices, and remain alert to any
conflict that may result in retaliation against your country and its citizens abroad.

❺ Using common sense and being aware of your surroundings are your best defenses against crime and
terrorism.

Chapter 8

SECURITY

England is a relatively safe place. The locals constantly complain about how the country is "not like it used to be," but in comparison with the United States, the risk of dangerous crime is very small.

Still, your basic house break-in and theft are common. I remember returning from a holiday to find my window boarded up and shards of glass scattered on the carpet. A note was left for me to call my neighbor. It did not take long to figure it out.

Well, my neighbor had heard a suspicious noise and had gone to check it out. In the process, she must have scared the burglars away, and she noticed the break-in. She called the police, cleaned up the mess, and had the window boarded up.

A few days after my return, the police came to interview me and brought along the fingerprint specialist. I was touched but stunned that they would take a routine theft so seriously. It felt like living in a small town in America. They were all so pleasant and professional. Of course, I did not expect anything to come of it. I did, however, receive a phone call from them a little later, saying that they had recovered some of my belongings (nonvaluables) in a local bar.

Exactly one year later, I received a letter from the local police department saying that I would be pleased to know that they had apprehended the criminals who had broken into my house. Although they did not recover any of the goods, they still wanted to let me know of their success.

Laws in most countries regarding conventional criminal behavior (i.e., bodily harm, theft, illegal substances, etc.) are relatively similar. Differences in punishment can vary widely, and being a foreigner does not exempt you from the host country's criminal-justice system. For instance, in Saudi Arabia, the punishment for theft is to cut off the criminal's hand, and capital crimes are punished by public beheading (Morrison et al., 1994). There are also laws that apply in the host country but would never be considered an infraction in the your home country. One example is the dress requirement, especially for women, in Muslim countries.

An expatriate is exposed to two types of crime when overseas — common unlawful incidents and terrorism (Piet-Pelon and Hornby, 1992). Each category has its own characteristics that affect an expatriate. In almost all cases, common sense is your best defense.

Fortunately, most countries do not have many violent incidents in everyday life.

Firearms are greatly restricted in many countries, as compared with the United States, so the threat of bodily harm is small. Unfortunately, violent crimes are on the increase in many countries, but still, the incidents (statistically) are much less common than in the United States.

Petty theft is prevalent in many countries.

A foreigner is perceived as a wealthy and easy target. You should always take the same precautions you would at home. Many expatriates, particularly those who live in cities, are cautious and "street-smart." This attitude should be very beneficial while you are abroad. Do not carry large sums of cash (yet always carry a small amount of local currency), and reduce the number of credit cards you carry.

Make a photocopy of the contents of your wallet, including the telephone numbers for lost or stolen credit cards. Most accounts will make you liable for only a small amount if you have reported your card stolen. When you are out, remember to guard your belongings and never leave them unattended. Airports, train stations, buses, and tourist attractions are common areas that thieves frequent.

To guard against pickpockets, women should carry handbags securely (i.e., around their chest instead of on the shoulder), and men should put their wallets in front pants pockets or inside jackets. Be alert to jostling in crowds and other attempts to distract you. To guard against thieves on motorcycles, walk on the inside of sidewalks, with watches and handbags away from the street side. Always look confident and as though you know where you are going when you walk around a city. Avoid the lost and dazed "tourist" look; tourists are common targets.

A common problem foreigners have is not knowing which areas to avoid. This is true in all cities but is more difficult in a foreign location. Before wandering around, talk with local nationals and expatriates to learn which areas are not appropriate. A knowledge of your local surroundings is essential, coupled with much common sense. Avoid bars and nightclubs until you are familiar with the area.

Another issue foreigners can face in foreign cities is "passive" theft, or cheating. Overcharging, extra charges, and other forms of cheating are all problems that an expatriate can face, particularly if there are language differences. In countries where bargaining is the accepted way of doing business and shopping, an expatriate unfamiliar with such a system can often be taken advantage of and pay more for goods than warranted. Being aware and observant is your best defense. Talk with your host national colleagues to find out the best practice. Do not be too upset if it happens to you; it even happens to the locals! Never exchange currency in the street or on the black market.

Always check receipts. For example, in Chile and Italy, it is illegal not to have a receipt after purchasing something, whether it is merchandise or food. When a receipt is not issued, it most likely implies that the merchant is not declaring the sale for tax purposes. These countries have special police that control this problem. If you are caught leaving the store without a receipt, both you and the store owner will be fined. If you are not given a proper receipt, ask for one.

To reduce the incidence of household intruders — also a common concern overseas — again, both common sense and a local knowledge of your surroundings are essential. Of course, the normal procedures — such as keeping the house secure and well lighted, canceling deliveries while you are out of town, having adequate locks and using them, and having neighbors watch your house — all go without saying. Depending on the potential magnitude of the problem, the installation of alarms, metal screens on windows, high walls, and security guards may be necessary. The need for these more extreme deterrents can be decided by observing what others around you are using.

Women should take the same precautions they would at home. Being aware of surroundings, avoiding dark or lonely areas, and keeping alert to potentially dangerous situations are all effective strategies. Some countries, particularly in the Middle East, will hold a woman responsible for any assault that may befall her if she dresses "provocatively" (de Kieffer, 1993).

There are several security measures you should observe when driving.

- Make sure your car is in good repair.
- Keep car doors locked at all times.
- Obey all traffic laws.
- Always wear seat belts.
- Never drink and drive.
- Avoid traveling alone at night.
- Avoid narrow alleys, poorly lighted streets, and suspect "shortcuts."
- Do not leave valuables in the car.
- Never pick up hitchhikers.
- Do not get out of the car if suspicious-looking individuals are nearby.
- If the police stop you, always be courteous and responsive to their questions.

One area that deserves special mention involves automobiles and roads. In some countries, you may be encouraged not to drive, such as in case of extreme traffic or liability concerns. For example, in some countries, if an expatriate is involved in an accident, even if he is not at fault, he will be considered by the authorities to be the guilty party. In these cases, your company often will provide you with a driver.

Where you are able to drive, make sure you understand the "rules of the road." Learn both the laws and customs pertaining to driving. Some countries have obvious differences, such as driving on the left side of the road, and you must be aware of these. "Roundabouts" (traffic circles) are also common in many countries, and you need to learn how to successfully navigate around them. Consider taking private driving lessons.

Although some countries have, by most standards, an incredibly controlled and organized (and some might say boring!) set of rules, many foreign countries seem a chaotic mess and free-for-all. Surprisingly enough, there is some sort of system, however disorganized it may appear! Whatever the case, *if appropriate,* do not be totally intimidated or avoid driving. Rather, take to the roads slowly, becoming accustomed to the driving styles and techniques. Ask a colleague to take you around.

Make a special point of finding out and adhering to the drinking-and-driving rules, because they can be quite strict. For example, in some countries, such as Norway, driving after having had only one drink is a serious infraction resulting in a large fine, loss of driver's license, and possibly a jail sentence. Police may stop drivers at random and require them to submit to alcohol tests. Bottom line — don't drink and drive.

Make sure you always wear your seat belt, have necessary driving documents, and are properly insured.

Off the road, as a pedestrian, you must take extra caution. *In practice,* the pedestrian *never* has the right of way in most countries. At crosswalks and signals, do not assume the car will stop. On the other hand, you will need to be somewhat offensive and "challenge" the car (always making sure that you are not directly in the way!). Often, drivers will try to "challenge" you by accelerating when they see you trying to cross the street! Usually, though, they will grudgingly stop or just weave behind you to let you cross. Make extra sure that your children understand the dangers, and never let them cross by themselves or play around the street. Happily, most drivers do seem to respect children and will stop to let them cross.

Both as a driver and a pedestrian, you must be aware of all the dangers and obstacles, but do not let them restrict your movements. The loss of freedom will only contribute to your frustration and loneliness.

Often, countries strictly forbid the possession of certain items.

Foreigners need to confront and accept the seemingly excessive punishments for criminal activities. Cutting off a hand for theft (Middle East), flogging for minor offenses (Far East), the death penalty for illegal drugs (Far East), and tolerated "honor killings" of women for having committed adultery (Middle East and Latin America) are common forms of punishments that many Westerners would feel are excessive, if not barbaric, considering the crimes. In some cultures, a woman who is raped is considered to be at fault. The apparent shame caused to her family can even result in her being sentenced to death.

Avoid all contact with and use of illicit drugs. Drug offenses are regarded seriously overseas. Even constitutional protections that we take for granted are simply not present. Penalties can include anything up to the death sentence in some countries such as Saudi Arabia, Malaysia, Singapore, Turkey, and Thailand (de Kieffer, 1993).

The main concern a foreigner faces in confronting common crime is lack of knowledge.

Terrorism, on the other hand, is a criminal activity that is mostly out of your control. Terrorism is frightening and even life threatening. Given your status overseas, it can also make you and your family a direct target in some countries.

There are in essence two types of terrorism — political or religious terrorism directed at the host country (e.g., IRA conflict in Great Britain) and terrorism directed against your home country. With the former, you are a random target; with the latter, you are a direct target.

Terrorist activity is on the rise all over the world, and you certainly cannot prevent it. You can take active steps to reduce your exposure and risks. For example, the U.S. Department of State cautions American citizens worldwide to remain vigilant with regard to personal safety. State Department officials advise Americans abroad to take appropriate steps to increase their security awareness. They recommend maintaining a low profile, varying routes and times for all travel, and treating mail from unfamiliar sources with suspicion. This advice is suggested for all expatriates abroad, regardless of nationality. You are urged to review your security practices and to remain alert to any conflict that may result in retaliation against your country or citizens abroad.

- Know the type of terrorist activity you could be exposed to in your host country and any places you plan to visit. Consult the **Bureau of Consular Affairs** in the U.S. State Department (see Resource 1, Appendix C) for information on your host country and the potential problems you may encounter. This federal organization provides current travel warnings. Your company should also be helpful in informing you.
- Avoid or reduce exposure to high-risk areas (e.g., airport terminals, crowded public places, bars, restaurants, and embassies), particularly places where Westerners congregate.
- Vary your route or schedule in countries where you could be a direct target. Avoid predictable times and routes of travel.
- Avoid dangerous or strange situations. Be wary of strangers who approach you.
- Do not look for trouble. Avoid the black-market economy, including purchasing items at unrealistically low prices or exchanging moneys at low rates.
- Do not carry firearms into areas of political unrest. In times of civil strife, the best protection you may have is your neutral status. If people with guns are unsure of your loyalties, your carrying a weapon can only further jeopardize your safety.
- Be cautious about what you discuss with (or what can be overheard by) strangers. Do not talk about your plans or itinerary. Keep your political and religious opinions to yourself.

- Avoid luggage tags, clothing, and behavior that can identify you as a foreigner.
- Keep a mental note of safe havens, such as embassies, police stations, hotels, and hospitals.
- Refuse unidentified packages.
- Continually contact your embassy for an update on terrorist activity.
- Have an evacuation plan, including easy access to cash and critical documents.
- Most of all, *use your common sense and be aware.*

Careful planning and precautions should minimize any encounter with terrorist activities.

The security of you and your family is always a concern.

For expatriates, particularly in certain locations, these concerns may be heightened. Careful planning and awareness will usually reduce the risks. Although expatriates can be specific targets, because of ignorance or wealthy status, most potential risks are no greater than in one's home country. Terrorism can be a problem in certain countries. Again, take certain precautions to reduce your exposure and risks. Common sense, awareness of surroundings, active preparation for an emergency (e.g., national disaster or civil unrest), and avoidance of obvious risks are your best defenses against crime and terrorism. Always review your security practices, and remain alert to any worldwide conflict that may result in security risks.

Chapter 9 (at a glance)

Culture Shock

In this chapter you will learn about ~

culture shock and the psychological and behavioral reactions to the phenomenon.

the definition of "culture shock."

the stages of culture shock.

possible psychological and behavioral reactions to culture shock.

the effects of culture shock on family and children.

effective adapting techniques for culture shock.

Some key points ~

❶ The differences and disorientation you encounter because of living in a foreign environment, and the resulting anxiety and stress, are what make up "culture shock."

② Culture shock in itself is not bad; rather, it is the individual's reaction to the issue.

❸ Nearly all expatriates suffer some degree of culture shock when going to a new country.

④ There are five stages of the culture-shock experience. The stages are both cyclical and predictable.

❺ The reactions to culture shock are very individualistic.

⑥ Change, uncertainty, and unsettledness are all part of being an expatriate.

❼ There are several effective techniques to help you handle your reactions to culture shock.

Chapter 9

CULTURE SHOCK

One of the main things an expatriate must confront when going overseas is the huge contrast in customer service. America is known throughout the world for its excellent and friendly approach to service. We have grown accustomed to it, and we expect it. Yet when we go to other countries, we are in for a shock.

The first thing one notices are that everything seems to take three times as long and involves as many trips to accomplish the task. Second, rather than being greeted by a friendly and helpful person, more often you will find someone who does not want to be bothered.

The other day, I went to the bank to do some routine transactions. My grasp of the local language is adequate, but certainly not fluent. After waiting in line for many minutes, I got to the counter to be faced by someone who clearly did not seem to enjoy his job. First, he abruptly and rudely told me that I had filled the form out incorrectly (I hadn't). He clearly did not want to help. Basically, he said I was stupid and to go away. The other transaction I wanted to do could not be done because "the computers are down" (that had been the same story the previous time I was in the bank).

I had entered the bank in a relatively good mood. I left feeling angry, frustrated, and inadequate. When I got home, I received a call from a friend back in the States, and I related my frustrating experience. She seemed surprised and even a bit disappointed in me. She perceived that my posting overseas was like an extended holiday, lacking any of the normal difficulties. She could not comprehend that I would have any problems. It is then that you realize that you have even lost your support system *from home because people do not understand you anymore.*

Moving to another country will mean giving up much that is familiar to you. This can lead to feelings of insecurity and helplessness. Simple tasks that are taken for granted, such as grocery shopping and going to the bank, become at the very least a challenge, and at worst a traumatic experience. Everyday tasks that are second nature to you will now involve having to learn new rules of social behavior.

Culture is the total way of life of society, and it includes everything that a group of people thinks, says, does, and makes.

It is learned and transmitted from generation to generation, shaping attitudes and responses. This culture enables society to meet its needs. Although people's needs are similar, it is inevitable that different groups will come up with different sets of solutions. For example, religion and government vary from culture to culture.

There are no intrinsically right or wrong solutions, no better or worse ones. Rather, they are just different ones. Logically, however, each society will believe that its way of solving problems is superior. This ethnocentric belief is passed along through the society. For the society to function properly, it is important that the society believes that its culture is overall the best *for itself.* It seems logical, then, that when you encounter other cultures and ways of solving problems, you will be disoriented.

The differences and disorientation you encounter because of living in a foreign environment — and the resulting anxiety and stress — are what make up *culture shock* (Munton et al., 1993). The *culture* represents the new way of life to which you are exposed, and the *shock* is the physical and emotional responses to the differences encountered (Pascoe, 1992). Adapting to a new culture requires obtaining new and unfamiliar responses to old and familiar habits, which can be disturbing and stressful (Roman, 1992). The emotional weight of constantly confronting new and challenging experiences generates the symptoms associated with culture shock.

The obstacles encountered can be stimulating and refreshing changes that present new experiences and opportunities for personal growth and development. These cultural differences are part of the excitement and adventure of an international relocation. You will experience all sorts of new and different things that an ordinary tourist or businessperson would never face. Perhaps your experiences will feel like an escape from your current routine, yet these cultural differences can be a source of major anxiety.

As with stress, culture shock in itself is not bad. Rather, it is the individual's reaction that is the issue. A negative reaction to culture shock can be a debilitating experience leading to isolation and depression. Even the most experienced travelers or those with an open and positive attitude will have negative reactions to some cultural differences. It is therefore essential that individuals transferring to an overseas post have an understanding of the culture, customs, and language. They must learn appropriate adapting techniques to minimize the negative reactions to culture shock.

There are several challenges an expatriate may face during an assignment. These can include:

- the sudden encounter with so many new and different things
- culture shock
- stereotypes toward you that you encounter from local nationals
- feelings of isolation and loneliness
- communication problems, including language and cultural differences
- distance from relatives and friends, and bad news from home
- children's adjustment problems
- loss of spousal network and possibly career
- disappointed expectations

All of these obstacles can affect your perceptions and attitudes as an expatriate.

The relocation process is very complex and unique. There are potential hazards and complications, and the aim of this chapter is to educate and give adapting techniques, not to frighten you. This chapter examines the relocation process, from the offer of the job through the premove, move, and postmove periods and finally to repatriation. The effects of culture shock and the related reactions to the expatriates will be explored.

Our own culture deeply affects our thinking, behavior, and values.

When we live in a foreign country, we come into contact with a completely and often radically different set of rules. Not only have the rules changed, no one has bothered to give you a copy of the new rulebook!

Sometimes one does not even realize the importance of culture until confronted with another. Culture to humans is like water to a fish (Hodge, 1997). The fish never stops to reflect on what it means to live in the water and how important water is to its survival. It just swims and goes about its normal routine. If you take the fish out of water, though, the water will take on a whole new importance!

This contrast between the two cultures can be significant, and the experience is termed *culture shock* (Piet-Pelon and Hornby, 1992). Nearly *all* expatriates, no matter how worldly or well traveled they may be, suffer some degree of culture shock when going to a new country. The experience of culture shock is similar to that of the "fish out of water." A main difference, though, is that we can learn effective managing techniques and alter our behavior so we can successfully adapt to our new environment.

An emotional reaction occurs when you find yourself suddenly immersed in an unfamiliar environment (Coyle and Shortland, 1992). The shock comes from the fact that the vast range of experiences, values, attitudes, and habitual behaviors that guides and provides you with security, stability, and control in your life is not transferable to the new culture. Most of your previous experiences are now inadequate for dealing with your new situation. All the familiar signs and symbols of social interaction of your own culture that instinctively control your everyday behavior and that you have take for granted are not available. Different sets of attitudes, values, and behaviors govern life in the new culture. The differences are sometimes obvious and large and other times very subtle.

When you enter a foreign culture, the simplest communication or a normally straightforward task can suddenly become a major obstacle. Everything is different, and you can no longer rely on previous knowledge alone or predict how people will respond. Even cultures that outwardly appear similar to America or a country with the same language, such as Great Britain, have their differences. Your reactions can be exacerbated because you do not expect culture shock to be a problem in those countries.

Everyday activities such as shopping can become monumental tasks when nothing is recognizable, and you may be unable or too intimidated to ask for assistance. Consequently, you can feel out of place, frustrated, and anxious. Anger, frustration, irritability, resentment, disdain, anxiety, insecurity, and even depression are all emotional responses to culture shock. People's reactions and their intensity will differ markedly and unpredictably. Further, your own reactions to a particular event will not be consistent. Your current state of mind has a large influence on the reaction.

Culture shock occurs in phases, each with its own unique characteristics.

Social psychologists have identified stages which a person living overseas will encounter. Several different models of culture shock are presented in the literature, yet they are all relatively similar. Whether in three stages or six, the feelings and reactions are common to all stages. *The important concept of the culture-shock model is that the stages are more or less cyclical, with each stage preceding the next.* The number of stages and the labels associated with each are academic.

The stages tend to be distinct and predictable, although sometimes they can overlap. The duration within each is highly individualistic and cannot be generalized. It depends on your personality and situation. One stage can last for only an hour, or it can last the whole length of the assignment. Research and observations suggests that for a three-year expatriate assignment, the whole process of culture shock, from the first phase to the final adjustment phase, takes about eighteen to twenty-four months. *For an international relocation to be successful and rewarding, the employee and family need to effectively enter the final stage.*

Even after successfully reaching the final stage, you will continually cycle through the culture-shock process because external effects will trigger the process. After successfully completing the cycle, you will learn to reach the final stage more easily and quickly.

The culture-shock model presented here includes five stages: honeymoon, anxiety, rejection, regression, and adjustment.

A brief description of each stage is discussed below.

Honeymoon stage

This is the first stage of the culture-shock cycle. It is a period of excitement and anticipation. Most people begin their assignment with great expectations and a positive mind-set, even mild euphoria. Everything seems exotic, new, exciting, and interesting. You feel like a tourist on an extended holiday. You are also focused on and involved with settling in and creating a home. In addition, the concerns of planning, packing, and saying good-byes are all behind you.

This stage can last from one day to one year. Typically, though, this stage lasts only *one or two months.* The length of this period depends a lot on the host country and your attitude when you begin your assignment. For instance, an expatriate assignment in Paris that you are excited about will most likely have a longer honeymoon period than an assignment in Lagos.

Anxiety stage

What once seemed quaint, exciting, and novel now seems dirty, crowded, inconvenient, inefficient, and low quality. It is at this second stage when everything seems to go wrong. Simple tasks seem insurmountable, delays are common, you feel that no one understands you, and communication is difficult. Enormous amounts of energy and time must suddenly be spent on small tasks that were second nature to you in your home country.

This is the stage that is commonly identified as culture shock. The cultural differences have a direct impact on day-to-day living. Your current coping techniques and experiences are now no longer valid. Familiarity is lacking, and you have a strong sense of being a foreigner and "a stranger in a strange land." North Americans, in particular, for whom day-to-day living in their home country is so convenient, may find that everyday chores become incredibly difficult and frustrating.

You begin to realize that you are no longer on holiday, and you now have to deal with living in your new environment. You begin to notice that your normal support groups and friendships are not available. You must begin to spend large amounts of effort and time rebuilding these support structures. You begin to feel disorientation and a sense of loss (i.e., home, familiar friends, foods, etc.). You react during this stage by feeling anxious, insecure, frustrated, and impatient.

This stage typically lasts for *three to six months*. Even the majority of expatriates, who successfully make it to the final stage of culture shock, will continually encounter difficult and new situations that will bring them back to the anxiety stage.

Rejection stage

In response to the anxiety stage, you become angry with what feels like the most obvious target — the local culture. You develop an intense dislike and even hostility toward the host country and its people. During this stage, you are hypercritical and very sensitive to your environment. You become annoyed with differences and are continually comparing them (typically unfavorably) with your home country. You are critical of and perhaps even reject the host country, people, and culture, with a tendency to be very nationalistic. In essence, you feel that everything about your home country is wonderful and everything in the host country is bad. You begin to judge the whole country and your assignment by the small issues and events in life.

Reaction stage

The fourth stage is the *turning point* in the success or failure of the assignment. Your reactions at this point can be either positive, which will propel you into the final stage of culture shock, or negative, which can lead to a "failed" assignment.

The feelings of anger and disapproval from the previous stage can serve as a form of assertiveness and help you to raise your self-esteem. By engaging in positive actions, such as meeting people and getting involved in the community, you begin to let go of some of your old experiences and come to terms with your new environment. This will then propel you into the final stage of culture shock.

However, if your reactions lead you to retreat from the new culture, you may begin to feel depressed, lonely, and isolated. You may try to avoid contact with the culture as much as possible, spending time solely with other expatriates. At this point, positive actions will probably help you recover and move forward. On the other hand, if your feelings continue to get worse, you may choose to cut short your assignment and return home or decide to complete the assignment but spend the remainder of the time feeling miserable and counting the days to returning home. In either case, you will not be able to reach the final stage of adjustment.

Typically, the process from the beginning of the rejection stage to its end takes *six to nine months.*

Adaptation stage

The final phase of culture shock is a period in which you have accepted, adjusted, adapted, and assimilated into your new culture. Although this stage is more of a slow, patient, and sometimes painful process, it is also the most enriching and rewarding. By entering this phase, you will find that your expatriate experience is most fulfilling, creating memories and experience that last a lifetime.

You may feel that the honeymoon stage is the most exciting, but in reality, holidays cannot last forever. More important, there is no way you can maintain the energy and heightened senses from the honeymoon stage for very long. In contrast, the feeling of being settled and part of your new environment is very uplifting and satisfying.

Adjustment begins when you start to feel comfortable and competent in your new surroundings. In the most basic sense, "you know where you are." You can get around in your environment, and you feel secure in undertaking everyday tasks. In essence, you have adapted to the lifestyle, learning to function well within the culture and its rules. Your self-confidence and self-esteem have improved dramatically.

At this stage, you have developed effective skills and confidence in your new environment. For instance, the food market that initially seemed foreign and confusing now seems rather normal and familiar. What used to take several hours of deciphering labels and trying to figure out what you are buying is now second nature. Everyday tasks no longer feel daunting, but are routine. You have much more control of your surroundings, and your competence in handling new situations has increased.

You have made new friends and expanded your social network. This can then help increase your knowledge base by the ability to share ideas and experiences, and also offer you support. You find that you are enjoying and accepting the new culture, with an increased tolerance and appreciation. Often, you even begin to find the positive attributes of your host country that are lacking in your home country!

The extent of assimilation can range from almost total immersion into the society to comfortable participation. Your degree of integration will depend on the length of your assignment and your personal situation.

By moving to a foreign country, you will automatically be exposed to a new environment and therefore a new set of values, attitudes, and behaviors.

The exposure is beyond your control, but you can have influence on your responses to the exposure. *The ability to control and influence events is perhaps your greatest asset in reducing the impact of culture shock.*

It seems that every day I live overseas, I am confronted with a new situation to contend with. After several years overseas, I am continually amazed that although I have successfully adapted to my new environment, I can be quickly thrown back into wanting to pack my bags and go home. Often, it is only the little things in life. What is so infuriating and frustrating is that I feel so lost and helpless. The simplest tasks that I took for granted now seem like such an ordeal and challenge.

I remember when we first moved to England sitting in a pub and trying to order 7-Up for my child. I asked the proprietor for a glass, and he said that they did not have 7-Up, but they had lemonade. Well, we had come from the South, where lemonade came in big cool glasses; sometimes it was lemon yellow and sometimes it was pink. But this time we wanted 7-Up. Again, the proprietor said they had only lemonade. This banter went on back and forth between us. I got continually frustrated, and he was fed up and disgusted with the "American fools." We ended up just walking out.

Here we were in a country that supposedly spoke the same language, yet we could not communicate. We later found out that the equivalent to 7-Up in Britain is called lemonade!

But the story is not over. On a return from our home leave in the States, my daughter, who was now "bilingual," asked the American airline attendant for a glass of "lemonade." Thinking I would cut off any potential problems, I politely told the attendant that she wanted 7-Up. In a very cross tone, the attendant said, "Don't tell her what she can have; she can have lemonade if she wants."

Culture shock, as does stress, relates to what your perception and responses are to an experience, and not the cause of a specific event. An individual's perception of the cause and his associated feelings are the determining factors in how he will react. For that reason, reactions are very individual. Some people will have severe reactions, others only an occasional irritation and confusion, and some will seem to thrive in the new environment, experiencing almost none of the effects of culture shock. Still others may adjust well to one culture but have a terrible time with another.

International relocation will involve a new lifestyle and change of roles. Our lives usually have prescribed and chosen roles and follow a defined and organized pattern. We are creatures of habit. The whole family must readjust and often redefine roles.

Holmes and Rahe's (1967) social readjustment scale, which rates each kind of potentially stressful event in terms of life changes, suggests that a relocation can be a very stressful period. Relocating one's home ranks among the top five most stressful life

experiences (Schell and Solomon, 1997). An international relocation introduces several major life changes all at once. For example, a typical, straightforward relocation would score about 215
points on the scale. To put this in perspective, scores significantly
above 150 points are considered hazardous to health, and a score
between 150 and 300 points implies a 50% greater chance of a
health breakdown. According to Wall (1996), a foreign assignment
carries at least a 60% risk of physical illness, emotional illness, or
both during the first year.

Given all the changes and differences you have encountered,
your responses could not be more natural. You may find yourself
exhibiting some of the following reactions, shown in Table 9.1.

Table 9.1 Psychological and Behavioral Responses to Culture Shock

Psychological	Behavioral
• anxiety	• loss of ability to concentrate
• frustration	• doubt of your own capabilities
• impatience	• difficulty working
• irritability	• difficulty making decisions
• quarrelsome	• excessive and compulsive behaviors
• fear	• exaggerated cleanliness
• discouragement	• need for excessive amounts of sleep
• apathy	• physical symptoms and ailment
• homesickness	• avoiding contact with host nationals
• unhappiness	• seeing only other expatriates
• withdrawal	• marital and family tension
• depression	• feelings of helplessness and confusion
• resentment	• feelings of isolation and loneliness

You may experience only a few of these reactions or many.
Sometimes the symptoms of culture shock can be mild and other
times severe. The reactions to culture shock are as diverse as the
people. Most of the responses to culture shock pass over time and
are part of the normal process of adjustment. *It is important to
know that your responses are normal and fairly inevitable.* You
should also expect to feel the effects of culture shock before you
actually identify the cause, yet it is important to be aware of the
signs and symptoms.

Table 9.2   Stages of Culture Shock and Associated Reactions

Stage	Perceptions	Feelings	Reactions	Causes	Approx. length	Shift to next stage
Honey-moon	differences are appealing	excitement, anticipation, euphoria	focused, curious, interested	everything is new, exotic, and fun (like a holiday)	1 to 3 months	exposing yourself to the culture and reality of day-to-day living
Anxiety	differences have a negative impact	anxious, insecure, frustrated, impatient, disoriented	low self-esteem, sense of loss	familiarity is lacking; no adequate support groups; current coping techniques and experiences no longer valid	3 to 6 months	continued immersion in culture
Rejection	differences are rejected	annoyed, critical, angry, hostile, anxious, frustrated	judgmental, rejection, sensitive, "bitching and moaning"	natural response resulting from the anxiety stage; criticism of host culture causes a preoccupation with differences	3 to 6 months	anger propels you to take action or retreat
Reaction	differences are understood	*productive feelings:* anger, nervous, anxious OR *unproductive feelings:* depressed, lonely, miserable	*positive reactions:* assertiveness, self-esteem rises, action OR *negative reactions:* retreat, avoidance	response to anger and anxiety propels you to take action OR to be overwhelmed and isolated	3 months	competence improves, allowing you to adapt OR to remain in reaction stage
Adaptation	differences are appreciated	confident, happy, self-assured, secure, relaxed, comfortable, competent, in control	settled, accepting, adjusted, assimilated, high self-esteem, tolerant, fulfilled	competence in daily tasks and situations has been achieved; social network has expanded	remainder of assignment	

(Adapted from Adler, 1975.)

Figure 9.1 Culture-shock Cycle

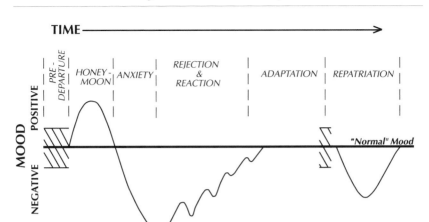

Your reactions also will be different for different situations. They will depend a great deal on your own personality, cultural background, and values. For example, pushing your way to the front of a line may bother one person but not another. Where one person may see a beautiful and picturesque piazza, another may see a dirty, rundown area.

It will be natural for you to experience wild mood swings, from euphoria to total despair (Pascoe, 1992). The excitement of the new culture and experiences can quickly be replaced by the anxiety felt over dealing with the new culture. For apparently no reason, you may break into fits of weeping. You may blow up small, seemingly insignificant challenges into major catastrophes. It is common to feel frustrated, inadequate, and stupid at times. You may even start thinking of the nationals as "them" and looking down at them and their culture. You may feel an intense longing for home.

Figure 9.1 illustrates a typical example of the mood swings you may experience during culture shock. Associated feelings and reactions are related to each stage. Time is on the horizontal scale, and your mood, both positive and negative, is on the vertical scale. The straight horizontal line represents your "normal" mood, or productivity. The cycle starts with predeparture, followed by five stages during the assignment, and concludes with repatriation. The magnitude of your feelings will depend on many factors (i.e., attitude toward assignment, stages of your life, etc.), and will vary from individual to individual. The length of the time scale is arbitrary. It seems to adapt to the length of the expatriation period!

Briefly, your mood for each stage will be as follows:

- **Predeparture** — Depending on your initial outlook toward the assignment, your mood will range between slightly positive and slightly negative.
- **Honeymoon** — Your mood is positive.
- **Anxiety** — Your mood becomes significantly negative.
- **Rejection and reaction** — Your mood remains negative at first, but begins to climb upward toward the normal baseline. The curve is not smooth because various setbacks will create a negative mood.
- **Adaptation** — Your mood returns to the "normal" baseline.
- **Repatriation** — Depending on your outlook toward repatriation, your initial mood will range between slightly positive and slightly negative. This is followed by a negative decline and then finally a return to the "normal" baseline with reintegration into your own culture. Note that the trough is not as extreme as it was while you were overseas.

You may find that there will be negative changes in your relationship with your family, with more arguments and loss of temper.

Before relocation, your lives were most likely settled, with a stable routine for the whole family. Roles were well defined and relatively straightforward. An international relocation will throw everything out of sync. It is common for your negative feelings to be vented on those closest to you — your spouse and children.

The family members are now being asked, sometimes against their wishes, to live in an unfamiliar environment where the climate, language, laws, customs, and people are all alien to their

normal lifestyle. Culture shock and added pressures can contribute to a temporary deterioration in relationships. Your frustrations and unhappiness are easy to take out on your spouse or children. It is important to realize that these changes are related to
culture shock, as compared with something inherently wrong with
your relationship.

As with adults, children experience culture shock.

Younger people generally have an easier time adjusting to new cultures and situations because they have not formed rigid views of
the world and how things should be done. Children are also somewhat sheltered by their parents from the daily confrontations of a
different culture, yet they still have a completely new and foreign
environment. Loneliness and anxieties about the unknown are
common feelings. It is easy to miss the signs your children may
convey concerning their feelings. Children, particularly younger
ones, do not express their feelings verbally; furthermore, you are
overwhelmed by the enormity of the culture and your own negative feelings.

Children can experience wide ranges of emotions and difficulties during relocation (Roman, 1992). The ages of your children,
their individual circumstances, and their personalities will create
different reactions and anxieties to the relocation. *Your goal is to
prepare them to perceive the move in the most positive and constructive way possible, and to help them adjust to their new environment.* Do not underestimate their concerns. Let your children
know that you do understand and care about their feelings and
concerns and that they are important to you.

It is important, therefore, that you are very aware of your
children's behavior and feelings and that you make the time to truly
listen to your children. Watch for signs of unhappiness and significant changes in their behavior or personality. Some clues of
these changes include: increased temper tantrums, mood swings,
changed behavior patterns (e.g., eating and sleeping), reading problems, discipline problems, withdrawal and sullenness, difficulty in
making new friends, and loss of appetite. These regressions may be
as short as a few days or as long as several months, depending on

the personality of the child and the parents (Ottaviano, 1994).

Watch carefully for any behavioral changes and attempt to address them before they become a major issue. Take time with your children to talk about their feelings and daily activities. You should expect regression in their behavior, but it will usually last for only a short time. Children are very resilient and quickly adapt to a new environment. They bounce back much faster than adults!

Be prepared for your children to go through the rejection stage of culture shock and to long for the familiar items, customs, and traditions of their home. As with adults, it is a natural reaction.

Next to spousal adjustment, teenagers pose the greatest risk to an expatriate assignment's success (Schell and Solomon, 1997). If teenagers are unhappy, their behavior can disrupt the family. The adolescent years are perhaps the most volatile and difficult time in a child's development. The changes and emotions they go through are dramatic, and an international assignment can overwhelm some teenagers.

Because teenagers are changing and developing so rapidly, it is hard for you to predict how your teenager will react to a specific move at a specific time. You may think an international move will be highly traumatic for your teenagers, yet it may turn out that they absolutely love it. In contrast, your expatriate child who thrived on your many previous assignments may now rebel and be miserable. The best advice here is to be very aware of and sensitive to your children's emotions and reactions. Help them to build self-esteem and confidence, and provide an outlet for their increased need for independence.

Teenagers' peer groups are the most important part of their lives. It is therefore important for you to help them meet friends. An international school can be a good environment for this because many of their peers will be in a similar situation. The downside is that an international school is more transient, and the peer groups change. You can also provide your child with the names of other teenagers in the host country. Community organizations that offer social or recreational events are another source of friends. Try to have your child talk with other expatriate teenagers to express concerns and fears.

Like adults who thirst for information, your children also have a strong need to know what is happening. Although their needs are more focused — school, friends, and home — their concerns are very real and definite. Whatever facts or information you learn, share them with your children. Information will have to be tailored to their age and maturity, of course. On the other hand, be careful not to overly project your own anxieties and unsettledness. Try to reduce constant discussions on the transfer, and remember that your children are very observant and are probably listening when you think they are not!

You can greatly help your children to adapt. Routine and security are very important to children, so you should do whatever you can to create such an environment. It is important to maintain stability and continuity in their lives. If they are entering school, a routine and schedule will be immediately available. Get them involved with activities and friends at school right away. Help them settle in their home as quickly as possible, unpacking their room and making it feel familiar. Involve them in the new culture and language, but at a slow pace.

Friends are very important to your children, and you will find that they miss their old friends. There are steps that you can take to help reduce their sad feelings. As adults, we sometimes tend to downplay how important relationships and friends are to children. Acknowledge their loss. Help them to keep in contact with their friends by writing letters (via post, fax, or E-mail) or even calling them on the phone. If your children are old enough, consider sending them back home by themselves during a school break to visit their best friends. Most children do make friends easily, however, and you can facilitate this by inviting new friends over to play.

Finally, allow your children time to adjust. As with yourself, do not expect them to immediately adapt to their new environment. Allow for some regression in their behavior. With your consistent love and caring, they will return to their normal selves. *The most important contributions you can make to your children are your love, understanding, patience, and communication (particularly listening!).* By having a positive attitude toward the move, you can help your children view the experience as being positive for themselves.

Often, parents wonder what the long-term effects of living

overseas will be on children. In most instances, the experience of a foreign posting is very positive. Expatriate children are more flexible, adaptable, and tolerant to change. They make friends quickly and can form solid friendships. Attending an international school enables them to cross cultural boundaries more easily. They learn to appreciate diversity and develop a sensitivity to others.

Children living overseas also develop a higher degree of independence because they see things from many points of view and are exposed to much more. They are more international and sophisticated in their perspective, realizing that their home country is not the only place in the world. Children living overseas are more verbal and pick up second and third languages readily. Studies show that nearly all of them, once they are grown, say they would not trade their international experience for anything (Kohls, 1996).

Interestingly, children living overseas tend to be well motivated and adjusted (Ottaviano, 1994). Those who do have adjustment or behavior problems tend to be from families in which the parents are having marital problems or difficulty adapting to their new environment.

On the other hand, expatriate children sometimes can have a hard time settling in one place as adults and remain more attached to their families for a longer time. Home is often thought of as where the family is rather than a specific place. The family unit is much stronger. Because the family members enter the new environment all together and have no immediate extended families nearby, children become even closer to their parents. This closeness extends into adulthood (Ottaviano, 1994). Relationships with their brothers and sisters can also be closer because they must rely on one another for support and companionship when overseas.

There is a four-step approach to dealing with culture shock.

First, you must *understand* what culture shock is and learn its related stages. Second, you must *be aware of* the patterns and ways in which circumstances can trigger negative responses. Third, you must *identify and analyze* the circumstances. Finally, you must *develop* effective techniques to minimize your reaction. Your goal is to cycle through all the stages of culture shock to the final adaptation stage.

There are also positive benefits of culture shock. The feelings associated with culture shock can lead to new opportunities for learning and growth. Learning always involves some form of change. The different situations you encounter as an expatriate will provide new opportunities. Further, the greatest amounts of learning actually occur when someone is motivated. The frustration and anxiety associated with culture shock certainly are an excellent catalyst!

As with any challenge, the understanding of the stages or process of relocation is essential so that effective practical and emotional adapting techniques can be applied. If you know what is happening, that it is a common occurrence, and that all expatriates are affected, it is much easier to deal with culture shock. When you are aware of the stages of culture shock and the associated potential responses, you will be better able to move through the stages. If you can then have an understanding of your own reactions to different stresses and how you manage changes, you will be well on the way to managing culture shock.

By taking charge, you can reduce the negative effects of culture shock. Many suggestions to alleviate the symptoms of culture shock and to help you progress quickly to the final adaptation stage are presented below (see Checklist 16, Appendix A). You will also be able to add more that work for you. Exercises 1 through 8 in Appendix B will also help you focus on culture-shock issues and give you some tools to help you reach the final stage of culture shock.

It is extremely important to realize that all of your reactions to culture shock are completely normal. You should accept that you will most likely suffer from some of the emotional and physical reactions to culture shock. There is nothing "wrong with you." Recognize and be aware of your feelings, even if you do not intellectually understand them. Do not judge them as good or bad, right or wrong. The feelings are normal.

Try to have realistic expectations about living overseas. A corollary to realizing that your reactions are perfectly normal is that your assignment will not always be a fabulous experience. Do not think that it is all going to be easy. Acknowledge that culture shock exists. There will be times when you are lonely, miserable, and homesick. That is normal! If your assignment is combined with another life-cycle change (i.e., new baby), realize that the adjustment may take longer.

Develop a positive attitude about your assignment. Probably the most effective technique in overcoming culture shock is having a positive and optimistic attitude. *It is probably the single most important factor for a successful relocation; it cannot be stressed enough.* Combining an optimistic philosophy with enthusiasm, opportunism, and even a sense of fatalism should make for a very successful assignment. Your positive attitude will be contagious as well. A sense of humor is essential. Be open to laughing at yourself and your mistakes.

Take concrete measures to adapt. Learn your way around your surroundings. Feelings of being hopelessly lost and potentially taken advantage of can be extremely stressful and frustrating. Explore outward from your home and office. Take a little extra time to investigate neighborhoods and routes around your house. Read the local newspapers, talk with your neighbors and shopkeepers, and ask for assistance and advice from others. Get basic information *before* you need it (i.e., doctors, dentists, emergency medical facilities, public transportation, shopping, etc.). These are techniques you would employ in a new city in your home country, but they are more complicated in a foreign location. By becoming familiar and comfortable with your environment, you will not only feel less anxious but also will be rewarded with many pleasant surprises, such as finding a wonderful bakery or café. This will make your life easier and more enjoyable.

Carry on with your hobbies and special interests. Investigate areas of interest or hobbies that are popular in the host country. You do not have to give up your special activities when you move overseas. Some hobbies are easy to continue, but you may need to find creative solutions. Look into various clubs or organizations that may have activities you enjoy. If you like playing sports, you may find other expatriates in your community who would like to play (e.g., form a Sunday-morning touch-football game). You may even find host nationals who would enjoy learning your sport!

To help reduce culture shock, learn more about the host country and culture. Learning about the culture, customs, and language is also part of finding your way around. Your new knowledge will help you to adapt and assimilate more easily and quickly. Do not forget to learn the local sense of humor! You must understand and accept the culture and people. Further, by taking control of the learning process, you will feel much more focused and less overwhelmed. Remember also that the local inhabitants are adjusting and learning about you as well. As you begin to gain confidence in your new environment, you will find that the everyday tasks become easier. Each new accomplishment is a small victory, and you need to remember to appreciate your successes. You will be amazed at how successfully attempting and accomplishing even the smallest tasks will give you a great sense of satisfaction and pride. You will be very pleased when you make that first dinner reservation in a foreign language.

Be prepared! Try to obtain detailed information on the host country. Your local library or a briefing seminar (see below) can be an excellent resource. Purchase a guidebook about the host country. Get yourself good country, local, and city maps. Some data you should try to learn include:

- climate — rainfall, temperature, humidity, and seasonal variations
- language — local language, local inhabitants' proficiency in English
- local inhabitants — attitudes toward business and social affairs, details on various ethnic groups
- food and drink — most popular dishes, normal meal schedule
- manners — customs for greeting, parties, gift giving
- communication — transport, telephone, postal systems
- politics — type of government and history, attitudes toward your home   country
- history — how the country developed, specific events that shaped its evolution, current issues, national affairs
- role models — identify the nation's heroes and heroines

- education — standard curriculum, educational attainment, technology availability, and sophistication
- cultural differences — styles of dress and local customs, unacceptable behaviors
- religion — local religion, national holidays
- laws — local laws and rules
- living conditions — housing, utilities, food, education, health and hygiene, security, travel
- health — inoculations required, local medical and emergency facilities, medical system
- economy — cost of living, local currency, taxation
- entertainment — local clubs, recreation facilities

Language training can be a major factor in adjusting successfully because communication is essential to a meaningful life. The ability to communicate will make the everyday tasks much easier and less intimidating. You also can ask for help from the locals. This increased competence will lead you to talking more with host nationals and thus learning about their culture, values, customs, and politics. This increased understanding will enable you to learn about the culture and why people and things are the way they are in the host country. There is a high correlation between those who learn the language and those who adjust best in the host country (Kohls, 1996). As you begin to view the values, attitudes, and behaviors of the culture as *different from yours, but not wrong,* you will approach everything much more objectively and open-mindedly. Furthermore, you can more appropriately evaluate the positive and negative aspects of the country. This cultural self-awareness, with an understanding of your own basic assumptions, values, and attitudes that lead to your behavior and reactions, will enable you to manage your responses in the new culture. Do not, however, be too hard on yourself if you do not master the language. Learning a foreign language is not easy. Even if you learn only the rudimentary words and phrases, you will have made great strides.

Attending a cultural-awareness training seminar is an important aid in understanding your host culture and learning effective adapting techniques. This training is essential, not only for the employee, but also for the spouse and children. It will help the employee to be more effective and efficient in the business environment and the whole family to assimilate and function better in day-to-day living. It is often assumed that such training is important only in the so-called difficult countries, but even in other countries, there are important differences. For example, a relocation to Great Britain from the States involves differences in the way business is done, cultural and social interactions, and day-to-day living. Culture shock between such "similar" countries is unexpected, and adjustment can prove to be surprisingly difficult.

Become in tune with the local rhythms of the host country. Realize that you *cannot* change the local attitudes and customs, and that you will need to either work around them or accept them. In many countries, you will be unable to accomplish a fraction of the amount of tasks that you can do in others, because things move more slowly and are more complicated (e.g., Saudi Arabia as compared with Canada). This acceptance will significantly reduce your stress level.

Appreciate the cultural differences. An important idea you must always remember is that "in matters of culture, there is not right or wrong — only different" (Pascoe, 1992). Your own culture is not inherently better. Cultures have been around a long time and deserve more than a superficial examination. Always try to consider cultural differences as something positive rather than negative. *Keep an open mind at all times.* We have found that although there are enormous differences between cultures, there is nothing inherently "good" or "bad." For the most part, cultures solve problems in ways that work for them. These solutions may not be transferable to other societies, but that does not make them wrong.

Explore your surroundings. Start with your home and work outward from there. Learn what is in the immediate vicinity (e.g., shops, services, restaurants, neighbors, etc.). When you feel more confident, explore even farther afield. You will be surprised at what you discover.

Set yourself small, short-term goals or projects. It is important not to set unrealistic goals or to expect to accomplish all new tasks immediately. For instance, set yourself the goal of opening your bank account or discovering a new food shop. Take pride in your accomplishments, no matter how little they may seem. It will boost your self-confidence. Yet also do not be afraid of not succeeding or making mistakes. It is inevitable that you will make mistakes, and this has no bearing on yourself. Do not forget to treat yourself to the small luxuries the host country has to offer; have that delicious-looking pastry you eyed in the shop window!

Distract yourself. Feelings of disorientation and inability to focus your thoughts are natural reactions to the anxiety and the overwhelming feelings you have. It is important to gain some relief from these feelings and to try to "distract" yourself. A healthy state of mind is essential for a successful assignment. Keep busy and active. Go sightseeing, visit a museum, go to a movie, read a novel. Whatever you enjoy, take time for yourself. Make sure that you resume your familiar hobbies or take up new ones. Join clubs. Explore opportunities that are available overseas. Do not neglect exercise. Regular exercise is essential for both your physical and mental well-being. Whatever activities you enjoy — walking, swimming, jogging, etc. — make the time for them.

Create a home. Make your life in the new area as pleasant as possible. Set up your new home to be as comfortable and homey as possible, including pictures, mementos, houseplants, and other personal belongings.

Make time for your family. Your family is your most significant and influential support group, particularly during the stressful times of an overseas assignment. It is important not to get too wrapped up in your work or social activities at the expense of your family unit. Remember not only to focus on the challenges and complexities of the relocation but also to enjoy the new surroundings. Children in particular need to be part of your life. They tend to keep many of their concerns and problems to themselves and express them with behavior changes. It is therefore essential to *keep the lines of communication continually open.* Develop an understanding of all the family members' concerns and problems.

Try to establish a support group outside the family. The family cannot and should not be expected to meet all your needs. Try to find a colleague or friend to share your experiences and concerns with, but avoid individuals who wish only to complain or gossip. Their attitudes are very detrimental to your successful adaptation. This is especially important for the nonworking spouse, who does not already have a built-up network at work or school.

Build your social network. Try to make friends immediately. Draw your friends from as wide a circle as possible, including local nationals. Friends are a foundation of life. They provide support, help, and companionship.

Consider the reasons why you and your family are accepting the international posting. Before you accept the assignment, everyone in the family should be clear about why you are transferring. Your acceptance should fit with your overall life goals (see below). Some questions you can ask yourself include: Why is the company sending me overseas? What are the benefits to my career? Who initiated the offer, my employer or me? What are some benefits, besides professional, that my family and I will realize? What will the opportunities be for my spouse and children? What do my family and I perceive as the main issues or difficulties resulting from the transfer? If I want to cut the assignment short or a member of my family does, what are our options and what will we do?

Establish goals. Both the employee and the spouse need clear and meaningful goals. Continually evaluate your short- and long-term goals, and understand how your current situation fits into your complete scheme. Make sure to put your life into perspective, and do not lose focus on what is really important to you and your life. You may want to reexamine your motives for accepting the assignment and may find that your priorities need to be reordered. Your assignment should not be treated as an extended holiday resulting in placing your previous life in suspended animation, but rather a major event in your life cycle.

Do not forget that a major benefit of your overseas assignment is that it gives you and your family the ability to travel, often an opportunity that would not have been available otherwise. Use your assignment as a chance to explore new sites. Remember to allow plenty of time for relaxation, and do not continually go to museums and tourist sites. Use this opportunity to explore some less-traveled areas. This will give you the added benefit of learning and understanding more about the country. Do not forget to plan short trips in your host country. It is all too easy to plan holidays in exotic and faraway locations and miss the chance to experience the local culture and sights where you are living.

Remember to ask for help! Whether it is asking for advice and suggestions or more serious counseling, seek assistance and do not try to tough it out by yourself. This is not an admission of failure. It is helpful to find a sympathetic listener so you can confide your feelings and fears. Focus on your emotions rather than just the perceived causes.

Learn stress-resistant attitudes and behaviors. These include, but are not limited to: exercise and a well-balanced diet; learning and practicing relaxation techniques; openness to learning and change; a positive attitude; appreciation of your accomplishments; avoiding perfectionism; taking control of, rather than responding passively to, your life; learning to relax; avoiding excess alcohol, smoking, or other drugs; learning to keep crises in perspective; lowering your expectations; and remembering to smile!

Keep in touch. It is important to keep in touch with your relatives and friends back home. This will continue to give you a sense of attachment to those close to you. Writing letters, sending electronic-mail messages, sending pictures, making telephone calls, etc., are all ways to keep in touch. Remember that this also applies to your children. It is also a good idea to keep a diary as a record of your experiences and as a chance to express your feelings. A picture album is also a good idea. Subscribe to or have sent to you newspapers and magazines from home. Do not forget to say proper good-byes to elderly relatives or special friends you think you may not see again, and make a special effort to keep in touch routinely.

If, through it all, you or someone in your family feels miserable and is not adapting, take action. First, you must recognize what you are feeling and that your feelings may be related to culture shock. Talk with someone you trust before the discomfort becomes unbearable. This may be a friend or a professional counselor. Getting help in dealing with your problems is simply recognizing that the techniques you use in problem solving at home are not adequate in your new location. Many expatriate communities and international clinic or schools have counselors who are trained to help with the problems associated with living overseas.

Maintain a problem-solving attitude. Rather than telling yourself how awful things are and how impossible it is to improve them, think in a positive way. For instance, however bad things may appear, there are always some activities that make you happy. Pay attention to the small pleasures in everyday living. Do good things for yourself and reward yourself for positive behavior. Maintain your interests and stay active on a daily basis. Stay in contact with friends; do not isolate yourself.

Finally, for some people, calling it quits and returning home may be the solution. This may make for a "failed" assignment, but it is not a personal failure. It is better for you and your family to alleviate the situation than to remain in an unbearable predicament.

There are some disadvantages of being an expatriate as they relate to the culture-shock stages.

These drawbacks will most likely be present throughout your assignment. They cannot be removed, but the impact can be mitigated. These are some of the issues:

- You will always feel *unsettled*, and therefore the culture-shock cycle will occur repeatedly, with little things tending to be more irritating than usual. This unsettled feeling will be the result of (a) continually being confronted with culture shock and (b) the tenuous status of your assignment (i.e., it has a finite period, tends to be short, and the subsequent assignment is often unknown).
- You will *continually cycle* through the culture-shock stages because you will be confronted with unfamiliar situations and differences. If you have reached the adaptation stage, the process will be easier and easier.
- You will be easily *rattled by events* that send you back to the anxiety stage. This relates strongly to the feeling of being unsettled and always being confronted with cultural differences.
- However nice your new home is, however well settled you may be, and however good your social life is, feeling

homesick will be normal and inevitable. With time, these feelings should fade, but most likely at different rates for each family member. Everyone, then, must be sensitive to this and provide support.

- You will always be a *foreigner.* Even as you make local friends, you will never be completely accepted by or truly understand the culture.

If you are a U.S. citizen, you must be aware of a few issues that will affect you when you are overseas.

The United States is perhaps the most influential country in the world — economically, politically, and culturally. America has a huge presence throughout the world, profoundly influencing different cultures.

The reputation of America will proceed you when you go to a foreign country. People's perception of the States, often negative, will be already formed. The news media and Hollywood create images that people in other countries believe to be true for all Americans. The press often portrays a negative image of the States, focusing on sensational and emotional issues. Media often will choose very unrepresentative features that display Americans as excessive, violent, and self-centered.

While attempting to understand the new culture in your host country, you will find yourself continually confronted with people's attitudes toward your own culture. You may be confronted with a negative attitude toward Americans, their politics, and their country. People's stereotypical attitudes run very deep and are difficult to counter. Because America is a very affluent and powerful country, compared with most others, you may be confronted with a negative attitude toward its excessiveness and wealth.

You will be considered an expert on all American politics and economics and will continually be expected to convey your thoughts on issues. This happens particularly when something extraordinary or traumatic occurs in the States. You may find yourself confronted with anger, and you may be accused of "misdeeds" perpetuated by your country, as if you were personally responsible.

To overcome the prejudices and discrimination, you must be patient and understanding of how these stereotypes form. By being open, friendly, and sensitive, you will find that in your own small way, you will positively affect foreigners' images of America. Small acts of kindness, respect, and appreciation of other cultures will have a large impression. Experience seems to show that most foreigners like the individual American. It is the politics, economics, and social system of the States that create resentment. Remember that you are not only the local "ambassador" of your company, but also of your country!

There are a few cultural components that you should be aware of when living in a foreign country.

By understanding these features and people's perspectives, you will have a powerful tool to adapt to the new culture. As an example, the perspectives of North Americans are presented below. See Chapter 13 for additional and more detailed discussion of these issues.

Time perspective

Westerners, particularly Americans, have a very different approach to time than most countries. Punctuality and efficiency are very important to Americans, and they have a strong emphasis on the "time value of money." They have a time orientation that focuses them on the short term. Many other cultures, however, have a very relaxed attitude toward time. You must realize that you will not change their approach to time. To avoid frustration and anxiety, you should try to adapt your own orientation.

Communication perspective

Americans are very direct and open. This contrasts significantly with people in countries which favor more indirect and subtle communication. Gestures and other forms of nonverbal communication are important in many cultures and can be a great source of confusion for expatriates. Although some are universal, you will need to learn others to avoid causing offense or embarrassment.

Interdependence perspective

The American society is highly individualistic, with a strong emphasis on personal freedom. Independence and self-reliance are considered virtues. Some cultures, on the other hand, have a very strong sense of community. In many cultures, the extended family is very important, and much of people's lives revolves around the family. For instance, you may find that an individual will need to consult his family before taking action. Connections and "who you know" are very important. Concerning socializing, often the evenings and Sundays are reserved for family occasions, and you may find it hard to get together with nationals during those times. On the other hand, if you are "adopted" and included in these gatherings, it will be a great honor.

Space perspective

Americans have a very strong need for a certain personal space. They dislike crowds, lines, and small spaces, and avoid physical contact with strangers. A strong premium is placed on personal space and privacy. This manifests itself in the size of offices, homes, and cars. Many cultures, however, have a very different attitude toward personal space, requiring very little distance between people to feel comfortable. In fact, people in certain cultures actually prefer a more crowded situation. Furthermore, foreign cities are more crowded and congested, with a much greater density of people in a smaller area. Their idea of personal space can be much different, and you must learn what is acceptable behavior. Related to his issue, you may also have household help that can lead to a sense of your privacy being violated.

Change perspective

Change is an integral part of the American culture. Newness and improvement are considered natural and positive processes. Tradition and the status quo are challenged, and Americans like to look for ways to improve the system. Other cultures, though, do not view change as a positive or natural force. Tradition and the status quo are the foundation of these cultures. People in these cultures will resist attempts to change.

Beyond Culture Shock

Change is an issue in and of itself. Relocation represents a major change. Many of the symptoms of culture shock will also appear when you make a major move, because of the stress of change. Change is stressful because human beings are essentially creatures of habit. Unfamiliar situations cause anxiety until people begin to adapt. Culture shock magnifies the issue of change. For example, moving across town causes a certain amount of distress. Moving to a different region of the country is incrementally more stressful. Moving to a foreign country, especially one where there is a language difference, is significantly more difficult.

Dealing with a foreign culture causes an individual to become disorientated in the ways outlined earlier in this chapter. Moving will not make long-standing personal issues go away. If you had a conflict in your life or marriage before you moved, moving may make it worse. Moving overseas is an additional stress in a relationship. That may be enough to cause something that was manageable to become a problem.

Moving overseas, for example, will not change your spouse's basic character and behavior. It may have been easier to handle these issues back home because you had a support network and a familiar culture to rely on.

Change, like stress, is not necessarily all bad, however. Some people actually thrive on change and love new challenges. Managing change and dealing with culture shock can enrich or strengthen an individual or a relationship. Most of us do not like change, but we emerge from the experience with a richer life.

Uncertainty is another issue that expatriates face. Whether your assignment is of a limited duration or is more open-ended, there will be unanswered questions about the future for everyone in the family. Assignments change, companies downsize, new offices open, and projects conclude. These and other issues are examples of how an overseas posting can change rapidly. Even if your assignment is completed in the contracted manner, you are still faced with what will happen next. It is not uncommon that a company will not decide your next move until very late in the assignment. You may know that your assignment is ending, but not where you will be going next or even if you have a job. Some expatriates must wait until the last moment to know which continent they will be moving to. This uncertainty adds to the stress of change.

Although you can be faced with all of the above changes when you are living in your own country, living overseas gives you a feeling of being more stranded and isolated. While your friends are envying your "glamorous" life, you may wistfully contemplate their settled existence.

There is not a whole lot one can do about the anxieties caused by change and the feelings of unsettledness. It may help to focus on what you are gaining from your overseas life and realize that there are trade-offs to any experience. Remember that change is a natural part of the life cycle and, more often than not, a positive experience. The associated anxious feelings are also normal.

Perhaps the biggest change you will face when living and working overseas is dealing with another culture.

The differences will undoubtedly affect you, and it is normal to experience culture shock. The stages of culture shock are fairly predictable and relatively short-lived. Even though the effects can be significant, most expatriates learn to adjust and even thrive in their new environments.

Chapter 10 (at a glance)
Day-to-Day Living

From this chapter you will understand ~

the day-to-day tasks you will face as an expatriate.

some coping techniques to make your life easier.

how to adapt and settle into your host country.

how to prepare for your new life.

aspects that impact your daily living, and how to manage them.

Some key points ~

❶ Perhaps the hardest part of any expatriate assignment is the necessity of functioning properly in your new environment.

② It is important that you learn and develop the necessary skills to participate in the host culture.

❸ You should do as much research about your new location as possible.

④ Remember to be confident and not to expect too much too quickly as you go about your daily routine.

❺ Be flexible and maintain your sense of humor, and you will be surprised at how quickly you adapt.

Relocation

Chapter 10

DAY-TO-DAY LIVING

Moving from London to Rome was quite an adventure when it came to getting behind the wheel of a car. Great Britain is a country of rules and unwritten codes of behavior concerning driving. In contrast, Italy appears to be a place of total chaos.

For example, in Britain, one stops at a "zebra" crossing (i.e., crosswalk). In Italy, sometimes it seems that a pedestrian in a crosswalk is fair game. The other day, I saw a rear-end collision because the front driver stopped for a pedestrian! The rear driver actually got out of his car and had the audacity to yell at the other driver for stopping!

Driving down the highway in England, most people stay within their assigned lanes, occasionally changing to pass. In Italy, the lane markings are only aesthetic, with the driver gently weaving in and out of the lane. In essence, the attitude is, "My space and concern are whatever is in front of me; those behind need to watch out for me." Then there is the "law of occupation of empty space." The basic rule seems to be to force your car as far as it will go into any opening in the traffic! The one I like perhaps best is watching someone back up on a busy motorway after having missed the exit. Another one that is fun is watching someone triple-park on a busy street to drop into a bar and have his espresso.

When I arrived in Italy, I was a bit uncertain about the rules regarding roundabouts (i.e., traffic circles) and right of way. In the U.K., it is the car that is in the roundabout that has the right of way. In comparison, the rule in France is the opposite (those who come into the roundabout have the right of way). So I asked an Italian colleague of mine who had lived and driven in Rome for forty years. He

*gave me this very quizzical look, clearly at a loss for the
answer, and said, "I really don't know. I just go." When
one looks at the Italian drivers in a roundabout, you can
understand the complete chaos. Yet surprisingly, whatever
it is, the system seems to work!*

*The British are a nation of extremely polite individuals.
They have a delightful custom of flashing their headlights
at you, which signifies their intention of letting you pass
(e.g., when you want to change lanes or pull out into an
intersection). In Italy, it is completely the opposite. When
they flash their headlights at you, it means, "Get out of my
way, because I am not stopping."*

Perhaps the hardest part of any expatriate assignment is the
ability to properly function in your new environment. So much of
one's life is made up of the little, routine tasks that one takes for
granted — grocery shopping, going to the bank, paying bills, and
commuting. Your ability to manage these tasks will have a significant impact on your outlook toward your assignment.

It is important that you as an expatriate learn and develop the
necessary skills to participate in the host culture. These skills
include learning the local language, mastering local customs, feeling relaxed and confident among local people, and making new
friends (both expatriate and nationals).

As you attempt daily tasks in your host country and begin to
settle into your new environment, you will find almost everything
different. Most errands will seem much more difficult. It is important to realize this at the outset and to be prepared for everything to
take three times as long and be many times more demanding! You
will be surprised, though, that in a relatively short period, you will
find these tasks much easier and less forbidding. You may even
begin to enjoy shopping as you get to know your local shopkeepers
and neighborhoods.

The purpose of this chapter is to give you an understanding of
the day-to-day issues you will face and to suggest some adapting
techniques to make your life easier. The suggestions here are just a
start. You will find your own techniques and what works for you.

The first step for a successful relocation is to "begin before you start."

You should do as much research about your new location as possible. Cultural sensitivity is one of the most important characteristics an expatriate can bring to the new environment. Preplanning and preparation are critical to adapting, and independent reading on the history, politics, and religion will greatly enhance this sensitivity. This new knowledge will give you the tools to help you understand and therefore manage the differences you encounter (see Checklist 2, Appendix A). Information you should find out about includes:

- climate
- language
- culture
- geography
- society and history
- national symbols and customs
- political system
- demographic information
- economics and major industries
- educational approach and system
- religion
- national and religious holidays
- laws and customs
- living conditions
- foods
- public transportation
- standard of dress
- social life
- fine arts and cultural achievements (past and present)
- communication networks
- recreation facilities and clubs
- sports
- entertainment
- cost of living
- medical practices and facilities
- inoculation requirements

- incidence and types of crime
- career and employment opportunities
- anything else that is of importance to you

If you can take a reconnaissance trip before commencing your assignment, all the better. As you begin your assignment, you will be better equipped to handle the changes. Fear of the unknown is often more paralyzing than the reality.

Each country is, of course, very different, and it would be impossible to cover all the aspects and details related to a particular host country.

One of the really special things about living overseas is the opportunity to experience aspects of day-to-day living that a tourist only gets to look at. I remember when I first traveled overseas on vacation, I longingly looked at the food shops, wishing I could buy something to cook that evening. I love going to the open-air markets and coming home with fabulous "bargains" or, at the very least, perfect-looking fruits and vegetables.

Recently, I shared a joke with one vendor, who told me that the luscious-looking strawberries she was selling came from her own garden! Yet when I was first learning Italian, the joke was on me. I could not understand why all the sellers were chuckling until one kindly explained that I had just asked for three fish instead of three peaches (in Italian, the word for peaches is pesche *and the word for fish is* pesce, *both pronounced very similarly)! I was embarrassed, of course, but the peaches were indeed delicious!*

Yet grocery shopping can indeed be a frustration and a scary proposition. All the items are so different and confusing. Often you must go to several stores to do all your shopping. I remember the first time I went grocery shopping and spent three hours slowly working my way through the store, which was about a quarter the size of a normal American one. I would stand there like an idiot trying to decipher labels I could not understand. I am sure

I looked totally bizarre to the locals. I went up to the deli counter and, after standing there for several minutes, I left, too intimidated to order anything. All the meats, cheeses, and breads seemed too unknown, and I didn't have a clue what I wanted and how to order it. It took several more trips to the store before I finally mustered up enough courage to order. With much pointing and gesturing, I was surprisingly successful!

It is strange how one adapts. Now I run through the store with ease, knowing my way around. I enjoy the small local stores and the ability to get to know the proprietor. In contrast, when I return to the States, grocery shopping takes forever! I stand in awe and bewilderment at the magnitude of the store and the maze of choices. A kindly shop clerk once came up to me to ask if I needed any help! And they bag your groceries and take them out to your car!

There are many issues that are common to all countries and that impact your daily living. The following discussion will touch on these subjects and offer suggestions to help you adapt to your new environment. Working through Exercises 9 through 12, in Appendix B, will give you useful tools to incorporate these points. There are also many resources you can consult, such as Craighead Publications, to learn more specific details of your host country. Remember to always "look, listen, and learn" when observing cultural customs. These are three key traits to being accepted in the host culture and not behaving offensively inadvertently.

Language

It is important for a successful transfer to a foreign location that you try to assimilate into the culture as much as possible. Your assignment will not only be much easier but also more rewarding. A fundamental method to achieve this aim is to learn the local language. English is commonly understood in many countries, but often only in tourist areas or among business professionals. For you to be able to talk in depth, make national friends, or complete daily tasks, a grasp of the local language is essential.

Language training is encouraged for the whole family. There are many ways to learn a language, and you will need to choose the best and most appropriate method for you. The four methods of choice are taking an intensive course, private tutoring, group lessons and speaking forums, and learning individually from books and tapes. All have their own pluses and minuses. It is also possible to combine some of these methods. Whichever method you choose, start immediately, and do not hesitate to use your new-found knowledge.

Not only is speaking the best way to learn, but you will also gain respect and acceptance from the locals. Most people are very tolerant and helpful when a foreigner is attempting to speak their language.

Health

Concerns of quality and cost in the host country are factors of anxiety for expatriates. In addition, health care is practiced differently throughout the world. These differences and the lack of knowledge about them are further worries. This topic is discussed in detail in Chapter 7.

Newness

Everything is new — job, house, acquaintances and friends, food, schools, environment, etc. This can be overwhelming. There is not much preparation you can do, but an awareness of the newness is helpful. It will help to explore your surroundings and try out new foods, products, and routines a little at a time. This is a time to not expect too much of yourself and to be less critical.

Personal life goals

When you and your family are entering a new phase of your lives, it is a good idea to reevaluate your long-term goals and values. Make sure your new assignment fits into your strategy, and consider how it will become a part of your future. An overseas assignment can also be accompanied by major personal life transitions unrelated to the transfer. These can include a new family member, career break, sick relative, or a child entering adolescence. The changes are stressful in themselves but can be exacerbated by the relocation. Again, there is not much preparation you can do. Just be aware that you are in a stressful time, and practice adapting techniques such as those outlined in Chapter 9.

Dress

Make sure you obtain preinformation on styles of dress in the host country. Differences can be quite small (e.g., between North Americans and Europeans) or quite large. Some countries have their own styles and even strict codes, particularly for women. A sensitivity to local dress customs will be very important. The best advice is to dress conservatively and inoffensively at first, until you learn the appropriate style. This shows respect for the culture and goes a long way toward helping you integrate into the society and be accepted.

Culture shock and nonverbal communication

Culture shock, resulting from your reactions to the different cultures, will continually confront you as you live in the host country. This issue is dealt with in detail in Chapter 9. In some countries such as India, you may see intense poverty, misery, and class distinctions, which can have a profound effect on you.

Physical characteristics

Your assignment may be in a country where your physical characteristics (i.e., color, physique, facial appearance) mark you as clearly different and as a minority (Piet-Pelon and Hornby, 1992). You may feel a discomfort from this that you have never experienced before. Remember that it takes time to get used to being different and to be accepted by local nationals.

Status of women

In some cultures, men and women have significantly different roles, rights, and privileges. From a Western perspective, women have secondary and restricted status in many societies (e.g., Muslim countries). Other countries still view women as less than equal to men, although not as overtly. Western women can also be treated as sex objects, an image perpetuated by American cinema. This can be a very frustrating and angering experience for women. For further discussion on this topic, refer to Chapter 14.

Loneliness

An expatriate assignment involves giving up the support network you and your family have developed in your home country. The paradox is that an international relocation is precisely the time you need the support group to help with practical matters and the emotional needs of adjusting. Loneliness can be particularly acute during the reaction stage of culture shock. See Chapters 9 and 11 for information on this issue.

Family emergencies back home

A family sickness or death back home is one of the hardest parts of living overseas. The normal stress and anxieties we feel when confronted with a family emergency are magnified by being overseas. The advent of global communications and travel do not make the world a smaller place when we are faced with a family crisis. Communication is made harder by time changes and, in remote locations, communication is not immediately reliable. Rarely can one instantly pick up and return home, given the extra complications and expense of international travel. The decision on when to return home is complicated. Do you return home when you first receive word of a severe illness (and how severe is severe?), on death, or for a funeral? Feelings of distress, guilt, and frustration are all compounded by the distance. The best advice is to not avoid the issue until confronted with it, but rather decide potential plans of action ahead of time, while you can be objective. Ignorance is not bliss. Be forewarned that no matter how much you plan ahead, this will still be a difficult and emotional time. You just have to do the best you can, and not expect too much of yourself.

Different perspectives

You and your family members will have different perspectives on living in a foreign culture, based on personal situations that will continually affect your emotional state and determine your actions. For instance, the nonworking spouse is confronted with the cultural differences and challenges, while the working spouse tends to be more insulated. Not only are the perspectives different for each family member, they will also change for the individuals during the course of the assignment. Continual communication among all family members is imperative. See Chapter 14 for more discussion on this issue.

Longer working hours

An expatriate employee usually has greater responsibility, more tasks with less support staff and, in some countries, even a six-day workweek. Further, some expatriates travel a great deal more for business. This travel will give them less time at home, often when their families greatly need their support and presence. (On their contrary, for some expatriates, an international assignment can actually shorten the amount of time they travel if, before their transfer, they were traveling extensively to the foreign office.) Communication and flexibility are again essential.

Climate and geography

Physical environment can greatly affect a person's attitude and morale. Extremes in heat or cold, particularly if they are different from your home country, can be a challenge. Of course, you cannot change the climate, but you can try to minimize its effects. This is where some premove research can pay off. If you know what to expect, you can prepare by having the appropriate dress for the climate and can purchase fans or heaters to bring with you (remember the voltage difference).

Shopping

Shopping is a major issue that you will continually be involved with in your day-to-day living, and it is very different in foreign countries. This is an area that you have most likely taken for granted in your home country, and therefore, it can be a trigger for the culture-shock symptoms discussed in Chapter 9.

> *For example, at the supermarket, the signs, packaging, instructions at the checkout, etc., are all different and most likely in a different language than yours. You may have to learn to price your own produce. In England, everyone patiently queues for service, while in an Italian bakery, you must assert yourself and catch the eye of the person behind the counter. Some host countries do not*

have large "one-stop" markets, but rather a series of smaller shops that sell only certain items. This can add greatly to the challenge, but also to the fun. Shopping can be more of a production and more inconvenient than in the your home country. Often, the produce and baked goods are fresher — a reward for your increased efforts.

Rely on neighbors and other expatriates to advise you on ood stores and what to expect (i.e., prices, hours, quality, etc.). Do not be afraid to explore, but do so only slowly. Investigate a small area, becoming familiar with what is available, how the people shop, and what prices to expect. Most shopkeepers in the Middle East and Asia will bargain, but you need to know the going rates before you can negotiate properly (Piet-Pelon and Hornby, 1992). In some stores, it is improper to touch or handle the merchandise for sale (e.g., fruits and vegetables). In other instances, even a slight interest in an item is an indication to the shopkeeper of a definite purchase. Watch other people, and ask your colleagues. Try not to be discouraged by delays.

Be aware of the business hours of shops and markets, because they are usually not continuous all day. Particularly notice the times for midday (i.e., lunchtime), weekends, early closing days, and local holidays. Sometimes there are surprises. Some stores may be open twenty-four hours (e.g., pharmacy or fresh bread dispenser!). Sunday is the traditional closing day for most Western cultures. In Muslim countries, Friday is the official closing day, and in Israel, it is Saturday.

No country in the world is as service oriented as the United States, with its convenience, flexibility, prices, and customer attitude. Most countries do not share the American idea of businesses adopting a policy that the customer is always right. Refunds and exchanges overseas are often difficult or not allowed, so you must be careful when making purchases. Sometimes you will find that you have made a mistake or made a wrong purchase in which you will end up losing money. Try not to let this rattle you, and look at it as part of the cost of being an expatriate.

You will most likely find that the cost of living is greater than what you are used to, particularly when you try to maintain a similar standard of living as before. There are ways in which you can lessen its impact. When possible, begin to think in the local currency and stop comparing prices with those in your home country.

Shop in the same way as the locals rather than trying to recreate your old environment. You will discover new and interesting things and will save money as well. Shopping at small shops, open-air markets, and bazaars and knowing your local shopkeepers are just a few of the differences that are part of the fun and experience of living overseas. However, although imported items are costly, an expensive jar of peanut butter is worth buying when you really miss it. Familiar things can provide much comfort. You may want to include some in your shipment and take advantage of buying your favorite items on trips back home.

It will be imperative that you "go with the flow" to keep your stress level to a minimum and to have a successful relocation. You will make mistakes, and some may even be costly, but try not to let them affect your attitude and self-confidence. Learn to go easy on yourself.

Food

In almost all cultures, great importance is placed on food and drink. Often, they are so integral to the culture that food and people are inseparable. You will want to learn as much as you can about the different types of food and varieties of dishes. Consider taking a cooking class in your host country. You will be pleasantly surprised at your increased cooking repertoire!

You most likely will find food shopping vastly different from back home. More countries are going toward the Western-style supermarket, but they are usually much smaller and the stock will be different.

Your host nationals will be very impressed if you embrace their cuisine. Your knowledge and appreciation of their food and drink will go a long way toward their acceptance of you, but be careful not to offend anyone by claiming expertise. For example, if you say to a Roman that you understand that the best Italian cuisine comes from northern Italy, expect some indignation!

Sometimes you may find yourself confronted with strange and unappetizing foods that may make you uncomfortable (e.g., dried lamb's blood, Iceland; camel meat, North Africa; duck feet and tongues, all laid in rows on platters, China; marinated and deep-fried scorpions, intact with stingers, and turtle heart and other unknown organs, in a green-and-red sauce, Far East; boiled duck egg with a half-incubated embryo inside, Philippines; snake blood in a shot glass, China). Sometimes the Chinese may test your fortitude on purpose. If you are adventurous, try the food; if it makes you uncomfortable, politely decline or take only a very small helping. In areas of questionable health standards, always be wary of some food (e.g., uncooked or poorly cooked meats; fruits and vegetables washed in dirty water, etc.).

Be sensitive to local table manners and take your cues from your hosts. For example, in Middle Eastern countries, it is impolite to eat with your left hand. In Japan, one never leaves one's chopsticks sticking up from the rice. Belching is acceptable behavior after a meal in Turkey. In Southeast Asia, leaving much food on one's plate at the end of the meal is not appropriate (de Kieffer, 1993).

Home and host-country customs

You will be confronted with two facets concerning customs. There will be host-country customs and holidays and your own.

For the most part, you will find the host country's customs very new and interesting. Local friends may invite you to join in their traditions and celebrations, which will make your relocation experience all the more rewarding and enriching. Even if you feel somewhat uncomfortable, do not shy away from participating.

You must also keep alive your own family traditions and customs, both religious and secular. These celebrations are often not celebrated, acknowledged, or understood by the host nationals. Expatriate groups may organize celebrations.

Sometimes you will find that people are interested and you can enrich your national friends by letting them be part of your celebrations. This can be a nice way to share some of your own culture and customs with the host nationals. For instance, sitting down to a quintessentially American Thanksgiving dinner can be a wonderful and rewarding experience for everyone. It could well be the first time your guests ever have had truly "American" food!

Depending on your host country, many religious festivities

such as Christmas and Passover are not celebrated. You must have strength and know that these observances come predominantly from within, and you must learn to be creative in your celebrations. It is important to keep your family traditions alive yet be flexible. Do not be too concerned if you cannot recreate the special occasions and holidays exactly as you would in your home country. You will be surprised how you can adapt to what is available in the local country. Seek out support from people of similar situations and beliefs, and consider celebrating as a group.

Mathematics

Most of the world uses the metric system, and if you are not familiar with it, you may find yourself frustrated and confused. In time, you will become more accustomed to the system. Refer to Resource 4 in Appendix C for handy conversion charts and tables.

Bureaucracy

Bureaucracy is a fact of life in all countries, and in some, it will be worse than others. *Patience and a positive attitude are essential.* In some countries, you may have to deal with doing business in person, in cash, and waiting in line. Things may take much longer and require several trips or phone calls to complete a task. A language barrier can further complicate matters. Dealing with documents such as a residence permit or a driver's license can be particularly challenging because you are unfamiliar with the local system. Take a deep breath and remember that the inevitable delays and confusion are part of the process. Seeking professional assistance or help from local colleagues can alleviate the frustration.

Lack of information about your home country

Feelings of being out of touch with your home country are common and can be disconcerting. See Chapter 12 for further discussion.

Travel

Traveling can be a great benefit of your life overseas. See Chapter 15 for more information.

Crime, violence, and personal safety

Although probably not significant factors in your everyday life, crime and terrorism are issues that need consideration. See Chapter 8 for more information.

You should be aware of personal safety and potential risks of accidents in some foreign countries. Although most industrialized nations have established procedures and safety nets, some countries are lacking in this area. For instance, potential fire hazards, structural deficiencies, and other dangers are typical, and you should use common sense and forethought.

Difficult postings

Some overseas locations, such as those in "developing" countries, pose significant challenges to you and your family. Some cities are very crowded, dirty, and noisy. Air and water pollution can be particularly bad or even dangerous. Public sanitation can be a concern. There are open sewers, insects, and rodents. Tap water is considered unsafe for drinking, fresh produce may be contaminated, and there are no regulations for food handling in restaurants or markets. Disease and sickness are widespread in the local community. Local hospitals do not meet North American or western European standards.

Adjustments to climate, diet, and local living conditions can be taxing, even for those in excellent health. Daily life can be challenging, and you will have many more things to cope with. You may face continual inconveniences such as power outages, water shortages, and delays that make daily living very stressful.

In some countries such as India, large class differences can be disconcerting. Beggars, invalids, lepers, and even bodies in the street can be common sights. People typically live in substandard conditions. Genuine poverty, something many Westerners are unaccustomed to, is not only normal but also very visible. Seeing and living among such poverty can be very depressing and stressful. Eventually, there is even a danger of becoming desensitized and uncaring, and finding that your values change. Corruption and bribery are also prevalent, and this can be another affront to your values and beliefs. Expatriates particularly are taken advantage of.

Living in a difficult posting location, although challenging, can be a rewarding and exciting experience. You can try to reduce the challenges but never to get rid of them. Always go on a familiarization trip to gain an understanding of the challenges you will face.

First and foremost, emphasis needs to be placed on rigorous family hygiene at all times (see Chapter 7). In these postings, the expatriate community is usually very strong and can provide much-needed advice and support. To help prevent your becoming desensitized to the poverty, try to keep it in perspective. Perhaps you can do volunteer work to help the community or can donate money, food, and clothing to local organizations and charities.

Unrealistic expectations

Most expatriates look forward to their new life and experiences with great anticipation, although perhaps with some misgivings and apprehension. Be forewarned that the day-to-day reality, although wonderful and rich, will not live up to the fantasy of guidebook descriptions or preconceived images. As in your home country, you will find times when your life seems difficult and frustrating. Be prepared for friends back home not to understand that there can be difficult moments. Often, their attitude is one of polite envy, and they cannot believe that your experience is anything but positive. Their attitude can seem very insensitive to you, but remember that it often stems from their ignorance of what it is like to live overseas.

Children

You may have to spend more time organizing your children's lives. Teenagers will probably be even more dependent on you because the opportunities to express their independence may be more limited. However, in some countries, particularly in western Europe, teenagers in groups may have more freedom of movement and safety than in other countries. Given that the teen years are a time when youngsters want to be more independent, you should be considerate of their needs and help them adjust. Teenagers tend not to make friends as easily as younger children, and they miss their established support group in their home country.

Younger children too pose a new set of challenges when living overseas. They can have trouble adjusting to their new life and have difficulty expressing their emotions. You must keep the lines of communication open and be sensitive to your children's feelings. See Chapter 4 for a more detailed discussion of children's issues.

Baby-sitters and day care

Finding good baby-sitters is always a challenge. Networking is the best way to find them. Try to recruit teenagers from an international school. Other parents are also a good source for recommendations. Older siblings of your children's friends, student teachers, and neighbors are other potential sitters. Sometimes your embassy may keep lists of potential baby-sitters. Some communities have professional agencies that provide baby-sitters, au pairs, and nannies. Live-in and live-out maids are sometimes used as child care-givers (see below).

Day-care centers, also called day nurseries, may be available. They can be operated privately or by the government. Some day-care facilities have certain restrictions and waiting lists, so it is best to check locally. Churches, local schools, and private and government agencies are a good place to look.

Career and business environment

There are two aspects to the business issue. First is how the transfer will affect the employee in his work, and second, how the relocation will influence the accompanying spouse. These points are covered in Chapters 13 and 14, respectively.

Household help

In some areas such as Southeast Asia, India, Africa, and Latin America, the use of household help will not only be readily available and inexpensive but also expected (Piet-Pelon and Hornby, 1992). Household tasks can include cleaning, cooking, child care, gardening, and security. In other countries, where household help is not prevalent, it may be prohibitively expensive.

There are many advantages of employing household workers. They can ease the burden of cleaning, shopping, cooking, caring for children, and other household tasks while you are learning to adapt in your new environment. This is particularly important in difficult posting locations, where the challenges of daily life can be overwhelming. In countries where shopping is done in open-air markets or bazaars, local workers are familiar with the markets and often can do the shopping more efficiently and get better prices.

Household helpers, though, can be a mixed blessing; they are there when you want them, but also when you *don't* want them (Pascoe, 1992). On the one hand, they remove much of the drudgery of household maintenance, yet they can provide another source of headaches. The experiences that many expatriates have regarding household help encompass the complete range from "wonderful, could not have managed without them" to "a nightmare."

A major concern when deciding whether to employ full-time help is lack of privacy. From your love life to your arguments, you will not have the type of privacy you used to enjoy.

Many Westerners have little experience managing and living with help beyond the weekly cleaning service or baby-sitters. The idea of servants is "foreign" and even considered demeaning. You may even feel a sense of guilt at having someone doing all the work you despise, for low wages. In these cultures, however, servants play an important role in the social and economic life and are considered to have respectable occupations. Always treat your helpers with dignity and respect. In some cultures, they may become almost like members of your family. In others, a certain distance is expected, and excessive familiarity can be confusing.

If you decide to have household help, there are several issues you must be aware of. Employing and managing household help involve common sense and standard employer-employee relationships. Unfortunately, it is easy to lose objectivity and firmness when dealing with others, particularly when the work is related to your family life. Below are some points to help guide you through key concerns.

• *Finding prospective help.* Finding competent, reliable, and trustworthy help can be challenging. The best way is usually through a friend, neighbor, or other expatriate who can vouch for the individual. Sometimes you can get a well-recommended person who has worked for an expatriate family which is leaving the area. Other resources for finding help are newsletters and bulletin boards of international schools and expatriate organizations.

• *Hiring prospective help.* Treat the hiring or prospective worker as you would in any potential employer-employee relationship. Discuss your expectations of hours, pay, responsibilities, duties, and holidays. Obtain letter of references and, if possible, verbal references. Be wary of fraudulent references or halfhearted endorsements. Interview prospective employees as if you were interviewing potential staff members for your business. Make sure you are comfortable with them. Trust your instincts. When you hire an individual, it is a good idea to request a medical examination (offer to pay), especially if you have young children.

• *Communication.* Communicating with the household staff can be demanding because of language and cultural differences. They may want to please you and are likely to agree with you or say yes no matter what you ask. You may find that they did not understand you at all. A patient attitude and a sense of humor will help greatly. Try to be explicit in all your instructions, and speak slowly if language is a problem. Learn some key words and phrases. It is preferable to show what you want and how you want tasks done, rather than tell them. They will definitely need close supervision at first.

• *Expectations.* Be conservative in your expectations of the quality of service (Pascoe, 1992). The helpers may not clean your house, cook your meals, or iron as you would like. First, you must show them how and what you want. Second, if it is not up to your standards, you have to decide if you can accept it or need to find someone else. Remember, however, that the next person may not be much better. If your current help is honest, trustworthy, and pleasant, that may offset the underperformance. Always be mindful of the relationship between the low wages you are paying and the standards you expect. It helps to be flexible and to keep your sense of humor.

• *Theft.* Although not as prevalent as in the stories you will hear, theft does occur, from outright stealing to not putting in a full day's work (i.e., "time" theft). Your standard of living is higher than that of most individuals in the host country, and the temptation and the perception that theft is not wrong will be present. Again, you must be firm in showing that theft is not tolerable, but also be aware of and generous toward the employee's needs. Be businesslike with your staff, keeping accounts of shopping money and supplies. Do not tempt fate; keep your valuables locked up. If something is lost, do not immediately blame the help. More often than not, the item will be found. As with any relationship, you must build up trust and confidence.

• *Salary advances.* Less economically advantaged people tend to have immediate needs and "disasters," and they may look to you for a salary advance or time off. You must find a comfortable position between refusing any advance and always giving in when requested. The important thing is to set and maintain consistent boundaries so that you do not feel taken advantage of, yet your employees feel they are being treated fairly. Be aware that if you are overly generous to your help, it will be a disservice to them in the long run. Your generosity will increase their standing and possibly their class. Yet when you leave, they will have no way of maintaining their new lifestyle. Not only is this financially difficult for them, but emotionally, they can "lose face" by going back to their previous class.

• *Benefits.* Always treat your employees fairly and with respect. Pay the going rate. Good help can be one of the best investments while living abroad, and this is not the area to economize in. Decide what benefits you will provide — time off, medical assistance, holidays, gifts, etc. — and tell that to your staff. Some countries have specific government regulations. For example, in Italy, domestic workers are required to be registered for tax, and the employee must pay holiday, tax, and even severance pay. You will need to tip at appropriate times. How much and when you tip will vary depending on which country you are in, so it is best to get advice from other expatriates or nationals who employ household help. You need to look into workmen's compensation for accidents, because you may be liable. Any "hand-me-downs" (e.g., clothes, toys, etc.) will usually be appreciated.

Your employees' families may become your dependents, looking to you for help in times of crisis. They also may welcome you as their guests at celebrations and festivities. Be aware of your responsibilities, but encourage self-reliance. Regarding medical care, it is a good idea to help with expenses for your staff and potentially for their families if the staff will be affected as well.

• *Raising your children.* The household help should remain only in a support role, and *not* act as a substitute parent. As a parent, you want to be the primary role model for your children.

Concerning the development of your children, you must make sure that you take an active role. The presence of a caretaker can create lazy and undisciplined children. In the first instance, the caregiver is always there to clean up after your children and to do the chores. The possibility of your children not learning the basics of good manners and personal responsibility and further developing patterns of laziness is something you need to avoid. Second, the household help may have discipline methods that conflict with yours, or they may not discipline at all, continually letting your children get away with anything. You must be firm about what you require and the way you want to raise your children.

Your greatest day-to-day challenges of living abroad are to function in and adapt to your new environment.

Your ability to successfully manage everyday tasks, ones that you took for granted in your home country, will make your life much easier. Remember to be confident, and do not expect too much too quickly as you go about your daily routine. Plan to take at least three to six months to feel settled. This perspective will enable you to feel less frustrated with the inevitable challenges and delays. By being flexible and maintaining your sense of humor, you will be surprised at how quickly you adapt!

Chapter 11 (at a glance)
Networking

In this chapter you will discover ~

how to meet people and establish a supportive environment in the host country.

how to rebuild your circle of friends and acquaintances with different social networks

potential benefits and concerns with making expatriate and national friends.

how to develop friendships.

where to meet new people.

effective adapting techniques.

Some key points ~

❶ To become comfortable and content in your new environment, it is important for you to create a network of friends and acquaintances to provide support, help, and companionship.

② You will need to get used to meeting new people and forming friendships in a short amount of time.

❸ There are, in essence, two groups of people you can build your social network with — fellow expatriates and nationals in your host country.

④ There are several avenues for you to explore in your host country to meet people.

❺ Once you build your social network, you will enjoy your assignment and develop a much deeper sense of appreciation than any tourist.

Chapter 11

NETWORKING

We arrived in England in July. The weather was absolutely glorious — six weeks of nonstop sunshine. We could not understand why everyone always complained about the British weather! "Just wait; you will see," they all said. But that is another story!

My biggest preoccupation was keeping our two daughters, then aged six and two, amused. We had a lovely, huge garden, and aside from a few stinging nettles, it was a perfect place to play. Yet even paradise can get lonely, and I was beginning to count the days until school would start. Then one day we heard voices on the other side of the fence — children!!

In search of potential playmates, I plucked up my courage and went around to knock on the neighbors' door. I had read all about the famous "British reserve" and how hard it was to meet people, but I figured mothers are always looking for playmates for their kids. Besides, I was desperate! The door slowly opened and I greeted my neighbor, saying that we had recently moved in next door, I had heard her children playing in their garden, and I wondered if they might like to play with mine. I was totally unprepared for what happened next.

She looked almost panic-stricken, wide-eyed, with jaws open. I began to apologize, saying that I did not mean to disturb her, but perhaps the children could come over and play sometime. "Oh yes, well . . . I . . . uh . . . I suppose I should invite you in," she exclaimed. I protested, "No, no. I did not want to disturb you," but we found ourselves following her into the kitchen. "Oh yes . . . I should offer you something to drink. A cup of tea?" she said, partly to herself and partly to me.

> *It was the first of many cups of tea I was offered in England. My neighbor and I became good friends despite the fact we were never formally introduced, and our children had a great time playing together. I learned that if I make the first move, people might be a bit surprised or caught off guard, but they will often respond positively.*
> *A few weeks later, the rains came — for eight months!*

To become comfortable and content in your new environment, it is important to create a network of friends and acquaintances to provide support, help, and companionship. These networks were most likely very strong in your home country. One difficulty of beginning your expatriate assignment is that this support group has disappeared.

Ironically, it is during this demanding period that practical and emotional support from other people is essential. Not only are you lacking local friendships, but also many of the basic skills needed for everyday living. Because your environment is new and unfamiliar, a good friend is very important. On the positive side, you will find people, both other expatriates and nationals, very sensitive to your new situation and very helpful and supportive. You must make sure to tap into this openness.

The aim of this chapter is to help you gain insight into some mechanisms and techniques available to rebuild your social network. You will learn how to nurture acquaintances and new friendships and how to handle the inevitable setbacks. The methods are very similar to what you would apply in moving to any new location. A major difference, though, is where you may focus or divide your energies. There are, in essence, two groups of people you can build your social network with: fellow expatriates and nationals in your host country. Each group can provide specific, yet different, support.

An expatriate community can be an excellent source of information and support during the early stages of a posting.

Most expatriates will understand what you are going through and will be very helpful and supportive. Furthermore, being with people from your own culture gives a sense of comfort, easing the adjustment to your new life.

It takes a relatively short period to become an "expert." Expatriates who have been in the host country for a year or so can provide information on good places to shop and eat, things to do, and how to circumvent the bureaucracy. This is a time for you to ask questions and listen. You can weed through all this new information to determine what is important to you, and then experiment yourself. Remember, though, not to be a pest and not to constantly bother your new contacts.

You will need to get used to meeting new people and forming friendships in a short amount of time. Do not be timid about calling people you have met only briefly or have never met but whose names you have been given. The international community is very receptive to such introductions. Friendships are accelerated in the expatriate time frame.

Usually, you will find people very open and you will make friends easily. Occasionally, you may run into some who are cold or remote. They may have their own solid network and have no interest in expanding it. If so, move on and do not take it personally. A word of caution: Do not put yourself in such a situation. Because expatriate communities are continually changing, you could find that your well-established network evaporates literally overnight. Cultivate as many new and interesting relationships as you can. This variety of relationships will make your assignment more rewarding (Kalb and Welch, 1992).

Associating solely with expatriates has a downside, however. If you rely solely on support from the expatriate community, you will find that this group is highly transient, which can lead to very brief relationships. You have assuredly felt the sadness in your home country when a good friend moves to a new location, but you still had a solid network of other friends, which lessens the impact. Expatriates, though, are a very ephemeral group. If all your friends are expatriates, you will find them leaving, and this can exacerbate the feelings of isolation and abandonment.

When meeting someone who is going to move on to a new posting or repatriate, there is a tendency not to put any energy into forming a friendship. This is natural, because it can be hard to put a lot of emotional energy into something that will end soon. Those who are leaving will also not be as open. They will not only be concerned with the enormous tasks ahead, but also will be trying to detach themselves emotionally. Given the shortness of many assignments, this pitfall will affect you both coming and going, literally!

Saying good-bye is part of the expatriate cycle, yet the friendships you make while overseas, however brief, are some of the most special encounters you can have. Rather than trying to shelter yourself from the sad moments and therefore deny yourself potentially rewarding friendships, be open and willing to make new friends. Remember that many of the bonds formed will last a lifetime.

Another concern with relying only on expatriates is that you run the risk of spending your time with individuals who are unhappy in their current situation overseas and continually complain about and criticize the host country. This can be a very depressing and destructive environment to be in.

Lastly, by associating only with expatriates, it will be harder for you to assimilate with the local community.

The advantage of building your social network with host-country nationals is that they are perhaps the best avenues to successfully integrating into the new culture.

They can provide not only a wealth of information about how to adapt in your new environment and deal with the day-to-day tasks, but they also can give you a sense of belonging. By having a network of national friends, you will feel more settled and part of the community. Another added benefit of these friends is that they are not as mobile as expatriates.

The difficulty of making national friends is most often related to language and cultural obstacles. You may find the nationals to be very friendly, courteous, and helpful, but they may be hard to approach beyond that. In a country where English is either the native language or very common, it will be much easier to meet people. Where language is a problem, you will find it more difficult. One wonderful exception is to find nationals who have previously lived in your home country. Not only will they have the language skills, but they also will have gained an appreciation and understanding of your own culture. This familiarity can be a good basis for a friendship.

Another complication to making national friends (one that is common in any new environment) is that they often will have their own social networks and not be as interested in forming new friendships. Many cultures are also very family oriented, and people spend a great deal of time with their extended family or close family friendships. In some cultures, people make sharp distinctions between socializing with those they are familiar with and with strangers, and foreigners often fall into the latter category. They may even have formed negative impressions of your culture, based on previous experiences.

Whomever you do meet, reserve decisions about making further commitments until you have settled somewhat.

Use your first contacts to gain insight and information into the new culture. Be wary of unloading all your problems and concerns on new friends, and avoid overwhelming or scaring off any potential friends. Try not to latch onto people, and certainly avoid individuals who want only to complain and be miserable.

When you meet someone, you should temper your first impressions and exercise some benefit of doubt. First impressions can often be negative because the person was uncomfortable for a variety of reasons. Therefore, give everyone a chance, and you may make a good friend. On the other hand, if on a subsequent two or three meetings your relationship does not jell, then certainly do not pursue a friendship.

Life in an expatriate community can seem at times like life in a small town or village.

It can become a tight-knit group of close friends and acquaintances, with everybody involved in everybody's business. Feelings can easily be hurt, and it can be hard to do things with just one or two friends or even alone. In some expatriate communities, most people live very close to one another in neighborhoods or compounds made up of mainly foreigners, and they have relatively little contact with the host community. For some expatriates, this can be very comforting and can ease the stress of living in a foreign country, but for others, it can be stifling and limiting. If your assignment leads you to an expatriate enclave, you will have to find your comfort level in terms of involvement in the community.

One benefit of living in an expatriate community is that there is a great deal of support close at hand. Friends become like an extended family. They can take the place of relatives, and you can often spend holidays, birthdays, and even vacations together. The close proximity is also a benefit for children who like to have their friends available.

The expatriate spouse usually has a surplus of unstructured time, and in expatriate communities, groups and clubs provide social involvement and activities. Overseas assignments often put spouses in the unique situation of having both time and money to spend, and thus the "shop 'til you drop" syndrome is born. Trips are organized to buy exotic items, and the assignment can begin to resemble a trophy hunt. It is easy to get caught up in a competitive atmosphere of weekend trips and purchases. Experiences can become part of a checklist of things to accomplish rather than part of the joy and uniqueness of living in a foreign country.

There are several avenues for you to explore in your host country to meet people.

Before you leave your home country, expand your network to find possible contacts in your host country. You will be surprised how successful this can be (i.e., a friend of a friend knows . . .). The world is indeed very small these days. Knowing someone "on the ground" when you arrive in your new and unfamiliar environment can be a great source of relief.

Whatever your particular circumstance, it is helpful to become as much of a "joiner" as you can, even if that is not your style (Kalb and Welch, 1992). This is a quick way to meet people and potentially make good friends.

Do not forget to take advantage of your local neighborhood. The local shops and markets are not only fun to explore and a way to learn about the culture, but also can give you opportunities to establish friendly relationships.

Some areas for you to explore to meet people (although certainly not limited to!) include (see Checklist 17, Appendix A):

- areas of mutual interests (i.e., hobbies)
- similar stages of life (i.e., young children)
- work
- national organizations with local branches (i.e., Rotary or Lions Club)
- religious organizations or church
- through your children (i.e., schools, parents' organizations)
- evening classes
- language training or conversation classes
- university
- volunteer organizations
- sports and social clubs
- professional and business networks
- embassy or consulate (i.e., Community Liaison Office)
- in-country resource services (i.e., such as FOCUS Information Service Ltd. in the U.K.)
- expatriate organizations or associations (i.e., American Women's Club)

Creating a network of friends and acquaintances is essential to successfully adapt to your overseas environment.

This network will provide support and friendship. Although it will take a proactive approach, building a network need not be particularly difficult. Friendships tend to develop quickly in an expatriate community. Host nationals should also be part of your social network. They may be harder to become friends with, but the effort is worth it. They will not only help you integrate into the local culture, but also will make your expatriate experience all the richer. Remember to persevere through it all. It may be slow at first, but you will make friends. Once you do, you will enjoy your assignment and will develop a much deeper sense of appreciation than any tourist.

Chapter 12 (at a glance)
Bridge: Keeping in Touch

In this chapter you will discover how to ~

maintain contact with relatives and friends back home.

manage guests.

make overseas phone calls and reduce the cost.

keep in touch with news and changes in your home country.

vote by absentee ballot in the United States.

Some key points ~

❶ It is important to maintain relationships with relatives and friends back home.

② The simple things, such as frequent phone calls, letter writing, and home visits, will help maintain contact.

❸ It is very easy to make an international phone call, and today's technology makes for excellent connections.

④ There are several avenues available for keeping in touch with news back home.

❺ It is often possible to vote in home-country elections while you are overseas.

Chapter 12

BRIDGE: KEEPING IN TOUCH

Thanksgiving can be a tough holiday to celebrate when you are overseas. I believe it is one of the nicest traditions in America, a time for families to share company and food. Yet it is a quintessential North American holiday. It is not celebrated anywhere else in the world, and therefore can be difficult to arrange a celebration.

I wanted to prepare for my family as traditional a Thanksgiving dinner as possible. My hope was to prepare turkey, stuffing, sweet potatoes, cranberry sauce, glazed carrots, spinach, pumpkin pie, and apple pie. I was prepared to divert from my menu, inspired by an article my mother-in-law sent me many years ago that, tongue in cheek, suggested the Pilgrims actually ate spaghetti carbonara on their first Thanksgiving! I set off in the morning to gather the ingredients for dinner.

With a little bit of luck and ingenuity, I succeeded. The turkey was fresh, complete with feathers that needed to be plucked and head and feet still attached — a bit different from what I was used to back home! I improvised on the sweet potatoes (used just plain), and even spotted a jar of cranberry sauce in the local grocery store. The pumpkin pie was the only casualty!

It was very comforting to know that I was successfully able to transport my customs with me to my overseas posting. We even invited a national family to join us in our celebration. They had never tasted "American" food and were duly impressed by both the meal and the tradition.

It is important to maintain relationships with relatives and friends back home.

This can be especially demanding with the significant geographic distance created by your being overseas. The oceans create a psychological as well as physical barrier. Second, one major benefit of being overseas is the prospect of international travel (see Chapter 15), and you may not want to return home for your vacation.

As with any move, an international relocation causes feelings of isolation and loneliness, made more acute when you leave the security of your home. Friends and family are always a comforting and helpful network, and leaving them will always be painful, particularly for families that frequently visit their relatives. You probably will even feel a tinge of guilt about leaving your parents, particularly if you have children or if your parents are not well. It is therefore essential that you keep in touch with them when you live overseas. It is more complicated and difficult, but possible.

The simple things, such as frequent phone calls, letter writing, and home visits, will help you to maintain contact. Encourage your parents to visit you. If they have never traveled overseas before, they may be very apprehensive, or they may be tremendously excited at the opportunity. In either case, be as supportive and helpful as possible. As your relatives get older, it may be harder for them to travel, and so you will need to make more of an effort to visit them.

Although more complicated, it is important for both your children and their relatives to see one another. You will need to be more creative to get them together. For example, have your children send regular letters, photos, and artwork. If possible, plan a vacation at an international location and include the grandparents. For instance, if you are an expatriate in Paris, you could organize a gathering of the whole family in London. If business brings you back to your home country, consider bringing your children with you and letting them visit their grandparents.

The holiday season can be a hard time, especially if you traditionally celebrate with the whole family. Often, it is not feasible to go home at these times, yet it is important for you to keep alive your own family traditions and customs (see Chapter 10). You will need to find other ways that can satisfy your emotional needs.

Friends are a more tricky issue. Usually, when you leave a city, your friends will miss you, but they tend to get on with their lives. Your departure, although sad, will not cause a significant change in their lifestyle. You, on the other hand, are facing major changes in your life and will have greater need of your friends. Do not be upset if they tend not to stay in touch, but rather understand the differences in needs.

Make a strong effort, therefore, to stay in touch through frequent letter writing and phone calls. Take the initiative; do not wait for them to contact you. The development of the Internet makes keeping in touch all that much simpler via E-mail, but remember to occasionally send a "real" letter with a foreign stamp. The ubiquitous Christmas card is an excellent way to keep in touch with friends and to reflect on the past year's events. If the timing is incorrect, consider sending an early card to notify your friends of the move.

If you can send letters via a courier service back to your home country, remember to bring along postage stamps. Purchase a small postal scale so you will know the correct amount for small packages and oversized envelopes. Have a friend or family member notify you of any rate increases.

Some of your more adventurous friends may come to visit. This can be a wonderful opportunity to include your friends in your life overseas. Do not feel compelled, however, to be their dedicated tour guide. Have guidebooks handy and prepare sightseeing itineraries with information on public transportation, so you can send them on their way by themselves. Most good friends will understand and will appreciate the chance to explore by themselves. If, on the other hand, they expect you to be a tour guide or never want to leave your home, the days will become very difficult and uncomfortable. In these cases, you will need to be very determined, and politely but firmly encourage them to venture out by themselves. Insist on time to yourself.

Part of the challenge of having friends and family come to visit is that, depending on the distance they have traveled, they will want to stay for a long time — perhaps as long as a month! Try to limit their stay to seven to ten days maximum. If you really do not want houseguests, you can always make sure that your home does not have any extra space for guests!

You may find that some casual friends, maybe even some vague acquaintances, will descend on you as their free "bed & breakfast." Do not feel obligated to let them stay with you, because a poor houseguest is an ordeal. Consider having on hand a list of inexpensive and nice hotels in the area. While exploring your local neighborhood during your settling-in period, keep an eye out for appropriate hotels.

Family visits can be the hardest, particularly if you have children. Relatives will almost certainly expect to stay with you, and their visits will be long. If it is the accompanying spouse's in-laws, the working spouse should definitely take some time off from work. As when friends visit, you must make time for yourself.

An area that is often intimidating for some people is making international phone calls.

It is actually very easy, and today's technology makes for excellent connections. Friends back home will be amazed at the quality of the connection and will be surprised that it is an overseas call. Remember to calculate the time difference when calling, to avoid making or receiving calls in the middle of the night!

International direct dialing is possible to almost all countries. To make an international call, you need only dial:

International code -> country code -> area code -> private number

The international code from the United States and Canada is **011**; from all other countries, it is **00**. Country codes and time differences are listed in Resource 3, in Appendix C.

One significant concern with international phone calls is that they are expensive. Exponential advances in technology, coupled with a similar increase in global demand and deregulation of national markets, have helped to make the range of telecommunication services more diverse and competitive.

The types of services available for international calls include the standard fixed line allowing for direct dial, phone cards and account-based products, callback services, and mobile phone services. As with any service, research the options, price, and quality. This is an area that is rapidly changing, and new options are continually being made available.

Direct-dial calls, where available, are probably the most convenient, but also the most expensive option.

There are also some companies that allow you to "call back to the States" on U.S. rates, based on the curious fact that it is cheaper to make some calls from a foreign country via the United States than by dialing direct. The *International Herald Tribune* has many advertisements for these companies. These companies allow you to have access to phone lines from the United States. Any calls you make will, in essence, "originate" from the States. Using this system can save as much as 80% from national phone-company rates. Charges can be billed directly to your credit card. Another advantage of the "callback" system, besides price, is that you can access toll-free numbers. Note, though, that unlike toll-free calls originating in your home country, the calls are not free. Two drawbacks of these services are that the connection is not always good, and it involves an extra step of calling the service, waiting for the "callback," and then dialing the number.

Some countries such as Great Britain have their own local services that can be competitive. Research local telephone rates and options for long-distance calls, and compare them with other alternatives.

Remember, even if the calls are expensive, it is an important avenue to keep in touch with your relatives and friends. Also, the calls can have a great therapeutic value!

The feeling of being out of touch with your home country is disconcerting.

You will find that life overseas will open new doors to understanding global politics, which will broaden your viewpoint. However, you probably will want to keep up with news from home, and often the local press will give only a very superficial and biased viewpoint of current affairs. You will find it difficult to be involved in politics and the national election process, and almost impossible at the local level. Updates from your favorite baseball, cricket, bas-ketball, soccer, American football, and rugby teams will be few and very erratic. Trying to keep a regular appraisal of your invest-ments can also be hard. You may find that you are losing touch with your own culture, arts, fashions, and trends.

There are some things that can be done to help remedy the sit-uation. The *Herald Tribune* and *USA Today International* editions have excellent coverage of the States. *USA Today* is particularly thorough on sports reporting. The *Wall Street Journal International* and the *Financial Times* have general news and a comprehensive current review of international financial markets. Most internation-al cities sell a selection of other major foreign newspapers. The *Times* (U.K.), *Le Monde* (France), *Corriere della Sera* (Italy), *El Pais* (Spain), and *Frankfurter Allgemeine* (Germany) are all examples of editions that may be available overseas.

Time and *Newsweek* have international magazine editions that are excellent and give similar coverage as their American counterparts. The *Economist* (U.K.) and *Der Spiegal* (Germany) are other magazines that are commonly seen in major international cities.

If you have a reliable courier service from your home country, consider subscribing to a local weekly news magazine. Consider asking a friend back home to send you clippings of relevant and interesting articles. Although not timely, it is fun to catch up. This technique is particularly successful with sporting articles and team standings.

Do not disregard local newspapers and magazines in your host country. You will find yourself learning about world affairs and local language and customs as well.

Another excellent source of information is the Internet. You can get news, weather, sports, and financial data in "real time." Both *USA Today* and CNN have excellent Web sites that can keep you occupied for hours. Besides a computer and modem, you must subscribe to a local Internet service provider to obtain access.

You may be able to hook up to satellite television, which in western Europe includes Sky (U.K.), CNN (U.S.A.), NBC (U.S.A.), Eurosport, and other European stations. The children will appreci-ate the Cartoon Network.

One area that is often overlooked or neglected is voting.

It is often possible to continue to vote in your home-country elections while you are overseas. All countries have their own rules and regulations, and you are advised to understand them before you leave.

For example, as an American citizen overseas, you are entitled to vote via the absentee-ballot system. You must contact your local county clerk's office in your home country where you are currently registered to obtain an application for an absentee ballot. *You will need to do this when you commence your assignment and then at the beginning of every year of your posting.*

The **Federal Voting Assistance Program (FVAP)** is your first stop in finding about national elections. It is a nonpartisan group that provides information on federal and local elections to all U.S. citizens overseas. See Resource 1, Appendix C.

You can contact the **League of Women Voters** to obtain information on upcoming U.S. elections, such as names of candidates and other issues. You can also communicate with the major parties' national committees to find information on candidates and issues.

Both the **Democratic** and **Republican National Committees** have E-mail addresses (see Resource 1, Appendix C). There are branches of Democrats or Republicans Abroad groups in major foreign cities. They can provide information and are an outlet for your political energies.

As an expatriate, you will be focusing your energies toward your present environment — settling in, dealing with daily tasks, working, and making new friends.

Yet it is also important to maintain contact with relatives, friends, and culture back home. Even though the distance may be great, you can keep in touch. The simple things, such as letters and telephone calls, and the more complicated, such as visits, are all ways to keep in touch. The advent of the Internet and the accessibility of news make keeping up with life in your home country much easier.

Chapter 13 (at a glance)
Business Issues

From this chapter you can understand ~

the issues and guidelines for becoming a successful international businessperson.

the expatriate business cycle.

traits that are common to a successful person overseas.

steps to take to prepare yourself for the expatriate assignment.

the effect of culture on conducting business overseas.

a business cultural model and how to apply it.

strategies to address cultural differences.

how to deal with daily business issues and work-related problems.

Some key points ~

❶ The expatriate business cycle has six related parts that correspond to the relocation process, each with its own implications.

② The most important traits for a successful overseas manager are flexibility and a positive attitude.

❸ You must take control of your transfer and new job assignment overseas.

④ You should expect at the beginning to have a lower level of job performance.

❺ Multicultural awareness is essential.

⑥ Potential conflicts occur when your cultural values and attitudes are different from those in the host country.

Relocation

Chapter 13

BUSINESS ISSUES

How exciting! My family and I were transferred to Rome. I was to work in an Italian joint venture. I am sorry, but two years in Rome does not seem like a hardship posting. And the work truly was exciting.

I was ready to hit the ground running when I arrived — introductions with the players, some small chitchat to get to know one another, but let's get on with it. The workload was tremendous, and the time frame was ridiculously small.

A joint venture means that you must work together as a team. Great. I always prided myself on my ability to successfully work in a team; it was one of my strengths.

Well, let's get to it. My Italian colleague was ready as well. We sat in his office, ready to tackle our first problem. I had many ideas and wanted to discuss them. "But wait," he says, "we need a coffee." Sounds good, I think — a wonderful Italian coffee. Afterward, he says he will be right back. He needs to talk with someone; only a few minutes, he assures me. I sit in his office, waiting for thirty minutes. He never shows up, and I get up and leave. The morning was shot. Oh well, after lunch.

I grab a sandwich and am ready to go at 1:00 P.M. He is just leaving for lunch. Two hours later, he wanders back into the office. Finally, we get back together and start to work. The phone rings. "Excuse me, this will just take a second," he says. Thirty minutes later, he hangs up. Meanwhile, someone walks in to discuss something. Again, he assures me that this will take only a minute.

I go home that day having accomplished nothing.

The same scenario plays out day after day. I try all sorts of ideas. We'll work in my office . . . he hears his phone

*and runs down to answer it. We'll make appointments
with the restriction of no interruptions . . . he finds it intol-
erable after about two days.*
    *Projects and tasks that should take a few hours take
weeks. I am totally frustrated. What am I to do?*

Working in the international arena requires you to deal with,
sell to, and/or buy from people in other countries. These people
probably speak a different language and most assuredly have different cultural attitudes. By nature, they will approach business
from a different perspective and cannot be treated in the same
way as your colleagues. What works in one culture may fail miser-
ably in another. For example, do not be fooled into thinking that
other countries are "Americanized" because of the presence of
modernization or people who have studied or worked in the
States.

The relocation process, as discussed earlier (see Chapter 1),
has a chronological order that commences with the initial offer and
finishes at repatriation. The actual business assignment also goes
through a similar process. This expatriate business cycle has six
related parts that correspond to the relocation process. Each part of
the cycle has its own implications to the business assignment, as
shown in Figure 13.1.

Figure 13.1 The Expatriate Business Cycle

RELOCATION PROCESS	BUSINESS CYCLE	IMPLICATIONS
decision	*selection*	successful traits
predeparture	*preparation*	job preparation
relocation	*commencement*	what to expect
settling In	*culture*	cultural perspective
assignment	*daily business*	business environment
repatriation	*future career*	new assignment

You will encounter a whole set of issues and challenges that
are not present in your home-country work environment. To be

successful in the international arena, you must become "globally astute." This implies being able to understand behaviors and to translate that knowledge of cultures into appropriate responses and winning tactics (Schell and Solomon, 1997). Failed assignments are costly, potentially resulting in loss of business and market share, poor customer relations, lower work-product quality, and bruised relationships.

This chapter will navigate you through the expatriate business cycle. You will gain an understanding of the implications and subtleties of working in the international marketplace. It will address the many differences you will face when working overseas and will offer solutions to help make your assignment more effective.

The business cycle and related experiences are similar to the culture-shock stages discussed earlier. Refer to the "culture-shock cycle" diagram in Chapter 9 (Figure 9.1). Here you can substitute business productivity on the vertical scale, with the straight horizontal line representing your "normal" productivity.

Almost 95% of all expatriate employees are selected by line managers based on technical and managerial skills (Schell and Solomon, 1997), yet technical skills are only part of the equation.

International experience and cultural adaptability are rarely considered as factors. Many expatriates have little or no experience abroad. Often, previous exposure to anything but their home country is limited.

Several traits are common to a successful expatriate experience (Coyle and Shortland, 1992). International personnel must be able to move, adapt, and work successfully in a new environment. An expatriate must have a fundamental base of technical, creative, interpersonal, and communication skills. Many attributes are common to any effective employee, but others are specific to an international posting. If you are being considered for an overseas assignment, you obviously are exceptional in your profession and possess many of the skills listed below. Yet this is no guarantee that you will function as well in an overseas assignment. Many of the challenges you will face during an international relocation are very different from those back home.

The characteristics of a successful expatriate can be subdivided into three categories: *global perspective, change orientation,* and *people skills* (see Checklist 19, Appendix A). The successful person must:

Global perspective

- have a global viewpoint
- understand international politics and economics
- have a deep understanding of cross-cultural issues and their impact
- be interested in foreign cultures
- have a sensitivity to different cultures and people
- be open to learning the language of the host country

Change orientation

- have an openness to change
- adapt easily
- be accepting of foreign cultures and realize that they are just as valid as his own
- be open-minded and able to consider issues from different perspectives
- have a tolerance of ambiguity
- be open to learning and have a deep curiosity about people and the world
- be at ease with different types of people

People skills

- be innovative
- have excellent communication skills, including *listening* and *observing*
- be sensitive to the feelings and beliefs of others
- be self-confident and positive
- be self-motivated
- be outgoing and willing to seek out contact with nationals and their culture
- be nonjudgmental and accepting of opposing views
- be patient
- be a problem solver

Last, and most important, a successful expatriate must be flexible and have a positive attitude!

By accepting a transfer overseas, you are also assuming a new job.

This may sound obvious, but there is a tendency to be so involved with the actual moving process that one can lose sight of this. It is important to be clear with your managers on whom you will report to, what your new job will entail, what the responsibilities and duties will include, what the goals of your assignment will be, and what will be expected of you.

Expatriates serve several purposes for an organization. Foremost is usually the need to perform a particular function and accomplish goals. Expatriates are also important in that they can establish the corporate culture and way of doing business within a different culture. They need to be aware of transferring their skills to the nationals. This is sometimes as important as the material support. When expatriates return home, they need to encourage hosts to develop a sense of ownership and way of doing business for projects and ideas.

As with preparing for the move overseas, you must take control of your transfer and new job assignment. Often, there is little support from your company in dealing with preparations and ongoing support. The cultural impact and differences also tend to be ignored.

You also will have many questions from your employer, such as:

- What human resource, personnel, and business support are available to you overseas?
- Can you get a preview of the job and new location?
- Do you need additional training?
- What about your current projects? Who will assume your duties?
- How long will the assignment last, and are there plans for your future career beyond the assignment?

These are all critical considerations, and you should have discussions with your current managers so you are clear in your mind *before* going overseas.

There are also many aspects of a personal nature that you must recognize and give careful consideration. Questions to ask yourself can include:

- What are your *expectations* of the assignment, including job and day-to-day living? Are they realistic? Are you aware of the challenges? Do you and your family look forward to the opportunity?
- Are you *open-minded?* Are you receptive to different beliefs and ideas?
- Do you *respect* other cultures and beliefs?
- Do you *trust* new contacts?
- Are you *tolerant* of foreign environments and living conditions?
- Do you feel that you have some *control* over your environment?
- Are you *flexible?* Do you consider alternate approaches and points of view?
- Are you *patient?*
- Can you comfortably *socialize* with new people? Are you openly interested in and accepting of others?
- Do you have *initiative?*
- Are you willing to *take risks?*
- Are you *tolerant of change?*
- Do you have a *sense of humor?* Can you learn from your mistakes?
- Are you and your family motivated by the transfer?

Review the section on successful traits of an expatriate businessperson, and highlight the areas you think you may need to enhance. Many of these skills can be learned and nurtured.

You must realize that you are beginning a new job, with significant responsibilities and perhaps unforeseen burdens.

The support and patronage you had in your previous assignment may be missing. Such support can range from the tangible, such as the infrastructure of the home office, to the more abstract, such as emotional and technical advice from colleagues. You and your family will be much more on your own and will have additional pressures.

You should expect to have a lower level of job performance at the beginning (i.e., 50–80% during the first year) than in your current position (Wall, 1996; Coyle and Shortland, 1992). You will feel more exhausted and stressed, and you may even feel lonely and "lost." These feelings will result from the changes in your work life and the complexities in your personal life. The added physical and emotional demands from work and home will be significant. After the initial excitement, you may find yourself feeling let down. Mixed up with all these emotions will be significant uncertainties and concerns involving both work and family life.

Most people are aware that they will be faced with unfamiliar customs and behaviors when they interact with others in another culture, yet they are relatively unprepared for the emotional impacts such cross-cultural encounters will have (Cushner and Brislin, 1996). Dealing with the unknown and with differences invariably results in anxiety.

Your new assignment will most likely add the physical demands of extra work and perhaps travel. This can be especially burdensome on the family members, who are also dealing with major changes and trying to build up a new network of friends. Your support is essential, and they may resent the time you spend away from them. Therefore, you must be aware of the challenges and try to lessen the impact during the beginning of your assignment. This, of course, is hard because you are trying to "get your feet on the ground" and make a favorable impression.

Perhaps most important, you should be aware that the beginning of your assignment will be a particularly difficult and stressful time. This awareness will help greatly because you will better understand your emotions. Practice appropriate stress-management skills (see Chapter 9) and make sure you allow time for yourself, whether through personal relaxation or hobbies. Do not forget to initiate and maintain an exercise program if that has been part of your routine. Also practice time management to improve your productivity and provide more time with your family.

It is important to set realistic, or perhaps even slightly lower, expectations of yourself and your success in your assignment. As an expatriate, you need to accept that you will go through an awkward learning stage and will make mistakes. If you realize that it is relatively normal, you will hasten your adjustment.

Also remember that you are not isolated in your feelings. Most other expatriates have experienced similar reactions to working overseas. Talk with them. Benefit from their experiences and learn from their encounters. Communicating to people that they are not alone in their feelings is a major contribution to their well-being (Cushner and Brislin, 1996).

Cultural Influences

Multicultural awareness is essential when conducting business internationally.

A simple idea, but not necessarily straightforward in practice!

But why is culture so important to the success of an expatriate business assignment? Culture is the patterns of thinking, feeling, and potential acting of a particular group (Hofstede, 1997). Learned and assimilated during childhood, reinforced by literature, history, religion, and media, symbolized by our role models, and expressed in our values and laws, culture is a powerful force (Schell and Solomon, 1997). Culture forms the fundamental framework on which a whole society is built and molds the way we view the world. It affects the way we perceive and judge events, how we respond and interpret them, and how we communicate to one another in spoken and unspoken language. Culture is one of the factors that forms an individual's values and beliefs and directly relates to actions and behaviors.

Further complicating matters, we subconsciously believe that our own behavioral norms are the same for everyone (Storti, 1994). Because we are not aware that our values and behaviors were not learned but rather were internalized over years, they become unconscious and instinctive. Many of our norms were acquired in early childhood, when we are most susceptible to learning and assimilating (Hofstede, 1997). That is the reason we do not have to think about what we do or say in a given situation.

Storti (1994) presents an argument that if we do not feel that we learned our cultural perspectives but think they are instinctive, we think everyone else should be the same! Perhaps more appropriately, the reason we probably attribute our perspectives to others is that we have always done so, and it usually works. In one's own culture, this is imperative. If you could not predict how people behave in particular situations, it would be very difficult to function in your daily life. Remember that a particular behavior or action has no meaning other than what people assign to it.

Problems arise when we come into contact with another culture. Here we learn that much of what we assumed was universal human behavior is peculiar to a particular group or culture (Storti, 1994). In essence, culture is the way people solve problems (Trompenaars, 1995). Perceptions and interpretation of the same data, events, etc., will be different depending on cultural orientation. People from different cultures can sometimes assign different meanings or interpretations to a particular behavior. Culture, with all its implications, *differs in every society!* These differences might be profound or subtle, obvious or ambiguous, but more often than not, they are hard for an outsider to interpret. It is important to remember that there is nothing inherently "good" or "bad" about these differences.

When you are confronted with a different culture and way of doing things, the tendency is to make comparative judgments with your own culture. The assumption is that yours is normal and natural, and the other culture is different, strange, or inferior. Actions by someone from another culture, therefore, can be perceived negatively. For example, an American's directness may be perceived as being rude by a Japanese, and Japanese indirectness could be perceived as evasive by the American.

Business, therefore, cannot be separated from people and their cultural background. More than any other aspect of international business, your sensitivity, knowledge, and understanding of culture will affect the outcome of business ventures. Without insight into the ways of others, you cannot effectively develop credibility, nurture goodwill, motivate and manage individuals, or build effective teams.

Not all cultural differences are visible. Language and dress are the most obvious contrasts. Less conspicuous are the values and beliefs that are often hard to recognize, but are every bit as critical to forming cultural perspectives. Even if people appear similar outwardly, their culture will have shaped them to behave and think differently than you.

Cultural differences manifest themselves in several ways, including symbols, heroes, rituals, and values (Hofstede, 1997). Symbols are the words, gestures, pictures, or objects that carry a particular meaning and are usually recognized only by the culture. Language, dress, and status symbols fall into this category. Heroes are persons, dead or alive, real or imaginary, who possess characteristics valued by a culture and are role models. Rituals are collective activities, such as social and religious ceremonies, that are considered socially essential by the culture. Finally, values are the core system that truly governs the culture's beliefs and attitudes. They form the underlying basis for a culture and are usually acquired by individuals at an early age. As an outsider to a culture, one can observe, learn, and accept different symbols, heroes, and rituals. This is often not so for values.

There are many attitudes and beliefs that shape an individual's behavior (see Checklist 20, Appendix A). The following questions address many different perspectives one can have.

- When people communicate, do they favor a direct approach or a more indirect style?
- Do they base their actions on faith (i.e., religion), fact, or emotions?
- What is more important, the project or building relationships among colleagues?
- Do rules universally apply to everyone?
- Does the society favor an individualistic or a communal approach?
- How are decisions made — collectively, immediate/ middle manager, or top level only?
- What motivates people — personal achievements, money, titles, etc.?
- How important is time?
- Are people punctual to meetings and appointments?
- How important are social ranking and hierarchy to the

workforce, and what is your position in the group?
- What is the employee's attitude toward authority?
- How do the people view others who are different (i.e., gender, race, religion, cultures)?
- Is the business environment formal or informal?
- Are the people tolerant of change and open to taking risks or is there a strong bias on following rules and established patterns?
- Are the people open- or closed-minded by nature?

These are all critical modes of behavior that will affect how an individual acts. Learning about the culture (i.e., history, government, religion, and language) and the people will help in forming your interpretation of people's actions and will make you more effective.

This section will expose you to how culture affects lives and manifests itself in business. Clearly, it is impossible to provide information for every culture or for every conceivable difference that you may encounter, yet a framework can be presented for understanding multicultural interactions. First, you will learn a cultural model in the context of business. The next step will be to see how your own cultural orientation fits into this model. We will then see how each component and related cultural perspectives combine to form a general organizational culture, which is, in essence, an extension of the society. You then will have a foundation to appreciate and answer the questions raised above. You will be able to predict results and behaviors in intercultural business encounters, developing general guidelines on how to modify your behavior and address the differences. By learning effective strategies and new skills for cross-cultural business dealings, you will be better able to address the cultural challenges in your assignment.

Cultural Model

Culture, like stress, is a complex and often misunderstood subject.

As with the culture-shock model (see Chapter 9), the concept of culture is best understood when separated into discrete parts. By then relating these components to the international business environment, expatriates will have a powerful tool to help in understanding people from other cultures and why they behave in specific ways. They can then adapt their own behavior to be more effective in business situations.

Several business-related cultural models have been developed (e.g., Schell and Solomon, 1997; Trompenaars, 1995; Hofstede, 1997; Hofstede, 1980; Seelye and Seelye-James, 1996; Piet-Pelon and Hornby, 1992; Hall and Hall, 1990), each breaking down culture into a varying number of segments (ranging from four to ten). When developing any cultural model, it is necessary to make some generalizations about human behavior. Clearly, people are individuals, and one cannot make specific predictions. Surprisingly, though, there are certain features that seem to cross all cultures, with each culture having a certain perspective.

Drawing heavily from others' work (in particular, Schell and Solomon, 1997; Trompenaars, 1995; and Seelye and Seelye-James, 1996) and incorporating our experiences, we have subdivided culture as it relates to the business environment into two parts, each with three components. It is an individual's perspective toward each component within a specific culture that affects his attitudes and responses. *Potential conflicts occur when the cultural perspective is different within a component.* Our model is intended to be practical and relatively simple, and easily applied in the business environment (see Checklist 21, Appendix A).

The six components fall into two segments: personal influence and outside influence.

Personal Influence	**Outside Influence**
• communication	• time
• relationships	• hierarchy
• interdependence	• change

The first group involves characteristics that are controllable by individuals. The second group refers to outside influences within the society and the individual's reaction to them. Clearly, many of these dimensions are interrelated and have characteristics that are common to one another. We will now discuss each component and how cultural perceptions differ.

Personal Influence

Communication

One of your first priorities in your assignment is to develop effective communication skills.

Communication is probably the most important aspect of a successful business enterprise, and its style is strongly influenced by culture. Your ability to communicate clearly and to understand others will be a key factor in your success as an international businessperson. Issues of poor communication are accentuated when dealing with a different language and culture. For example:

Ford got it wrong in Brazil with the unsuccessful marketing of the Ford Pinto automobile. *Pinto* is a slang term in Portuguese for "small male appendage." Not surprisingly, the car was not a hit with Brazilian men (Morrison et al., 1994).

General Motors did not learn from its competitor's mistake. The GM Nova was not a success when introduced in Mexico. *No va* means "no go" in Spanish — not a stellar name for a car (Seelye and Seelye-James, 1996)!

These are perhaps extreme examples, but they show that miscommunication and lack of cultural awareness can ruin an overseas business operation.

> *The other day, I was in the most interesting meeting in our overseas office, with a group of partners involved in a project with my company. The meeting was convened to try to reach an agreement between the two companies. Our positions on a certain issue were exactly opposite. The attendees consisted of managerial and technical staff members from both companies. All were local Italian nationals except myself, the only American.*
>
> *As the meeting progressed, it became more and more contentious and argumentative. People were shouting, slamming fists on the table, posturing for position, and basically being downright hostile. Except for me, everyone was yelling and openly showing anger. Such behavior would be considered rude, aggressive, and unprofessional in a meeting in the United States. I was truly astonished.*
>
> *In contrast, I presented my company's position in a very*

controlled and calm, but direct and firm, manner. My tone, although not confrontational, was such that they knew I was serious. The partners were truly taken aback and did not know how to handle my presentation.

After the meeting, I was told by the manager from the partner company that he considered me "an aggressive manager." His tone was both complimentary and disapproving. I later learned that the shouting and dramatics displayed by my Italian colleagues were the expected way of making a point and were not taken as indications of hostility. In contrast, my "quiet firmness" appeared to them as a much more serious display of anger and distance.

Effective communication is essential in any business environment. English is often the language used in business settings, even if it is the second language of all the participants. It may be the only common language. Therefore, a good command of English is important. If English is not the official business language, you should make a significant effort to learn the appropriate language. Even if English is the dominant language in the office, knowledge and use of the local language will go a long way toward your earning your host colleagues' respect and acceptance. The ability to speak a local language will greatly add to your understanding of the host culture.

It is recommended that you take an intensive language immersion course. After that, continue with weekly language lessons throughout your assignment. The time and money invested in language training quickly pay for themselves. Recommendations from friends are probably your best source for finding a good instructor. Be careful in your choice of language instructors. As with any service, there are good ones and bad ones. Do not be afraid to dismiss someone you are not learning from or who does not seem interested in your successfully learning the language.

Language learning can be a very rewarding process, but you should keep in mind that slow progress is part of learning and should not be taken too seriously (Cushner and Brislin, 1996). Your efforts will usually be greatly appreciated by your hosts, however clumsily you come across.

Although English is spoken in many countries and is often the language used in many business communications, it is not usually their first language. You must recognize that although they may speak well, the comprehension of nonnative English speakers is not necessarily good. Speaking in English may be difficult for them. It is a good idea to avoid business jargon (e.g., *bottom line, MBO,* etc.) because these may be unfamiliar expressions.

Many Western cultures, particularly the United States, favor the direct and open form of communication in business dealings, ascribing a low value to communication. These cultures prefer to get right to the point. Nonverbal communication, emotion, flowery discussion, and eloquence are not considered particularly admirable traits and often detract from the business dealings. Those cultures value logic, clarity, and simplicity in discussion. Content is more important than details.

This contrasts significantly with other countries (i.e., Far Eastern cultures) which place a high value on form and favor more indirect and subtle communication. Being very forward can severely damage business negotiations. Stating your business needs at the wrong time may be viewed unenthusiastically by your hosts. Often, what is not said or how it is presented is more important to the sense of the conversation than the actual words.

Cultural attitudes toward expressing emotions in a business environment vary considerably. North Americans tend to exhibit emotion but usually separate it from objective and rational discussion. Southern European cultures such as Spain and Italy tend to show emotion and not separate them from business. Finally, many northern European cultures, such as the British and Swiss, tend not to show emotion and never would consider them to be a part of a business meeting (Trompenaars, 1995).

In some cultures, it is impolite or threatening to disagree, particularly with a superior. The employees may say whatever they think will please their manager. Such an attitude occurs in some Far East, Latin American, and former Soviet Union countries. For instance, Japanese society values harmony, civility, and the avoidance of confrontation. This can be related to a cultural bias of wanting to shield superiors from "bad news," wanting to avoid conflict, wishing to please, or not wanting to be blamed for problems. The Indonesians actually have a term for this trait, *asal bapak senang,* which broadly translates as "keeping father happy" (Morrison et al., 1994). Whatever the reason, in these cultures it can be difficult to receive accurate reports or the truth.

An example of a more indirect style of communication is in the many ways certain cultures have devised of not quite saying yes. Storti (1994) lists seven potential responses that may mean no: 1) to ask a question; 2) to say they do not understand; 3) to change the subject; 4) to say they cannot answer at this time; 5) to give a conditional yes; 6) to say that the question is very difficult; and 7) to claim that this question is not within their authority to answer.

You can also learn some qualifiers and gestures in conversation that may suggest a negative response. For instance, sentences with "Yes, but . . .," "Maybe," "We will see," "Possibly," or "It might be difficult" are all red-flag qualifiers that could signal "no." Excessive politeness or evasiveness can also indicate a negative. In a desire to please, you may get the answer they think you want to hear. To individuals from cultures that are more direct, these responses can be confusing and can lead to incorrect interpretations. Therefore, be careful how you phrase questions. For example, put your questions to people so that they require more detailed answers rather than just a simple yes or no.

One solution to not receiving the truth is to sponsor regular one-on-one visits with your coworkers. You can also try to rely on employees who have previously worked in your home country. They may understand that if managers are aware of problems, steps can be taken to solve them rather than placing blame.

In some countries, personal identity is directly tied into all aspects of their life. The issue of "saving face" is a very important and delicate matter. This is particularly the case in some Far Eastern, Middle Eastern, and Latin American countries. Loss of face can signify loss of honor, trust, or respect for an individual.

> *We were having a technical meeting in our conference room. There were several attendees but not enough chairs. Our Arab colleague went next door to his manager's office to borrow one of his chairs. The manager came into the office just as Hassan was wheeling out one of the chairs. The manager, sarcastically but in jest, said to him, "Stealing chairs again?"*

> *All during the meeting, Hassan, who was a primary contributor to the meeting, was very silent and sullen. After the meeting, he seemed unable to contain himself and went to see his manager. In a very proud and dignified manner, Hassan told him, "I am not a thief."*
>
> *What was meant as a very innocent joke by the manager turned out to be taken very personally by Hassan. He felt that his honor and reputation had been called into question.*

"Face" means the image one presents to the world, including one's reputation and self-esteem (Storti, 1994). Obviously, one wants the image or reputation to be positive, particularly in public. Left alone, one can look after one's own self-worth, so the issue is usually the need to be careful to preserve the face of others. Therefore, public criticism, shame, embarrassment, or disapproval of someone in front of others can be devastating. Any criticism should be handled with extreme care, sensitivity, and discretion. Discreetly saying no, as discussed above, relates to the issue of saving face. By outright saying no or even implying displeasure or disappointment, one risks humiliating the other person.

Another seemingly innocuous area you must look out for is the friendly or sarcastic insult. In cultures where the concept of face is important, a sarcastic joke or comment, even if meant merely as a joke, can be taken literally. This, of course, will lead to serious misunderstandings.

Many languages have two forms of the word *you*, a familiar one and a formal one (e.g., *tu* and *vous*, respectively, in French). The appropriate time to use either one is very significant. English, on the other hand, does not distinguish between formal and familiar relationships. In other languages, inappropriately addressing someone with the informal *you* can be highly offensive.

> *I had just moved to Italy and was struggling to learn the language. In the Italian language, there are two ways of greeting someone,* buon giorno *and* ciao. *The English equivalents are* hello *and* hi. *I was attending a high-level meeting with several Italian government officials, and as I was introducing myself to the chairman, I said, "Ciao." He looked at me ever so strangely and said in a highly sarcas-*

tic tone, "I do not recall, but we must have met before."
Obviously, I did not make a favorable impression!

There are many figures of speech and slang expressions in any language and culture. Even an English-speaking country such as Great Britain has its unique differences. If your daughter's British male friend calls to tell that he "will knock her up around noon and bring along his rubber," do not be too concerned (translation: her friend will come over to visit at noon and bring his eraser)! It is probably unavoidable to make a misstep, but if you do, try to keep your sense of humor.

There are other important aspects of communication besides verbal. These include written language, gestures, and body language. Research has shown that at least 75% of all communication is nonverbal (Trompenaars, 1995). Researchers have found approximately one thousand distinct units of nonverbal communication (Storti, 1999). People around the world use body movements or gestures to convey specific messages. Nonverbal cues — such as body language, eye contact, hand and body gestures, and seating positions in business meetings — are all important.

Although members of different cultures use the same gestures, they often have different meanings. Misunderstandings over gestures occur frequently in cross-cultural communications, and their misinterpretation can lead to business complications and embarrassment. Words or gestures conveyed inappropriately can send the wrong message. Your posture, stance, or distance from a foreigner can also convey unintentional messages. For example, putting your feet up with the soles exposed to an Arab or Southeast Asian is insulting, and taking off your coat without an invitation in a Japanese negotiating session confirms you as unsophisticated (de Kieffer, 1993). You will need to learn the appropriate as well as inappropriate ways of language and behavior. Foreigners are often judged by the same standards that host nationals apply to themselves.

It is impossible even to make generalizations regarding behavior. For instance, in most countries, spitting in public is considered vulgar, yet in Russia, spitting three times over the shoulder is believed to prevent bad news. In Spain, the "OK" gesture used in the United States (circle with thumb and forefinger) is rude; in Japan, it is a symbol for money; in France, it means "zero."

Throughout Arab countries, the thumbs-up gesture, which connotes approval in the United States, is offensive. In Sri Lanka, the nonverbal signals for agreement are reversed. A nod of the head means no, and shaking your head from side to side means yes. In Turkey, the gesture for yes is the same as in the United States, yet the U.S. "no" gesture of shaking your head from side to side means "I do not understand." In some countries (i.e., Muslim), the left hand is considered unclean and taboo because it is used for personal toilet hygienic purposes. When in these countries, do not use this hand when eating, passing food or objects, touching another person, or accepting gifts. (The above examples are cited in Morrison et al., 1994.)

Something as innocuous as a smile can be interpreted incorrectly. In many cultures, a smile is a good way to establish rapport, yet Russians do not customarily smile at strangers. Smiling at strangers would show an inappropriate amount of familiarity (Seelye and Seelye-James, 1996).

Just because you have *recognized* a given behavior, do not assume you have therefore *understood* it.

Do not forget the correct titles for the host-country people. They most likely have great pride in their country and are very nationalistic. Simple mistakes can upset people. For example, someone with an "American" accent may not necessarily be from the United States but may be Canadian. And certainly, everyone in North, Central, and South America is American, not just those in the United States!

People in other countries are very sensitive about their history and culture. This pride is quite strong and reflects on self-image. Furthermore, they can get very touchy when not respected. Many foreigners innocently call all people from Great Britain "English." This is an insult to the Scots, Welsh, and Irish, who do not have a close affinity to the English. (When the English team was in the World Cup, some Scottish and Irish people supported the opponent, which was Germany!). Some Far Eastern countries, such as South Korea and Taiwan, are extremely proud of their history. References to Japan and the People's Republic of China, respectively, can be upsetting. Before embarking on your assignment, read about the host country's history. Your hosts will appreciate your knowledge, and you will gain some insights into their culture.

Seelye and Seelye-James (1996) present several signs for recognizing the symptoms of communication misunderstandings. Blank stares, unnatural stopping points in a conversation, embarrassment in the other person, and feelings of "not connecting" are all common indications that someone does not understand you. They suggest that to optimize your communication, you should reinforce important points by rewording them in different ways, use visual aids and numbers, ask questions to check understanding, avoid the use of idiomatic expressions and slang, ascertain the real meaning of nods and verbal assents, and follow up on any agreement or plans.

No matter how well versed you are in the appropriate and inappropriate behaviors in a specific country, you are still bound to make mistakes. Most likely, as a foreigner, you will not greatly offend people the first time. Apologizing and admitting your error go a long way toward smoothing relationships.

Relationships

There are two types of behavior (Trompenaars, 1995).

The first involves a responsibility to adhere to ethics and rules of the culture. The other extreme refers to an obligation to people. The former is focused on rules and the second on relationships and individuals.

> In the Latin American country I was working in, I had the fortune to observe two different styles of negotiations with the local government. Both American companies, one a large multinational and the other a smaller company with a local office in that country, were trying to obtain approval to drill an oil well in their prospective licenses.
>
> The first company sent top managers from the States to present the company's position to the top country officials. They gave a very polished and solid presentation over a two-day period. They very convincingly presented their ideas and recommendations. During the first evening, they hosted a very elaborate dinner for the country representatives.
>
> In contrast, the other company sent their local national

representative to meet with midlevel officials. The meetings took place over several weeks and were more informal. The company's position was presented and potential problems and concerns were resolved. The next step involved the company managers meeting with the local and top country officials. They flew in from the States the day before to host a dinner. This enabled them to meet the individuals in a more informal manner and establish personal relationships. The next day, the meeting was relatively short, with only brief presentations. There was much support of the company's position by the local nationals.

Although the first company's meeting was very direct and time-effective, the company never seemed to obtain approval for its project. It encountered continual opposition and requests for additional work. In the end, it was more than two years before the company could move forward with its project.

In contrast, the second company, although it had spent a few months in negotiating and nurturing relationships in the country, obtained approval with minimal problems.

The concept of "Thou shall not lie" is held as an accepted "rule" by the first cultural type. In the second culture, it can also be an accepted behavior, but more because it would be hurtful to their friends. Notice that these different points of view sometimes complement each other, but at other times they can be in conflict. For instance, in the relationship-oriented culture, the above concept may apply to someone's friend but not to a perceived threat (e.g., official, competitor, etc.).

It is predominantly Protestant cultures, where religion focuses on obedience to God and his written laws, that have the rules-oriented approach (Trompenaars, 1995) in which "truths" are universally applied. In a relationship-oriented society, it is the person and not the rules that is the central issue. The former society's attitude toward the latter may be, "They cannot be trusted because the rules do not apply evenly." In the latter culture, they may think, "They cannot be trusted because they would not even help a friend." Notice the conflicts that can occur when individuals from the two cultures interact.

Many countries in the world have an emphasis on relationships rather than on rules. The focus is on the person and, by association, the nature of personal circumstances. Personal relationships are often more important than technical expertise and business competence. In relationship-focused cultures, human interactions are resilient, develop slowly over time, and are viewed as long term. By their nature, it is therefore inconceivable to conduct business with someone you do not know. Trust must be built and nurtured between individuals over time and is essential for initial and future business dealings.

The importance of forming a personal relationship *before* moving directly into business dealings in a relationship-oriented culture cannot be understated. Trust, personal bond, and even friendship must be built before effective business can be undertaken. Whereas business in a rules-oriented society can be engaged in almost immediately, it takes much longer in a relationship-oriented culture. Interest in the individual is as important, if not more so, than business issues. Business dealings are considered to be with the individual and not the company. "Getting down to business" instantly is not appreciated and can impede relationships. In the short term, business dealings appear to take a long time, but eventually they will be more successful and rewarding. If people take the time to build relationships, they will be forged forever and will serve to avoid potential problems in the future.

It is important to create a sound and trustworthy basis that equates the quality of the product or task with the quality of the personal relationship. This may entail entertaining, social conversation, and other nonbusiness relations. Initial dealings should be focused on the individual and family rather than the business. It is only after the friendship and trust have been formed that successful business can be undertaken.

In contrast, in a rule-oriented culture in which standards apply universally to everyone, the need for building long-standing relationships is not necessary. Partnerships and alliances are based on opportunity and circumstance and are protected by rules or laws. Trust is not a prerequisite to business dealings because it is protected by rules. Written contracts are therefore more important. In contrast, contracts are not a significant issue in a relationship-oriented culture and are often very vague or general. Cultures that have a low emphasis on relationships will therefore predominantly focus on the business, with little emphasis on the individual. Getting to know the individual is considered mostly irrelevant to the business.

Interdependence

The group-dependence issue concerns the differences between cultures that focus on individuality and individual achievement and those that emphasize conformity with a group or team.

> I was part of a team sent to China to negotiate a contract to establish a joint venture with our company and the Chinese government. Our team consisted of upper-level managers and technical staff members.
>
> As the meeting progressed, every Chinese would express opinions. Any ideas or decisions were clearly a consensus. There was a strong sense that they were working and cooperating together. Although our team wished to progress the meeting at a faster pace, it was clear that patience was a virtue in this situation.
>
> On one particular issue, one of the Chinese expressed some reservations. He seemed almost apologetic, and at a superficial glance, it was not a major problem for him. Although the majority of the delegation appeared to be ready to compromise on this point, they all supported the minority opinion because of one member's dissent. It was as if the harmony of the group would have been affected adversely. A majority agreement was not sufficient.

The United States and Japan are two classic examples showing these differences. For example, compare the differences in proverbs from one culture to another. In the States, people say, "The squeaky wheel gets the grease." In other words, if you stand out (in a group), your needs are more likely to be noticed. In Asia, the sayings are, "The nail that stands out gets pounded down" and "The pig that squeals goes to slaughter." Both show reference to the need to conform and the dangers of being different (Schell and

Solomon, 1997). In Japan, youngsters grow up learning that they cannot exist on their own as individuals but only as members of a group (Grove and Hallowell, 1996). Fitting in and maintaining harmonious relationships in all aspects of life, including work, are paramount.

The attitude toward the individual and group determines how people are motivated and rewarded. The issues you need to consider when managing and working within teams include:

- How are project assignments made?
- Are problems solved individually or by the group?
- Is decision making to be a group process?
- Is the reward structure based on individual performance or the success of the group as a whole?
- Is compensation based on skills, achievement, and experience or on a person's loyalty, sensitivity, and ability to work in a group?

Most business environments value the group approach to problem solving and encourage teamwork. Yet the actual carrying out of problem solving by the team is quite different, depending on how cultures view "group dependence." For instance, in the United States, teams are formed to achieve an objective, yet the team is considered to be made up of individuals. They usually work on their own, often getting together to share ideas. Individual performance and success are valued and rewarded accordingly.

In contrast, in cultures that are more group oriented, it is the complete group effort that is important. The group moves ahead *as a group*. Loyalty to and harmony within the team (and corporation) are paramount. Often, the functioning of the group takes precedence over its business achievements. In Japan, for example, groups compete seriously with one another, but individuals within groups experience communal feeling and do not compete with one another (Stewart and Bennett, 1991). Incentive plans and other personal-motivation schemes, therefore, will not work in Japan. Rather, incentives must be applied equally to all members of the group. This can be confusing to people from cultures with low interdependence, in which it is assumed that corporate competition is paralleled by open competition at the individual level.

In dependent groups, decision making will take longer because everyone in the group must be heard. Meetings, therefore, will take a significantly longer time. Meetings in a more individualistic society tend to focus on specific objectives, decision making, and exchange of information. In group-dependent cultures, meetings are more of a forum for team members to express their thoughts and ideas. Many meetings are required to make decisions. Although consensus decision making is slow, implementation of a decision with consensus in place is quite rapid. In comparison, in cultures with a low-interdependence perspective, decisions are reached faster, but much effort is needed to garner support for the decisions (Stewart and Bennett, 1991). A close look at the decision-making styles and expectations of all parties is necessary for good cross-cultural adjustments in the workplace (Cushner and Brislin, 1996).

Outside Influence

Time

Cultures view time in different ways.

Essentially, there are two basic attitudes toward time. The United States, Far Eastern countries, and much of northern Europe view time as a valuable commodity (i.e., the concept that "time is money"). These cultures view time as finite, controllable, and not to be "wasted." In contrast, other cultures, such as countries in southern Europe, Latin America, and the Middle East, believe that time is unaccountable. Time is viewed more fluidly.

> *I was sent to a meeting at our West African regional office to help prepare for a major presentation to the government ministry. We were hoping to gain a major industrial contract.*
>
> *I left the States on Saturday morning, hoping to arrive Sunday afternoon. Meetings were scheduled for the whole week. I felt that we had a fairly ambitious agenda, but with a bit of focus, we would have plenty of time. I was even hoping that I might be able to make a quick visit to the local museum.*
>
> *The journey was horrendous. My flight was delayed by*

several hours, and in the confusion, my bags were lost. I arrived at my hotel late Sunday evening, exhausted.

The next morning, as I rode from the hotel to the office, I was stuck in a huge traffic backup. The heat and humidity were stifling. Through the exhaustion, I felt my stress level rising, and I was very upset that I was late. It was not an auspicious beginning.

At the office, I was greeted happily by the local staff members. I was told that both the general and assistant managers would not be available until late afternoon, and a key technical member was attending his son's music recital. Regrettably, we would have to postpone our meetings until the following day. I was flustered. In fact, I was incensed. Surely they all knew I was making the long journey to help them with their critical planning.

The next day, my driver took a "shortcut" to avoid the construction responsible for yesterday's delay, yet the drive seemed to take just as long. I could again feel my stress level rising and the time slipping away.

I entered the office ready to begin work immediately and make up for lost time, but my hosts would have none of that. We spent the whole morning socializing, more or less. Although I was presenting a polite front, I was seething on the inside.

Finally, after a long lunch, it seemed that we would start our meetings. About forty-five minutes into our discussions, a colleague of the general manager's stopped by his office. Rather than politely asking him to return at a more convenient time, the manager welcomed him with open arms. They sat and talked for an hour about nothing particularly urgent. Other members of the team drifted in and out of the conference room, and before I knew it, any semblance of organization had broken down into disarray. I was almost halfway through my trip and had accomplished nothing.

The next three day were much the same. All my careful plans and ideas seemed to be for nothing. Although my hosts seemed overjoyed at our "successful" meetings and felt that we had made great progress, I left feeling that nothing had been accomplished. I was frustrated and exhausted, and dreaded explaining my "failure" to my boss back home.

In the "time-is-money" scenario, scheduling, prioritizing, deadlines, and planning are critical. Time is viewed most frequently with reference to the future. Commitments such as deadlines and schedules are taken seriously. Punctuality and promptness are highly valued, and people in these cultures have great difficulty understanding how business can be effectively run without this orientation. Circumstances and unforeseen events are considered to be a nuisance and should not be allowed to interfere with plans. Individuals who place a high value on time prefer to do one task at a time and are dedicated to its rapid completion. They show great respect for people's time and are concerned about disturbing others. Interruptions are frowned on.

The working unit of time in these cultures is the five-minute block; any amount of time smaller than that is not considered very important (Cushner and Brislin, 1996). Therefore, if an individual is late to a meeting by only a few minutes, he is considered to be "on time." If he is late by five or ten minutes, a brief apology is expected, and if late by more than fifteen minutes, a lengthy and sincere apology is required, often with a phone call to the waiting party to announce the delay.

In contrast, in cultures with less emphasis on time, more importance is attached to building relationships. Obligations to family and friends take precedence over work concerns. Plans are expected to change, and lateness (e.g., to a meeting) does not reflect negatively on a person's ability or character. Time commitments are more of an objective to be achieved rather than a "quasi-legal" contract (Seelye and Seelye-James, 1996). Everyday events and chance circumstances (e.g., traffic, running into a colleague) are considered normal interruptions. There is also a tendency to do several things at once, to appear to be unfocused, and to welcome interruptions (e.g., phone calls, other people). The comparable working unit of time, approximately fifteen minutes, is a much larger block than in high-time cultures (Cushner and Brislin, 1996). It is not uncommon for someone to be late to an appointment by an hour yet not consider himself to be "late" from his perspective.

These cultures tend to view time in reference to the past or present. In Pakistan, for instance, the word *kal* in the Urdu language describes both "yesterday" and "tomorrow"; in Indonesia, the term *jam karet* translates as "rubber time" (Morrison et al., 1994). A historical perspective is very important, and current or future issues often will be viewed in this context. Tradition is often used for guidance.

A culture's attitude toward preventive medicine is an example of different time perspectives. Cultures with a future outlook find significant value in preventive medicine. Essentially, preventive medicine requires individuals to anticipate a future event and connect it with present conditions and actions by means of a cause-and-effect relationship (Stewart and Bennett, 1991). This outlook requires an orientation to the future and faith in the ability to control it through measures taken in the present. In contrast, in cultures with a past or present time perspective, people's attitude is more like, "If it isn't broken, why fix it?" People in such cultures often believe that one cannot control the future or one's environment, and therefore it makes little sense to try to alter the course of nature.

The potential conflicts between people operating with different time perspectives can be great. Misunderstanding, stress, and frustration are all possible results. Imagine the anger building inside a person who views time as precious when meeting with a colleague who does not. While the former person is trying to focus on a specific project, the latter is answering phones, talking with others, and seems quite distracted and unfocused. The impression is that he does not value or respect the other individual's time and may even take offense at his colleague's "pushiness" and obsession with time. The perception would be that such behavior is rude and insulting. The idea of not taking time for others would be unthinkable.

The pace of business in some countries is much slower than in the United States, for example. You may encounter lots of verbosity, exaggeration, poetics, flowery language, and emotion when working with others, particularly in meetings. There can be constant interruptions. People answer telephones and other people walk in.

If you have a high-time perspective, you may find yourself getting very frustrated and angry with a slower pace. Take several deep breaths when you find yourself in this situation, and realize that you cannot change others' attitudes. Try to keep sight of the goal and of forming trusting relationships, as compared with always being "time-efficient." Above all, be patient.

Punctuality is highly emphasized in the United States and is an important factor in forming impressions of individuals, yet this concept is not consistent throughout all countries. It is important for you to understand your host culture's attitude toward punctuality. For instance, in northern European and some Far Eastern countries, there is a strong emphasis on punctuality. It is considered an insult and very impolite to keep executives waiting. Yet in other places, including Russia, Saudi Arabia, and Latin American countries, delays and lateness to appointments are the norm, with punctuality not considered a virtue.

Even if punctuality is not followed in daily life or business settings, it is often expected of foreigners, North Americans in particular (Morrison et al., 1994). You should strive to be on time for all appointments. Remember to consider the commute time, because traffic congestion in many cities is terrible.

If you find yourself waiting for someone in an office, for example, use the time to develop a good interpersonal relationship with the secretary or other people in the office. As discussed above, the importance of building relationships in certain cultures cannot be underestimated, and you may find that these relationships can help you in your business dealings. In these situations, it is a good idea to schedule only one or two meetings in a day to reduce your anxieties about being late to appointments.

Hierarchy

How we view authority and power varies based on the cultural framework.

There are essentially two ends of the spectrum: Authority clearly separates individuals, and people are more nearly equal and authority is less of a defining factor.

> *I was transferred by my American company to Thailand to become the general manager. On my arrival, I was offered the previous GM's company car, a Mercedes-*

Benz. In the States, I drove a luxury Japanese car and always thought that a Mercedes was a nice status symbol. I knew that the traffic in Bangkok is terrible, so I opted for a practical, small car. I left it to the local Thai finance manager to handle the details. He looked slightly puzzled at my request, but I didn't think much of it.

During the next weeks, I continued to use the Mercedes, with much difficulty, while waiting for the arrival of my new company car. After a month, I asked the finance manager about the status of my order. The Thai looked uncomfortable and said, "We can get you a new Mercedes by tomorrow, but the Toyotas take much, much longer." Slightly annoyed, I asked him to speed up the process.

After several more weeks with no delivery, I brought up the issue during a management meeting and asked for an explanation. Somewhat shyly, the Thai managers explained that they could hardly come to work on bicycles.

A lightbulb went on. I remembered from the cultural training I had attended before moving overseas that Thai people are very status conscious. In this case, the status of each individual in the organization is interdependent. If I were to drive a "lesser" car, then each member below my level would have to turn in his current car and order a lower-level car. By asking for a Toyota, I had disturbed the delicate balance. With this understanding, I continued to drive the Mercedes.

(Story adapted from Trompenaars, 1995.)

In societies that view authority as more fluid, people believe in individualism and equal rights. An individual has more control of his life and "rank." Advancement and power are available to all people in society. Business organizations tend to be less hierarchical, with flatter structures. Employers empower their people, giving them more authority and responsibility. Business relationships are often more informal. In low-hierarchical cultures, people believe that they control their destiny in life. Accomplishments are personally achieved and rewarded accordingly; hard work, intelligence, and ability will lead to success.

In contrast, societies that place a large emphasis on authority and rank have very different relationships. People view rank as fixed and unlikely to change. For instance, the Japanese society places enormous importance on rank and hierarchy. Indonesia is a nation that values rules and respects authority. The ramification of this idea is that people feel they have little control over their lives. They show great deference and respect to authority and do not challenge it. Confrontation is avoided. Usually, subordinates do not make decisions or expect to. Middle managers who are most familiar with a project are not always the ones who are the decision makers. They do not bear much responsibility beyond their direct jobs. The business organization is much more pyramidal, with a strict management chain of command. Relationships are more formal. Status symbols, such as office size and location, titles, and cars, are very important.

People view their lives as something related to whom you know and your place at birth. Connections and whom you know are critical and are the basis for any accomplishments. Seniority is very important. In such cultures, networking and relationships are key in any business environment. Hierarchies are more clearly defined, and corporate structures are more rigid. One's position in society tends to be fixed. Recognition and rewards are based more on proper connections and position, with less emphasis on individual accomplishments. In those cultures, you must always be aware of the social and business hierarchy. Class distinctions are considered normal, appropriate, and socially useful (Grove and Hallowell, 1996).

It can sometimes be hard to understand the criteria for placement in a hierarchy, because it can vary from culture to culture. For example, in Japan, teaching in elementary or high school is a very respected occupation and is rewarded with high status. In contrast, teaching is not an especially respected profession in the United States (Cushner and Brislin, 1996). An American teacher working in Japan, therefore, would experience an increase in status, whereas a expatriate Japanese teacher in America would experience a decrease.

Interestingly, cultures that are very hierarchical tend to be very group oriented, and cultures with a flat business structure tend to employ more individualistic people (Hofstede, 1997). In other words, the interdependence cultural component is correlated positively with the hierarchy component. However, there are exceptions, such as France and Germany.

Good management practices in one culture, therefore, will not necessarily work in another. For instance, a casual egalitarian approach to business can fail in a class society. It is therefore critical to know the employer-employee relationship when doing business.

Change

Tolerance to change refers to people's attitudes toward change, newness, and doing things differently.

A culture's view toward risk taking strongly relates to this attribute as well. In essence, some societies view change as an inevitable and even a positive force. Others perceive change as something to be avoided.

> *A major U.S. multinational corporation purchased a small and successful German company. The purchasing company was very impressed with both the operation and personnel and wanted to retain much of the original structure. The company officials felt it was important, though, to integrate the home-office corporate style and culture. To that end, a few expatriates were established in the country.*
>
> *One area in particular that needed consolidating and improving was the finance department, and thus one of the expatriates was a finance manager. Her interpersonal skills were outstanding, and she considered herself culturally astute.*
>
> *After her arrival, she spent many weeks building trusting relationships with her national staff, and held numerous meetings to establish the new accounting procedures. She went over the many benefits and reasons for the changes.*
>
> *Although the staff members seemed receptive and interested in the changes, the manager noticed intense resis-*

tance to adopting them. She was frustrated that the employees were all very skeptical and cautious, even though they acknowledged the potential advantages of the new system. They viewed any changes as suspect, much preferring their original procedures.

Partly because they did not want to disagree with their superior, they would nod their heads in agreement and commit to making the changes, yet in practice, they would continue with the old ways. Their reluctance to express honest views on issues led to wasted discussions and wasted time, and ultimately to failure to achieve objectives.

Some cultures thrive on and encourage change, creativity, and ingenuity. Risk taking in these cultures is encouraged, and it is considered good to challenge the accepted practices; "new is better." Note, however, that although some *societies* embrace change, many *individuals* feel uncomfortable with it (see Chapter 9). Human beings tend to be creatures of habit who find change difficult.

A good example of this difference between society and individuals is the recent corporate tendency of downsizing staffs. Lifetime employment in North American corporations used to be normal and expected. When companies began to lay off employees, their first reactions were obviously fear and anger. Yet they began to adapt, and have replaced job security with career security. Changing jobs is now viewed as a desirable way to broaden one's knowledge and skills. The relationship between companies and employees has been changed forever. The expectations are now completely different.

Cultures that do not view change as a positive or natural force hold onto tradition, even at the expense of progress or profits. History and tradition govern their lives. Change often represents a threat to these cultures. They are risk-adverse societies, and their attitude to new ideas is commonly, "We have always done it this way; why change?" They follow rules and restrictions, even if they seem nonsensical or dysfunctional (Hofstede, 1997). These organizations have clearly defined systems with very little flexibility. Jobs and responsibilities are very detailed and spelled out. How well you work in this environment is partly a function of *your* flexibility.

An interesting paradox is that although cultures that view change as a positive factor do not like rigid rules and establish them only out of necessity, they are generally more respected (Hofstede, 1997).

Doing business in low-risk-taking cultures means that conducting business negotiations and meetings takes much longer. Individuals need continual confirmation of new ideas, with corroborating data. They need to be comfortable with a new idea before they will accept and act on it. Often, people will micromanage projects. They feel they must be part of all aspects and cannot release any control. The underlying basis of this need relates to their difficulty in accepting change or risk. This can be frustrating and can slow the project down if, for instance, you must share responsibilities. The person will find it impossible to let go of any control and will insist on being part of your work, or may not accept any of your individual work or ideas. The best way to handle this is to be patient, continually communicate with your colleagues, and involve them as much as possible.

Table 13.1 summarizes the differences among different cultural perspectives and presents a general guideline for understanding people's perceptions of other cultural values.

The following table is intended to give you a general guideline of the perceptions individuals have of people with a different cultural perspective than their own. The first column indicates the cultural perspective of an individual, and the following columns are possible perceptions of others. For example, an individual with a high communication value may view someone who is from a low communication value as impersonal, etc. An individual from a low communication value may view someone who is from a high communication value as evasive, etc.

Table 13.1 Cultural Perceptions

Cultural perspective of people with ↓	possible interpretation of people with	
	HIGH **Communication** VALUE	LOW **Communication** VALUE
HIGH **Communication** VALUE	—	impersonal, untrustworthy, blunt, transparent, confrontational
LOW **Communication** VALUE	evasive, circuitous, secretive, emotional, distracted	—

Cultural perspective of people with ↓	possible interpretation of people with	
	HIGH **Relationship** VALUE	LOW **Relationship** VALUE
HIGH **relationship** VALUE	—	apprehensive, impersonal, superficial
LOW **Relationship** VALUE	wasteful, inconsistent	—

Cultural perspective of people with ↓	possible interpretation of people with	
	HIGH **Interdependence** VALUE	LOW **Interdependence** VALUE
HIGH **Interdependence** VALUE	—	disloyal, disrespectful, confrontational
LOW **Interdependence** VALUE	indecisive	—

Table 13.1   Cultural Perceptions

Cultural perspective of people with ↓	possible interpretation of people with	
	HIGH **Time** VALUE	LOW **Time** VALUE
HIGH **Time** VALUE	—	unfocused, rude
LOW **Time** VALUE	rude, pushy	—

Cultural perspective of people with ↓	possible interpretation of people with	
	HIGH **Hierarchy** VALUE	LOW **Hierarchy** VALUE
HIGH **Hierarchy** VALUE	—	disorderly, informal, disrespectful, undedicated
LOW **Hierarchy** VALUE	unequal, formal, pretentious, lacking initiative	—

Cultural perspective of people with ↓	possible interpretation of people with	
	HIGH **Change** VALUE	LOW **Change** VALUE
HIGH **Change** VALUE	—	inflexible
LOW **Change** VALUE	impulsive	—

A Word of Caution

It is important to realize when studying cultures that you are also dealing with individuals, *and there are always exceptions to any custom or cultural perspective.*

Many ideas presented above are generalizations about particular cultures. Although a particular cultural attitude may govern a society's behavior, individuals will react differently, depending on their personalities and experiences. Generalized ideas will not replace the need for getting to know the people you are working with. You can complete and "score" the Exercise 12 questionnaire in Appendix B to better understand your host culture and people.

Even with all these generalities about culture and allowing for individual differences, you must also be aware of contradictions within the culture. For instance, a classic example is with France and Italy. They are very risk-adverse societies when it comes to change in labor practices (i.e., continual strikes), yet the world looks to them for fashion change. Thus, there is a danger of oversimplifying and stereotyping cultures (Schell and Solomon, 1997). A person's culture is only one of the factors that will influence how he acts in a given situation.

Still, making an oversimplified and generalized opinion of others is not wrong. Such opinions often capture characteristics that are generally representative. Cultural generalizations imply a potential of how people from a particular culture *may* behave in a given situation, but not how they *will* behave (Storti, 1999). It can enable you to form a model of other cultures. The danger is that generalizations can lead to stereotyping. Looking at a culture in terms of stereotypes can further lead to prejudice and negative opinions. Be careful not to fall into the trap of judging or criticizing others based on your own cultural perspectives. Differences are not something better or worse; they are only differences. In the end, being judgmental is detrimental to your business relations and your ability to adapt successfully to your new environment.

Cultural components and perspectives by country

Table 13.2 is meant to be a companion to the discussion on cultural components and related perspectives. The intention is to give a *general* idea of different countries' and societies' predispositions to the cultural components discussed earlier. You can then form the basis of your host country's cultural model and compare it with your own perspectives.

The results draw heavily on the work of the following: personal communications and research (see Exercise 12, Appendix B); Hofstede, 1997; Hofstede, 1980; Morrison et al., 1994; Seelye and Seelye-James, 1996; Storti, 1994; and Trompenaars, 1995.

Table 13.2   Cultural Components and Related Values

	Communication	Relationships	Interdependence	Time	Hierarchy	Change
Angola	high	high	high	low	high	low
Argentina	high	high	high	low	high	low
Australia	low	low	low	high	low	high
Austria	low	low	low	high	high	low
Belarus	high	high	high	low	high	low
Belgium	low	low	low	high	high	low
Bolivia	high	high	high	low	high	low
Brazil	high	high	high	low	high	low
Bulgaria	high	high	low	low	high	low
Canada	low	low	low	high	low	high
Chile	high	high	high	low	high	low
China	high	high	high	high	high	low
Colombia	high	high	high	low	high	low
Costa Rica	high	high	high	low	high	low
Czech Republic	high	low	low	low	low	high
Denmark	low	low	low	high	low	low
Ecuador	high	high	high	low	high	low
Egypt	high	high	high	low	high	low
El Salvador	high	high	high	low	high	low
Ethiopia	high	high	high	low	high	low
Finland	low	low	low	high	low	low

Table 13.2   Cultural Components and Related Values

	Communication	Relationships	Interdependence	Time	Hierarchy	Change
France	high	high	low	low	high	low
Gabon	high	high	high	low	high	low
Germany	low	low	low	high	high	low
Ghana	high	high	high	low	high	low
Greece	high	high	high	low	high	low
Guatemala	high	high	high	low	high	low
Honduras	high	high	high	low	high	high
Hong Kong	high	high	high	high	high	low
Hungary	high	high	high	high	high	high
India	high	high	high	low	high	high
Indonesia	high	high	high	low	high	low
Iran	high	high	high	low	high	low
Iraq	high	high	high	low	high	low
Ireland	high	high	low	low	low	low
Israel	low	high	low	low	low	low
Italy	high	high	low	low	high	low
Jamaica	low	high	high	low	low	high
Japan	high	high	high	high	high	low
Kazakhstan	high	high	low	low	high	low
Kenya	–	high	high	–	high	low
Kuwait	high	high	high	low	high	low
Lebanon	high	–	high	–	high	low
Libya	high	–	high	–	high	low
Malaysia	high	high	high	low	high	low
Mexico	high	high	high	low	high	low
Nepal	–	high	high	–	high	–
Netherlands	low	low	high	high	low	low
New Zealand	low	low	low	high	low	high
Nicaragua	high	high	high	low	high	–
Nigeria	high	high	high	low	high	low
Norway	low	low	low	high	low	low
Oman	high	high	high	low	high	low
Pakistan	high	high	low	low	high	low
Panama	high	high	high	low	high	low

Table 13.2   Cultural Components and Related Values

	Communication	Relationships	Interdependence	Time	Hierarchy	Change
Paraguay	high	high	high	low	high	–
Peru	high	high	high	low	high	low
Philippines	high	high	high	high	high	high
Poland	low	high	low	low	high	high
Portugal	high	high	high	low	high	low
Romania	low	high	low	high	low	high
Russia	high	high	low	low	high	low
Saudi Arabia	high	high	high	low	high	low
Sierra Leone	–	–	high	–	high	low
Singapore	high	high	high	high	high	low
South Africa	low	low	low	high	low	high
South Korea	high	high	high	high	high	low
Spain	high	high	high	low	high	low
Sri Lanka	–	high	high	low	high	high
Sweden	low	high	low	high	low	high
Switzerland	low	low	low	high	low	low
Taiwan	high	high	high	high	high	low
Tanzania	–	–	high	–	high	low
Thailand	high	high	high	low	high	low
Tunisia	high	high	high	low	high	low
Turkey	high	high	high	low	high	low
U.A.E.	high	high	high	low	high	low
Ukraine	high	high	low	low	high	low
United Kingdom	low	low	low	high	low	low
Uruguay	high	high	high	low	high	low
U.S.A.	low	low	low	high	low	high
Venezuela	high	high	high	low	high	low
Yemen	high	high	high	low	high	low
Yugoslavia	–	–	high	–	high	low
Zambia	high	–	high	low	high	low

Editor's note: A dash signifies no data are currently available.

It is important to realize that the results are a comparison of cultural tendencies for each country and not for individuals. The usefulness of this table is that it describes the dominant values and perspectives toward each cultural component of the majority within a specific country. You can then better appreciate different cultures, yet never assume that these results apply to a particular individual from a country (i.e., stereotyping). They are only a *general predictor* of behavior. There is no better substitute for learning about the people you are doing business with than to get to know them personally.

Note that you must refer to this table with care.

- In all relationships, you are dealing with individuals. They may or may not subscribe to the general cultural observations (see above).
- Cultures go through continual changes in perspectives. For example, the former Soviet Union countries are struggling between their obligation to the collective unit and individual freedom. Some countries are breaking away from traditions and making changes that do not fit with previous perspectives (e.g., companies in Japan are instituting individual "pay-for-performance" incentives).
- Several countries consist of different subcultures which may have different value systems and beliefs. For example, Belgium is made up of Dutch, French, and German cultures; Switzerland consists of Germans, French, and Italians; and in Malaysia, the ethnic Malay and Chinese cultures dominate.
- There are differing intensities or degrees of cultural perspectives within a society. It is very difficult to generalize about all cultures and their perspectives; be wary of them. For instance, both Switzerland and Canada are "high-time" cultures and would answer "**a**" for Question 5 in the "Culture and Business Environment" questionnaire. Yet the degree in which each culture values time is different, with Switzerland placing a greater emphasis on time than Canada. Possibly a Swiss evaluating Canada might answer "**b**"!
- Individuals may act differently within their own culture

than without. For example, the Japanese tend to close all doors to outside influence (i.e., change cultural component), but are open to ideas within their group.

- Most of the research and observations come from a Western perspective. Further, even the best of researchers tend to approach cross-cultural research with their own cultural biases. Given that the results are intended for a North American audience, the observations are valid, yet you must keep this bias in mind.

One should evaluate each country individually, but a general inference can be made by region (see Table 13.3). In general, Arab, Latin American, and Mediterranean countries are all relatively similar, except for the interdependence component in the latter cultures. The Far Eastern countries are similar as well, except that they have high interdependence and time components. The northern European countries are similar in all components except for hierarchy and change, which are more specific by country. For example, Germany places high value on the hierarchy component but low value on change. In contrast, Sweden places low value on hierarchy but high value on change.

Table 13.3   Cultural Components and Values by Region: Generalizations

	Arab Countries	Latin American Countries	Mediterranean Countries	Northern European Countries	North American Countries	Far Eastern Countries
Communication	high	high	high	low	low	high
Relationship	high	high	high	low	low	high
Interdependence	high	high	low	low	low	high
Time	low	low	low	high	high	high
Hierarchy	high	high	high	*	low	high
Change	low	low	low	*	high	low

Note: Components noted with an asterisk are specific by country rather than region.

Perhaps what stands out most is that North American countries *are not the norm but rather the exception.* The United States is actually an anomaly compared with most of the countries in the world! Although the United States has a huge influence in the global business environment, very few cultures share its cultural values. This understanding of differences is essential in intercultural business dealings.

Cultural Model and the United States

To complete your comprehension of the cultural model presented above, it is helpful to focus on your own culture.

By understanding yourself and why you act in certain manners, you will be better equipped to understand others and the subtle and not so subtle cultural nuances. Keep in mind that any generalizations are just that. They do not allow for individual or organizational differences within a culture. To determine your own perspective on each of the cultural components, complete and "score" the Exercise 12 questionnaire in Appendix B *as you see yourself.*

As an example, the breakdown of the behavior and attitudes of the United States culture is given below, and is meant only to be a guideline. Remember, though, that there are always exceptions and differences within any culture. To explore U.S. cultural patterns in detail, Stewart and Bennett (1991) is an excellent resource.

Personal Influence (United States)

Communication

The United States ascribes low value to communication.

Americans are very direct and open, preferring to get right to the point. They generally avoid long greetings and rituals, preferring to exchange only minimal pleasantries before conducting business. Content is more important than details (Schell and Solomon, 1997). Americans in business stress facts, logical analysis, and practical results. They value objectivity over subjectivity. The concept of "saving face" is not an important issue.

Verbal symbols (i.e., words) are much more important than nonverbal signals (i.e., gestures, facial expressions, tone of voice) in America. Substance of a conversation is based more on what is stated than on what is not (Stewart and Bennett, 1991). Nonverbal communication or flowery discussion and eloquence is not considered a particularly admirable trait and often detracts from business dealings. Americans are often poorly prepared to cope with the significance of nonverbal communication in cultures where it is important. Americans value logic, clarity, and simplicity in discussions.

Relationships

In the United States, Americans place low value on business relationships.

Although most organizations say that "people are their greatest asset," what is important are the products, results, success, and the project . . . the "bottom line." Results and action are considered more significant than being people oriented and building relationships (Schell and Solomon, 1997). Teamwork is considered important, but often, little emphasis is placed on building a team. The project is considered the focus, and it is felt that the "team" will come together during the course of the work.

Associations may develop quickly, but they often last for only a short period. Usually, no obligation is attached to relationships. One result is that people in the United States expect to engage in business immediately, spending a superficial amount of energy on social issues. They want to "get to the point" quickly and prefer short, focused meetings. One does not need to like or truly trust someone to have business dealings with that person in the United States.

Interdependence

In the United States, independence and self-reliance are considered virtues.

Hofstede (1980) suggests that the United States is the most individualistic of all societies in the world. Americans are encouraged to be self-sufficient from childhood, and individual accomplishment is recognized and rewarded (Schell and Solomon, 1997). Motivation and reward are usually centered around the individual rather than the group. Indeed, "the squeaky wheel gets the grease." Loyalty is with the individual and not the group or organization. People tend to work alone, even when working in a team. Ideas, concepts, and problems are all shared in the team, but there is much greater emphasis on the project and individual. Americans consider success to result from individual effort, competence, and originality (Stewart and Bennett, 1991). Failure is usually considered a personal responsibility rather than an outcome of life circumstances.

Outside Influence (United States)

Time

The United States places high value on time.

Time is viewed as a precious commodity and is a very important concept. Time management is critical, and there are countless books and seminars on how to effectively use your time. Schedules, plans, appointments, deadlines, and punctuality are all very important. Americans prefer to focus on one thing at time and are very organized.

Hierarchy

In the United States, hierarchy does not play an important role.

Certainly, individuals in positions of authority and power are treated with respect, but they are not regarded with total awe and deference. American employers give their staff members more authority and responsibility and expect them to "challenge the system." Managers encourage ideas from subordinates. Aggressiveness and independence are met with more toleration and may be encouraged.

An American's core ideal is that the same opportunities, rights, and obligations apply to everyone (Grove and Hallowell, 1996). In theory, all Americans are felt to have an equal opportunity to be successful. Individuals are rewarded according to abilities rather than ascribed characteristics (e.g., age, gender, ethnicity, parental social rank, class distinction, etc.). Others are judged by what they achieve and not "who they are." Status is based much more on personal achievements. Americans dislike authority and do not appreciate it when people in positions of power flaunt it.

Americans are much more individualistic than most societies. They identify less strongly with groups (i.e., family, friends, work colleagues) than people in other cultures do. One result of this in the business environment is that Americans may speak, act, and dress informally. People typically are on a first-name basis. Often, the supervisor will have an open-door policy, and it is acceptable for employees to enter. Meetings are usually "open" and participation is encouraged from everyone. This degree of informality is uncommon in most other cultures (Stewart and Bennett, 1991).

Of course, with increased authority and responsibility also comes greater accountability. Americans believe that hard work, intelligence, and achievement lead to success. Furthermore, anyone can be successful if he possesses these traits. Accomplishments are expected to be rewarded and recognized. Therefore, accomplishments and related rewards define a person's importance and status.

Change

In the United States, Americans are future oriented, and they value change.

They believe that the future holds opportunity. Change, transition, newness, improvement, opportunity, and risk are all considered vital and natural parts of the business cycle. Tradition and the status quo in business are not particularly valued, and Americans are often looking for ways to improve the system. Creativity, innovation, and effort are an integral part of this change process. Americans are receptive to new ideas, innovation, and alternate ways of doing things (Schell and Solomon, 1997). A common marketing technique for a product is to slap "new and improved" on the label. Americans thrive on taking risks because they believe it increases the chance for greater success and rewards. Change is a way of life for Americans. Moving to a new location and changing jobs are considered normal and even encouraged.

Cultural Model within the Business Organization

For the past several pages, we have discussed different components of culture and their impact on the business world.

We have also seen how North Americans perceive each of these aspects, and that they are the exception rather than the norm. These national cultural dimensions, which permeate throughout a society, will form to build an organizational culture. Certainly, corporate culture is very dependent on the type of business and the personality of the leaders, but it is surprising how much influence cultural perspectives have on the organization. Although certain corporate attitudes and practices do transcend national boundaries, thereby creating a body of shared expectations, they affect only a small percentage of the most common interactions (Storti, 1994). It is the national culture that has the greatest impact. In essence, business enterprises are actually a "mixed" organization, with selected cultural components dominating and forming the basis of the corporate culture.

Just as national cultures conflict, leading to problems, so do corporate cultures. An obvious example is the culture clash in the foreign satellite office of a company. These offices are usually filled with a predominance of nationals and a few expatriates. Often, the home office wants the expatriates to bring the corporate culture to the foreign location. Such things as ways of doing business, reward strategy, policies and procedures, and communication are all key areas the central office is planning to imprint on the foreign office. Naively, the home-office leaders may expect it to be a simple change and are surprised when it is not. It can be much like swimming against the tide.

Let us look at these potential conflicts by considering an example.

A large German company has just purchased a successful

Spanish firm. The German company wants to maintain the organization and plans to keep the office intact, with all the Spanish employees, and send a German expatriate to manage the office.

Looking at the cultural components and the different perspectives of each society, we see that a German organization tends to have these values:

> communication — low value
> relationship — low value
> interdependence — low value
> time — high value
> hierarchy — high value
> change — low value

In contrast, the Spanish perspectives to each of the cultural components are:

> communication — high value
> relationship — high value
> interdependence — high value
> time — low value
> hierarchy — high value
> change — low value

Referring to the implications of each perspective discussed earlier, imagine the conflicts and challenges that the German expatriate manager could encounter if he is not sensitive to cultural differences. The difficulties could even be compounded, because both cultures are not particularly open to change!

(References: Hofstede, 1997; Hofstede, 1980; Morrison et al., 1994; Seelye and Seelye-James, 1996; Storti, 1994; Trompenaars, 1995; and personal communication and research.)

Trompenaars (1995) has identified four types of corporate cultures. We can consider each of the cultural components identified above to see how the perspectives and values fit into each corporate culture. This is a valuable way to look at organizations, but it is, again, a generalization.

Type I: personal, yet hierarchical, corporate culture (like a family):

> communication — high value
> relationships — high value

        interdependence — high value
        time — variable
        hierarchy — high value
        change — low value

Examples of countries that fit this corporate culture include Japan, South Korea, Spain, Greece, Venezuela, and India.

Type II: very hierarchical, formal, and bureaucratic corporate culture:

        communication — low value
        relationships — low value
        interdependence — low value
        time — high value
        hierarchy — high value
        change — low value

Examples of countries that fit this corporate culture include Germany, Austria, and Belgium.

Type III: egalitarian, impersonal, and task-oriented corporate culture:

        communication — low value
        relationships — low value
        interdependence — low value
        time — high value
        hierarchy — medium to low value
        change — high value

Examples of countries that fit this corporate culture include the United States, Canada, and Australia.

Type IV: egalitarian, personal, and nonhierarchical corporate culture:

        communication — low value
        relationships — high value
        interdependence — low value
        time — high value
        hierarchy — low value
        change — high value

An example of a country that fits this corporate culture is Sweden.

What is seen from these broad organizational models is that there is considerable overlap between a corporate culture and a national one. Furthermore, there are many similarities among organizational models. The problems arise when there are differences. Working style and individual interactive style are critical factors that must be identified and understood if workers from two cultures are to interact effectively (Cushner and Brislin, 1996).

Effective Strategies to address cultural differences

With your understanding of each cultural dimension, you will need practical guidelines to be successful in your multicultural business interactions.

In the first section, tips are presented for each cultural component to help you interact in cultures that have a different orientation than the United States or similar countries. The second section presents strategies for working in cultures with a similar orientation to the United States. Remember that behaviors that are both appropriate and sensitive by your own standards may not be perceived as such in other cultures. Before you project your norms onto another person, consider that yours may not be the most appropriate.

Personal Influence

Communication
In cultures that place a high value on communication:
- Learn the local language.
- Do not get impatient when people are indirect or circuitous.
- Let meetings flow.
- Avoid being direct.
- Do not be uncomfortable with expressing emotions.
- "Listen" to both the verbal and nonverbal communication.

- Be aware of the signs of communication misunderstandings.

Relationships

In cultures with a high emphasis on building relationships:

- Build informal networks and trusting relationships.
- Take time to get to know the individuals you are working with, and show an interest in their lives.
- Engage in small talk and after-hours entertainment.
- Always have face-to-face meetings.
- Focus on people and relationships rather than tasks.
- Show empathy, and be sensitive to others' suffering and discomfort.
- Be flexible and open to new ideas, other beliefs, and points of view.

Interdependence

In cultures that are strongly group oriented:

- Seek to get a group consensus; listen to all opinions.
- Reward the group rather than the individual.
- Acknowledge the importance of interaction of individuals in a group.
- Avoid favoritism.
- Encourage team meetings, if only to share information and concerns.
- Make sure that all team members understand the project's goals and their participation in the process.

Outside Influence

Time

In cultures with a low value on time:

- Be prepared for meetings, appointments, etc., not to begin on time and to take longer than you may expect.
- Agree on future projects' completion targets in principle, but do not fix precise deadlines for completion.
- Emphasize the history, tradition, and rich cultural heritage of those you deal with as evidence of their potential.
- Remember that projects and tasks are generally subordinate to relationships.

- Spend more time discussing issues with people to help facilitate the decision-making process.
- Tolerate interruptions.
- Schedule only one or two meetings in a day.

Hierarchy

In cultures where there is a large emphasis on authority and rules:

- Be familiar with people's positions and rank within the organization.
- Show respect and deference to people at or above your perceived level.
- Never overtly challenge anyone, and be aware of people's need to "save face."
- Use titles extensively.
- Remember the importance of age and seniority.
- Be aware that decisions are challenged only by people with higher authority.
- Always consult with your superiors, and keep them informed at all times.
- Dress appropriately for your respective position in the organization.
- Do not expect individuals at lower levels to take responsibility.
- Be polite.
- Realize that money is not a prime motivator.
- Remember that employees' personal time (e.g., family, vacation, weekends, etc.) is highly valued.
- Value connections and personal characteristics.

Change

In cultures with a low tolerance for change or risk taking:

- Avoid grand or swift changes in the organization or policy.
- Realize that the status quo is preferred, and any changes in behavior or attitudes will come slowly.
- Respect company loyalty.
- Be clear and concise with outlines of requirements, rules, and instructions.

- Honor history and tradition.
- Respect the wisdom of continuity; new and different are not always better.
- If you encourage others to take risks, then reward the risk taking regardless of whether it works out.

In this section, tips are presented for each cultural component to help you interact in cultures that have an orientation typical of the United States or similar countries.

Personal Influence

Communication

In cultures that place a low value on communication:

- Learn the local language.
- Do not take confrontational discussion or criticism personally.
- Remember that content is more important than form.
- Be clear, precise, and direct.
- Get directly to the point in meetings, and expect to be taken at your word.
- Do not be afraid to say no or that you do not understand something or to admit mistakes.
- Give less meaning to body language than to actual words.
- Be aware of the signs of communication misunderstandings.

Relationships

In cultures with a low emphasis on building relationships:

- Do not be apprehensive of doing business with someone you do not know.
- Remember that you do not have to like or trust someone you are doing business with.
- Do not engage excessively in small talk, but focus on business issues.
- Do much business by phone, fax, letter, etc.
- Focus on tasks and rules rather than the relationship.
- Be sensitive to others, but not to the extent that it impedes business.

- Be flexible and open to new ideas, other beliefs, and other points of view.

Interdependence

In cultures that are strongly independent:
- Do not be afraid to express your own opinion.
- Reward the individual rather than the group.
- Acknowledge the importance of an individual's contribution.
- Take responsibility for your own actions.
- Recognize that teams are important but are a means to an end.
- Do not be reluctant to make decisions without a group consensus or full discussion.
- Allow for personal freedom and individual initiatives.
- Be prepared to work independently, with a minimum of supervision.

Outside Influence

Time

In cultures with a high value on time:
- Be punctual to all meetings, appointments, etc.
- Plan, organize, and complete projects in a timely manner or by an agreed-upon deadline.
- Emphasize future potentials, aspirations, and goals.
- Practice time management.
- Respect others' time.
- Schedule events and adhere to plans.
- Remember that time is considered to be a precious and valued "commodity."

Hierarchy

In cultures where there is a lower emphasis on authority and rules:
- Respect people's position and rank, but do not defer to them.
- Treat individuals at all levels with the same rights.

- Do not be afraid to challenge or question a superior.
- Do not view status symbols as significantly important.
- Be direct and informal.
- Avoid extensive use of titles.
- Remember that power is determined by competence and achievement and not by seniority, age, or status.
- Do not be afraid to take responsibility or make decisions.
- Be prepared to be accountable for your actions.

Change

In cultures with a high tolerance for change or risk taking:

- Be open to new and different ideas.
- Do not be afraid to take risks, even if you may not receive the expected results.
- Be creative and innovative and receptive to new ideas.
- Make broad plans and guidelines, leaving room for change.
- Recognize that uncertainty and ambiguity are normal.
- Always question the status quo and look for a better solution.
- Break new projects into small increments, if feasible.

A successful expatriate cannot try to force a foreign national to conform to another way of thinking and doing. One cannot give universal advice that will apply to all cultures and businesses; the world is too complex. However, by understanding people and different cultural perspectives, you can go a long way toward building successful relationships. It is important to realize that the issues and problems are the same for everyone; it is just that cultures differ markedly in how they approach and solve them. Generating and using cultural generalizations effectively, while avoiding stereotyping, are some of the most demanding skills of intercultural interactions. Cultural self-awareness, combined with some knowledge of predominant perspectives of other cultures, is the first step toward achieving this goal.

Begin by understanding and having a healthy respect for the dominant beliefs of other cultures. Do not judge other people's behavior, particularly from your own perspective, but find out what it signifies from their cultural perspective. It is a good idea to first describe a particular behavior before interpreting and assigning a meaning to it. By taking a moment to think about it, you have a better chance of not making a mistake.

Each culture possesses integrity and is neither inferior nor superior to any other culture. In a business setting, one cultural perspective may work better than another. Try to combine the strengths of your own culture with the positive attributes of the host cultural style, and downplay or avoid the ones that cause problems or that you do not like. Build on the cultural differences for mutual growth and accomplishment. There are many successful pathways to reach a goal. You will make mistakes and often will feel frustrated and confused. As you learn from your mistakes and find your own solutions, you will have come a long way toward being a successful international businessperson.

Daily Business

The more you can reduce surprises and create greater predictability through awareness and understanding, the more you can lessen the effects of cultural differences for you and your coworkers in your work environment. If you are oblivious to the differences, it will be impossible for your business assignment to be successful.

Your daily business interactions as an expatriate can be subdivided into three categories: the *daily business environment, basic business practices,* and *work-related concerns.* The business environment that the expatriate finds himself in is unique. The expatriate needs to understand and be sensitive to the differences from the home country. As in any new situation, there are basic business practices that one needs to be aware of when working in a new situation. Finally, there are specific job-related issues that can accompany an overseas assignment.

The daily business environment

The expatriate is sometimes caught in a double bind. The expatriate represents the home office, but simultaneously faces the difficult task of winning the "hearts and minds" of the local staff members (Munton et al., 1993). The expatriate employee must instill the feeling of a common goal and a sense of teamwork between the nationals and the expatriate staff, avoiding an "us versus them" atmosphere. While promoting the corporate culture, the expatriate also must be sensitive to cultural differences and not impose beliefs on the host-country nationals.

Expatriates can find themselves caught in a conflict between corporate policy and goals versus local interests. A successful manager must walk the fine line between corporate bully and local ally. The manager often can face resentment and resistance from the local employees, particularly when trying to enforce the head office's culture and climate, and getting pressure from the home office. Although the expatriate ensures the continuity of corporate managerial style and organizational culture in the foreign office, he must also be aware of internal and external conflicts that may arise from these dichotomies.

International business implies that people from more than one culture must interact regularly to accomplish corporate goals and objectives. When people's behavior is influenced by the different values and attitudes of their culture, basic elements of communication and expectations can be in conflict. Values and styles of work are different by definition. The perspective on employer/employee relationships, group behavior, leadership, conflict resolution, and motivation will all be regulated by cultural orientation.

It is important not to assume that your business techniques are the best. Always presume that there is a difference in approach unless a similarity in perspective is obvious (Munton et al., 1993). As the expatriate and therefore perhaps the "outsider," you should approach a situation with tact, openness, and sensitivity. Try to gain a perspective of foreign colleagues based on *their* cultural viewpoint. Try to see the situation through their eyes. For example, never say, "In America, we do it this way. . . ."

One advantage of being a foreigner is that you can be more assertive than a native. You will often be unaware of the social strata, background, and education that impede successful business practices, and this can enable you to cross boundaries and be more effective. In some cultures, you will have more room to maneuver because it is harder to place you in the hierarchy. Your "social blunders" may be excused simply because you are a foreigner.

The stereotype of the "ugly American" still exists in some

places (Shannonhouse, 1996), and your expatriate status can work against you. The nationals may resent your presence and not want you or, by association, your company. What you may think is a "virtue" may be considered a liability by another society.

If you experience prejudice, discrimination, or resistance from the local staff, try to understand the attitudes and beliefs that create those feelings. It will be difficult, but you can work to balance their negative feelings toward your culture with the positive ones reflecting on you as an individual. Stereotypes can go both ways. Many foreigners also have a very favorable impression of American business sense, for example.

North Americans tend to tie their identity into their careers and what they do for a living. This attitude does not hold as much importance in other cultures. Although their work and related successful performance are very important to them, many foreign nationals do not necessarily regard their jobs as the most important factor in their lives. Family, friends, and leisure time take on a more important role. Holidays are an integral part of their lives, and they will regard them quite seriously. The U.S. standard of two weeks of vacation will be seen as almost barbaric or certainly ridiculous.

If your office in the host country has other expatriates in place, you must be very careful and sensitive to the impact this will have on the nationals. There is a tendency for fellow expatriates to gravitate toward one another, forming a tight-knit group. This is normal because familiarity is comfortable, particularly when people are in a new and foreign environment. This inclination should be reduced. It will take a conscious effort on your part to achieve this.

This accentuation of the separation between yourself and nationals may cause resentment and isolation, which lead to poor working relations and ineffective team integration. The nationals are most likely already threatened by the company's presence and sometimes may be concerned about losing some identity and authority. Excluding them will serve only to heighten their fears.

As you effectively adjust and adapt to the host culture, you can react to situations much more confidently, allowing for increased effectiveness and improved productivity. Cultural diversity creates many challenges but offers the opportunity to make the most of the unique differences and strengths among staff members.

Basic business practices

You must learn the basic business practices in the host country. For instance, you must know the basic rules of punctuality and time orientation, negotiating, business entertaining, and when it is inappropriate to conduct business. Learn the business hours, when it is appropriate to work outside normal working time, and when national holidays occur.

Review the six cultural perspectives presented above, and make sure you are familiar with the particular cultural styles of behavior. You need to learn the appropriate protocols when dealing with people. How do you greet someone? What are the titles and forms of address to use? Which forms of gestures are appropriate and which are not? What is the appropriate form of dress? Do you offer gifts to a business associate? These are just a few examples of questions you need to answer. Simply being aware that there are customs that foster rapport and, equally, that there are behaviors that discourage friendships will help you to establish satisfying relationships.

The more you know about a given society, the more you can assume individuals' behaviors. Fortunately, there are ways to predict behaviors in a culture you know little about. The best ways to learn the specific behavioral routines and protocols that are appropriate and inappropriate in a certain culture are to observe people and their interactions, read about the culture, and ask questions.

It is more effective in many cultures, however, to ask open-ended or indirect questions (Seelye and Seelye-James, 1996). Observe people's reactions. You may unintentionally do or say the wrong thing, and your hosts may be polite and not mention anything. Yet often, by observing them, you can get an idea that you made a mistake. If so, politely ask what the more appropriate behavior is.

The purpose of the following sections is to give you a brief idea of some issues that you may face during your expatriate assignment. Of course, it is not possible to touch on all the points, and you should research the specifics of your host country. Attending a briefing seminar on your specific host country is an excellent way to familiarize yourself with the culture.

Business hours

In North America, work can often dominate an individual's life. American businesses are notorious for giving a small amount of vacation time, but still, some employees do not take all of their allotted holidays. This work ethic is not prevalent in all countries. It is important, therefore, to understand your host culture's attitude toward work and play, and to try to follow that pace.

People in low-hierarchical cultures believe that they have more control over their positions and that achievement is recognized, and they will be more willing to work long hours. Working nights, weekends, and taking only short holidays or even canceling some are all acceptable behaviors. The family tolerates these demands on the employee's personal life.

In other cultures, there is a stronger distinction between work and leisure time. The employee sees no reward to working longer hours or weekends. In many cultures, this would be unacceptable business behavior. It is important to recognize, though, that this does not mean that the employee does not take the job seriously or is unmotivated.

You must learn the appropriate business hours and workweek length. Most countries have a roughly similar schedule, but there are differences. North Americans tend to begin work earlier in the morning than most. The length of the working day varies from country to country. Some people work very long hours but others do not. The daily rituals are different as well. For instance, in many countries, lunchtime is very important, and business lunches can last several hours. The "weekend" (e.g., Saturday and Sunday) is not the same in all countries.

Be aware of the national holidays and the popular vacation periods. Every country in the world celebrates holidays, and little or no work is conducted during these celebrations. For instance, in Northern Hemisphere countries, many people take vacations in August. In Italy, for instance, much of the country shuts down for the last two weeks in August. In Southern Hemisphere countries, January and February are popular times to take a vacation. Just to complicate things, in Thailand, April and May are the traditional holiday months.

The role of the Islamic religion is singularly important in daily life in the Indian subcontinent and Middle Eastern countries. There will be implications of these religious traditions on local nationals, such as stopping work during daily prayer times. One significant national holiday celebrated throughout the Muslim countries is Ramadan, the Holy Month. Observers of this holiday fast from dawn until dusk for one month. If you are working in a country that celebrates this holiday, be prepared for business patterns to be interrupted, and be sensitive to a workforce facing mental discipline and perhaps physical fatigue.

Business cards

There is an etiquette associated with business cards in some countries. For instance, in countries such as Japan, South Korea, and Indonesia, business cards are taken very seriously. The cards contain a great deal of information beyond the normal titles and contact numbers. They may include specific qualifications and memberships in professional societies. The cards should be printed, and preferably embossed, in the local language, and on the reverse, translated into English. When you receive the card, take a moment to view and treat it with respect (e.g., do not put in your back pocket or write on it). In contrast, Italy has an understated approach to business cards. The more important the person, the less information is on the card.

Appearances

The working environment in the United States is one of the most informal in the world. It is important, therefore, to understand the correct procedures in the country you are working in. Proper use of titles, names, and dress are all aspects you must learn. Appearances are essential. Of course, most individuals develop first impressions on meeting new people, but in many countries, one's "presentation" is paramount. The Italians actually have a phrase, *bella figura,* that refers to making a good impression. It permeates all facets of life, from fashion to material goods to attitudes and opinions.

Your clothes are a sign of status in some countries. In China, people may wear suits with designer labels sewed on their sleeves. For Italians, clothes are very fashionable and elegant. Businesspeople in Argentina dress quite conservatively, but in Australia they are more informal. You should dress on the more conservative side until you learn the appropriate attire to wear and the degree of formality expected. Do not adopt native or traditional clothing, even if you think you are honoring the local culture.

Negotiations

How you negotiate an agreement depends on where you are and whom you are negotiating with. Know whom you are dealing with and what the cultural perspectives and negotiation styles are. Review the different cultural components discussed above. For instance, in cultures that are very hierarchical and status conscious, it is important to send persons with appropriate power, status, and rank, even if the actual negotiations are done by someone lower down (Hofstede, 1997). Group consensus is very important in Japan, for example. To disagree openly or to change one's position in a final negotiation setting is not appropriate, and the Japanese would not be prepared to change their position (Fisher, 1980). Long pauses and silence are normal in Far Eastern negotiations, both before responding and in the middle of developing thought (Fisher, 1980). This is often very uncomfortable for North Americans, and they may say things just to fill the conversation void. This is disconcerting and can lead to a reduction in negotiating position.

Seelye and Seelye-James (1996) list twenty practical rules for international negotiations. For instance, you must have a strategy and know what you are willing to concede and not to concede. Allow plenty of time!

Perhaps just as important are guidelines for negotiating with people who have styles different from your own. Some people negotiate from a factual style, in which the facts are the most important issue. Similar to the factual style is the logical style, in which logic is the persuasive argument. Others have a more intuitive style, in which they focus on the situation as a whole. Finally, there is the normative style, in which conclusions are based on intense bargaining. Establishing relationships and identifying cultural perspectives are of prime importance in negotiations.

The ability to understand the motivations behind the behaviors of others is an essential element of productive negotiations and joint ventures across cultures. What may be thought of as a common goal or understanding could be considerably different and should be investigated and understood (Cushner and Brislin, 1996). A key to obtaining your goals is to learn the underlying reason for others' behaviors and then make appropriate changes in your own behavior. Sometimes these changes will lead to actions quite different from what you feel is appropriate in your own culture.

Nonbusiness discussions

Small talk is prevalent in all societies. A positive relationship with an individual is essential in almost all societies when conducting business. In the United States, for example, social conversation usually precedes business dealings, but it is polite and short. In other countries, personal relationships are imperative, and effective business interactions will not be undertaken unless a "connection" is made. Building natural trust and compatibility in relationships is essential. Social conversation is an important means in forming rapport.

You need to know which topics you can discuss in social conversations and which ones to avoid. In most cultures, the following are usually good topics of conversation:

- sports (often football/soccer is the passionate sport throughout the world)
- travel plans (e.g., vacations)
- local cultural events
- local cuisine
- genuine questions about the country

It is a good idea to learn about the history and culture of the country. If you have a cursory knowledge of the country, you will impress your hosts and can ask intelligent questions. For instance, if you can understand the rules of cricket, you will greatly impress the British!

There are also topics of discussion to avoid. You can run the risk of offending and alienating your hosts. Topics to avoid include:

- religion
- politics
- home-country influence on host country
- "hot" issues related to country (e.g., human rights, gender roles)

Be careful not to criticize the country or things related to it. This is even more important in less technologically developed societies than in the highly industrialized nations most expatriates come from. They are often very sensitive to any "negative" or critical comments. You may find that your hosts will sometimes criticize their own country. Avoid agreeing with them, nod politely, and change the subject. If you need to let out frustrations about the country, share them with other expatriates!

Compensation and motivation

The national culture dictates the appropriate compensation. In the United States, for example, attempts are made to measure individual performance, and monetary reward is accorded. In complete contrast, in the Japanese society, the reward structure is linked to the success of the *entire* company. Age and length of service play much more important roles in the reward structure than in the United States. Perquisites (e.g., company car, larger office, etc.) have a much greater role in many cultures. These benefits, even if their cost is lower, can have a greater value than a monetary bonus.

"Pay for performance" is not very popular in high group-dependence cultures. The implication of such a reward system is that you alone are responsible for your results. Yet in cultures that are strongly group oriented, to be rewarded solely for an accomplishment is considered not to recognize the importance of relationships and group involvement.

Again, what works successfully in one culture can cause a complete disaster in another. The key to business success is to be aware of the impact that your corporate culture, business practices, and home-country culture will have in the host country. Rather than totally change, you must learn to adapt and be flexible.

Bureaucracy

Hierarchies among people are a fact. A natural extension of hierarchies is the existence of bureaucracies. All countries have bureaucracies. The challenge is to figure out the differences and how to "cut through the red tape." Most likely, you are relatively familiar and tolerant of the bureaucratic roadblocks and know how to work within the system. In an overseas setting, in the business environment and day-to-day living, you are confronted with new and unfamiliar bureaucracies. It is this unfamiliarity, rather than the bureaucracy itself, which is frustrating (Cushner and Brislin, 1996).

Individuals in any one hierarchy are very protective about the activities that give them their "powerful" positions. For instance, the right to approve or disapprove a proposal or even to be the source of information (the old adage that knowledge is power) can become part of self-concept. In some societies, this sense of status can be very strong and can be carried to extremes.

The best advice for an expatriate to learn how to work through the bureaucracy is to solicit help from a national or trained professional consultant who knows the system and perhaps even has personal contacts in a particular hierarchy. Usually, the basic ways of approaching and entering bureaucracies are not written down but are just learned. As someone not exposed to a lifetime in that culture, you have not had this exposure.

Rituals

Rituals pervade some aspects of all societies, to varying degrees. They may serve as social communication (e.g., shaking hands or bowing), invoking of power (e.g., calling on the assistance of supernatural forces), or creating of order in an otherwise seemingly chaotic world (e.g., religious rituals) (Cushner and Brislin, 1996). Rituals are therefore not based on facts but rather on symbolic concepts.

You should be aware of the importance of rituals to other cultures. Do not be judgmental or ridicule such beliefs as irrational or backward. Recognize the force that rituals may hold for the host culture, and be prepared to make allowances for this influence (Cushner and Brislin, 1996). You need to cultivate openness and develop patience in new situations. Keep an open mind.

Women in business

Some societies value diversity and equality, but others see more defined roles. This attitude will further manifest itself in how the society views, values, and encourages diversity. Diverse cultures believe that personal differences enhance the business and social environment and consider diversity an asset, yet they also feel that success and ability are not dependent on a person's personal status (i.e., gender, ethnic background, religion, nationality, etc.). Other cultures believe that uniformity and homogeneity are important and do not value diversity.

How a culture views diversity will greatly affect how women are perceived and what opportunities are afforded to them. In countries that value diversity, women's roles are not as clearly delineated. They will tend to have equal access to professions and activities. Cultures that are more rigid believe that gender roles are strictly defined and certain jobs are inappropriate for a specific gender. For women, this means that their roles are confined to raising children, maintaining households, and other nurturing, helping professions. In these cultures, professional women will have the additional challenge of overcoming gender stereotypes.

Some countries, such as those following the religious beliefs of Islam, have particularly stringent restrictions for and biases against women. Working women may encounter resistance and prejudice. There may be specific regulations regarding appropriate behavior and dress. For instance, it is forbidden for women to drive and to give public presentations, and the standards of dress are very specific. To be successful, the Western businesswoman must be aware of these constraints and be careful to follow them even if the regulations seem archaic or demeaning. You cannot change the culture single-handedly!

In deference to Muslim and Hindu cultures, women should always dress conservatively and modestly. Blouses should have high necklines and cover at least the upper arms, and skirts should cover the knees. Never dress provocatively. It is also wise to keep a scarf handy to cover your head.

Other miscellaneous points

There are certain customs and rules that are very specific to a country and will be very different for you. You need to learn these from the nationals and other expatriates, and sometimes from experience. Personal connections often matter more than business plans, and "rules" are open to interpretation. A negotiating tactic or sales technique that works in one country may be offensive in a second country and illegal in a third.

Certain cultures, particularly those that have a strong religious influence, have restrictions that you must know. For instance,

Hindus do not eat beef, Muslims do not eat pork, Buddhists are vegetarians, and followers of Islam do not have physical contact in public with members of the opposite sex.

Individuals in different cultures have different perceptions of personal and physical space. North Americans, who come from countries with large and expansive areas, prefer large personal space. This manifests itself throughout the spectrum, from the need for large houses and cars to a greater distance between people when speaking and interacting with others. A strong premium is placed on personal space and privacy. Look at an elevator or subway. In the United States, there is an unwritten code in which people would rather wait for an emptier compartment than violate space.

In other societies, personal space has a much different significance. The amount of personal space between people is much less. People do not need much personal space to feel comfortable and may even prefer a crowded situation. Individual offices have much less importance in these cultures. People comfortably cram themselves into elevators or subways.

Almost all countries in the world use the metric system. Make sure you are familiar with this system! Most countries write the day first, followed by the month and then the year, when expressing the date (i.e., 10/4/98 rather than 4/10/98 for April 10, 1998). This style can be confusing for North Americans, particularly when writing checks or buying milk that you assume is good for months!

You will find that you are continually confronted by values or norms that are different from those you are accustomed to. Your value system is deeply ingrained in your own cultural identity, and when you are faced with something different, you will have an emotional response based on your own values. By becoming aware of your own values, you can manage things that may cause you discomfort.

In some instances, you may be able to look at a situation from a slightly different perspective, which lessens the value conflict. Some adjustments can be relatively straightforward. For example, in some countries, the practice of giving officials small amounts of money to expedite bureaucracy is common. From a Western cultural perspective, this can seem unethical and is referred to as a bribe. Yet if looked at from another viewpoint, this supplementary payment (most likely to a very low income) is similar to the practice of tipping for service (e.g., in a restaurant), which is not considered unethical.

Other adjustments are more difficult, and total acceptance of values will be rare. For example, coming to terms with the large discrepancy in income between the few wealthy and many poverty-stricken people in India or accepting the limitations placed on opportunities for women in Arab countries can be hard for many expatriates. Total acceptance of these values will be rare. By understanding your own values and how important they are to you, you can have an appreciation of how important a differing set of values can be for another culture.

By using your acquired knowledge of the culture and business practices, you will find yourself successful and effective in your new working environment.

Work-related Concerns for an Expatriate

There are obviously many reasons why an expatriate is transferred overseas. Potentially, you may be brought over as a manager to oversee the entire operation (e.g., general manager) or only a part (e.g., finance manager). The expatriate may be brought over to work on a particular project as a technical "expert" or specialist and may be expected to transfer expertise to the local staff. The size and makeup of the office can vary as well. The office can be relatively large, made up of many nationals and only a few expatriates, or it can be a small office primarily run by expatriates. Possibly the specific circumstances will contribute to how the local staff perceives your presence

As an expatriate manager, you may face some resentment from the local staff. You will be perceived as the corporate representative brought in from the outside. Possibly, you have been brought into a problem situation that the corporation wants you to rectify, and this can intensify the local bitterness. You can find yourself faced with hindrances, skepticism, and resistance. It is essential in these situations that you stress your position of authority but also be sensitive to others' concerns and needs.

Another concern for the expatriate manager is that the local staff members may have high expectations of you and anticipate immediate results. As far as they are concerned, if the company is transferring you to an overseas post, you must be highly talented and proficient. No matter what your skills are, it may be difficult to live up to such high expectations.

Usually, the technician will have an easier time adapting to the business environment that the manager. As a technical specialist, though, you may experience ostracism. The locals may resent the corporation implying that they need expertise (i.e., they do not have it). On the other hand, they may welcome your experience and the sharing of technical knowledge. It is best in these situations to try to fit into their working environment and approach the work professionally but tactfully.

The expatriate manager must be sensitive to the increased standard of living as compared with that of the host-country employees. Your increased benefits can be a source of envy, and you would be advised to try to downplay your status. Keep your expatriate financial benefits low-key. Do not flaunt your status in front of the national staff, because this will cause severe resentment and later problems in the working environment.

Expatriate housing, although equivalent to (or perhaps lesser than) the standard you are used to, may be very expensive and exclusive by local standards. Similarly, international private schools cater to a more affluent population than the average public school. You may find yourself meeting and socializing with a very elite segment of both the local and expatriate population. It is not unusual for your child to go to school with children whose parents are ambassadors, CEOs, politicians, famous designers, pop musicians, etc.

Finally, do not forget your family. You may have more responsibility, greater workload, longer work hours, and perhaps even greater travel requirements. You may also find yourself being caught up in the excitement and aura of your expatriate position. You must put it all into perspective and create an appropriate balance between work and personal life.

Future Career

An overseas posting can be challenging for the employee because of loss of contact with the home office. "Out of sight, out of mind" is often the attitude of the home office. Often, managers in the home office will forget you, particularly if you are doing a successful job overseas. You may feel isolated and out of touch, and think opportunities are passing you by. As with your personal life in your home country, business goes on in the home office. Your managers will often give only minimal, if any, support to your needs and work.

It is important for you and your employer to realize that there has been a considerable investment in your assignment, both in monetary and emotional expense. Both you and your company must capitalize on this corporate investment, using your accumulated knowledge and experience.

There are several things you can do to make your repatriation more successful and to further your career:

- Take control of your own career.
- Identify a mentor who will be involved with your career.
- Stay current with your company and what is going on.
- Make people in the home office aware of your accomplishments.
- Visit the home office frequently.
- Keep in contact with your colleagues, including those in other companies.
- Keep your skills up to date.

See Chapter 16 for additional information on your career and repatriation.

Any reorganization or change in the home office will leave you feeling isolated and alone. Inadequate communication, particularly exacerbated by time-zone differences and poor quality, can further aggravate the situation. It can be a very unsettling period.

It is essential, therefore, that you maintain sufficient contacts with your home office. As with your friends back home, you must make most of the effort. Frequent phone calls to your manager and colleagues are critical. Even if you do not have anything significant to report or talk about, just a brief call to touch base is important. You will find yourself very busy and tempted to neglect this communication. Consider setting aside a regular time once or twice a week to make telephone calls.

The end of your assignment is also a very stressful time. It is important to understand how an overseas assignment will affect your career expectations and related growth. For example, an overseas assignment may or may not immediately propel you into a high-level position on your return.

Often, the home office, which may have neglected or forgotten about you, will not have a specific job for you. You will have gained significant experience and enjoyed your more autonomous business life, and thus find it hard to return to a more traditional and less demanding role. An overseas post is filled with increased diversity, stimulus, and responsibility, often lacking in the home office. You may have developed new business skills, acquiring a nontraditional approach and a shift away from the corporate culture and "party line."

It is important to realize how you have changed. Your return job will likely be vastly different from your expatriate posting. It may even be less demanding and rewarding at first. Eventually, your new experience should lead to a challenging and rewarding career.

The message of this chapter has been that culture plays a dominant role in all business dealings.

Everybody looks at the world from his own cultural perspective, believing that his viewpoint is normal. This is not to imply that every encounter with people from another culture will automatically be a challenge, but rather that the potential for misunderstandings is greater. Yet the principle of surviving in a multicultural environment is that people do not need to think, feel, and act the same way to agree on practical issues. People from very dissimilar cultures can cooperate and work together successfully.

Chapter 14 (at a glance)
Concerns of Special Groups

This chapter reveals ~

the special concerns related to the accompanying expatriate spouse or partner and to the single expatriate.

what the accompanying spouse should expect.

the implications an international transfer has on the spouse's career.

the different concerns of the accompanying spouse, depending on gender.

the issues related to being an expatriate single employee or single parent.

Some key points ~

❶ The success of an expatriate assignment is contingent on the ability of the spouse and children to adjust to and be happy in the new culture.

② The more enthusiastic and willing the spouse is to accept an assignment, the more likely it will be a success.

❸ The accompanying spouse is confronted with the practical and emotional adjustments associated with the new home and culture.

④ It is important to involve the spouse in all the relocation issues from the start.

❺ Dual-career families present the husband and wife with perhaps the greatest challenge of an overseas assignment.

Chapter 14

CONCERNS OF SPECIAL GROUPS

I have nearly lost track of how many places I've lived and how many jobs I have left behind while following my husband around the globe. Often, it has been exciting and has provided me with new opportunities.

When we moved from Houston to England, for example, I took a welcome break from work. Eventually, when I was ready, I found an even more enjoyable job than the one I had left in Texas. Yet before that, moving within the United States, I had to leave my job and establish myself in a new city, all with a three-month-old baby.

Essentially, each move has been both a setback and an opportunity for me. When we moved again from England to Italy, I left behind the most enjoyable job of my career. I have not even been able to find another job (let alone one I enjoy). It has given me the chance to do some consulting, learn a new language, and explore a new environment and culture, but it is not as deeply satisfying as my challenging and interesting career.

A great difficulty for my career is piecing together a coherent résumé and trying to explain all the moves and gaps. I have definitely missed the fast track, and it is probably too late for even a vaguely high-powered career. I have left behind unfinished accreditations, certificates, and qualifications on two continents. Yet looking beyond my frustrations and slight resentment toward my husband, I find that my experiences have been so varied and rich. Although they are not good for climbing the corporate ladder, they have been immensely satisfying and rewarding. If I had to do it all over, I would not have missed those opportunities for anything.

This chapter considers some special concerns and situations that have not been covered earlier. Perhaps the chapter would be more aptly titled "Special Concerns — the Spouse or Partner," because the following discussion will deal mainly with the concerns and issues that the spouse or partner will encounter in an international relocation. This topic is truly crucial to the success of the assignment. It is becoming an even more prominent issue as more families have dual careers. The chapter will conclude with issues that concern the single expatriate and single parent.

> *It has been documented by countless researchers that the spouse or partner is a critically important aspect of a successful expatriate assignment (Schell and Solomon, 1997).*

The best predictor of satisfaction and adjustment is the extent to which the expatriate's spouse is happy with the move (Munton et al., 1993). To put it bluntly, if the spouse is not happy, then the family and employee will not be happy. If they are not happy, the relocation will be difficult on everyone at best, and will not succeed, at worst. More than any other single factor, the success of an expatriate assignment is contingent on the ability of the spouse and children to adjust to the new culture (Schell and Solomon, 1997). The family is the crucial source of stability and support for the employee.

Relocation is often the most demanding for the accompanying spouse or partner. The employee is generally transferring to a specific function with a built-in network. Apart from accounting for a large part of the employee's time, the job also provides social contact and support. The children, if they are of school age, are also moving to a structured environment. The transferring spouse, in contrast, must often rebuild a new structure, routine, and social-support network in an otherwise empty space. That is an overwhelming task, made even more acute in a foreign location. Perhaps the spouse has even had to sideline a career and will experience a dramatic change in role in the household and in society.

The accompanying spouse is usually the woman, although that is slowly changing as women take on more expatriate positions. There are special concerns when the spouse is male, and those will be discussed later. For simplicity, the term *spouse* is used here to refer to either the accompanying husband/wife or partner.

The employee is usually the sole focus of the company's attention and is often the only one communicated with by the employer and personnel department (Munton et al., 1993).

The employee must then relay all the details of the transfer arrangement and the relocation to the spouse and family. Most companies do not even interview or assess the spouse when the employee is recruited for an international assignment. This can heighten the spouse's feelings of lack of control, which can lead to strong resistance and even refusal to relocate, thus jeopardizing the assignment. Often, the employee and family have no idea of the challenges they will face or the unique skills needed to be successful in a foreign culture.

Because the success of an expatriate assignment is directly related to the spouse, both the employer and employee should recognize and acknowledge the spouse's contribution. The spouse and children, if appropriate, should be involved in all the relocation issues from the start. They should be included in all preassignment meetings and discussions about the company's expatriate package. Spouses should be allowed to ask questions and express concerns and to expect support from not only the employee but also the company. The employee should insist that the family be involved in the whole process.

Most companies understand the importance of spousal and family satisfaction, but their concern is not matched by action. Only a few employers seem to have official support for the spouse in their relocation packages. This deficiency is related to tradition, cost savings, and concern about interfering with family life. Therefore, if the company is not active regarding spousal support, the employee must take control. The help given will foster goodwill and will make the company-employee-family relationship stronger and more meaningful (Roman, 1992). The spouse's perception of the company's attitude can greatly influence the sense of control and view of the relocation.

Even if the transferring employee's company does not have an established relocation program for the spouse or partner, consider asking for help. The company probably recognizes the challenges and difficulties a trailing spouse faces and will be happy to provide assistance (Schell and Solomon, 1997). Companies' philosophies differ, but it would probably be best to approach with specific proposals. Request language and cultural training and compensation for child-care costs relating to pretransfer preparations. Ask for spousal employment assistance, which *could* include:

- career counseling
- life planning
- self-marketing
- networking ideas and contacts
- job-application techniques and help with preparation of a résumé
- employment within the relocating employee's company
- assistance with obtaining a work permit
- financial compensation for loss of the spouse's salary
- retraining or tuition reimbursement for continuing education

The company may not directly provide help but may be willing to pay for the charges of qualified consultants.

When the spouse is emotionally dedicated to going overseas, the assignment has an excellent chance of being successful.

If the spouse is not "signed up" initially, the challenges of the transfer may overwhelm the family. The extent to which spouses feel happy about an international move is the single most important factor in determining how satisfied expatriate managers are with their posting and how successfully they adjust (Munton et al.,

1993). The more enthusiastic and willing a spouse is to accept an assignment, the more likely the employee will successfully complete the overseas job (Schell and Solomon, 1997).

It is essential that short-term needs are properly taken care of, both in assistance and practical help. Areas to focus on are accommodation, food, transport, shopping, medical care, baby-sitters, and friends.

Spouses are confronted very quickly with the realities of the host country. The demands on the expatriate employee are usually great, particularly with a new job and greater responsibilities. Therefore, the spouse tends to be responsible for most of the practical (e.g., shopping and taking care of the home) and emotional (e.g., making friends and building networks) adjustments associated with the new home and culture. They are most affected by the major changes in day-to-day living (see Chapter 10) and all the associated tasks and challenges. The spouse faces the further difficulties of learning a new language, enduring enforced idleness, and dealing with the disruption of the family's lives and career.

Even after a few months in the host country, the spouse can experience anxiety, isolation, loneliness, loss of identity and, in extreme cases, depression (see Chapter 9 and the discussion of symptoms of culture shock). If the spouse has temporarily discontinued a career, a lack of mental energy or drive may result. This "nothing-to-do" syndrome (Pascoe, 1992) may cause apathy, boredom, and loneliness. The sudden lack of structure makes it hard to motivate oneself. Expatriate spouses can often feel more socially and culturally isolated than their working spouses, who have a supporting network during the workday.

Yet as with the phases of culture shock, the accompanying spouse usually successfully adapts to the new life and environment. The spouse is more involved with day-to-day tasks, and thus can become more aware of the culture and enjoy and experience it. Whereas the employee has less contact with the culture, the spouse has the opportunity to appreciate the new environment. This is perhaps the most enriching and memorable aspect of living overseas.

The spouse can use the time to learn a new language or skill, prepare for a career change, or take a needed break. The important thing is to find a sense of meaning in whatever the spouse chooses to do. Once a sense of purpose and satisfaction are established, the assignment can be successful (Bond, 1997).

Moving overseas can also strengthen the bond among the husband, wife, and children, particularly when the move is viewed as a beneficial change (Coyle and Shortland, 1992). The family unit often gets closer overseas. This is particularly true when communication is open and constructive within the marriage and family. Siblings even tend to get closer as they rely on one another for support and companionship.

Even in a healthy partnership, feelings of resentment toward the relocating spouse and the company are natural (Pascoe, 1992). They are the most obvious targets for anxieties and frustrations, even if the accompanying spouse is a willing participant in the transfer. Your independence has seemingly been taken away, and you may feel completely dependent on your spouse and at the whim of the company. You need to be open with each other and make sure that you understand each other's expectations.

Isolation and boredom are probably the biggest factors contributing to resentment and antagonism (Pascoe, 1992). Rather than place blame, the best solution is to take action and gain control of your life. Explore and learn about your new environment, establish a routine, and build your social network (see Chapters 9, 10, and 11). You will be surprised at how the little discoveries and new friends will make a profound difference. Finally, remember to lower your expectations of yourself, spouse, and family.

Continual communication between you and your spouse, with openness about feelings, is critical throughout the assignment. Each spouse needs to share concerns and anxieties. This is especially important for the accompanying spouse in the beginning of the assignment, when the only source of support is from the family. Make sure that you attend to each other's needs and always make quality time for each other. The employee should try to keep longer working hours and business travel to a minimum during the early phase of the assignment. For some couples, the services of a professional counselor may be warranted.

Dual-career families present the husband and wife with perhaps the greatest challenge, particularly if the accompanying spouse is reluctant to interrupt and possibly jeopardize a career.

The loss of a career and financial independence is significant. Dual careers can be a major barrier to international mobility.

There are many practical implications involved for the spouse when deferring a career. Besides the obvious loss of income, there are several other concerns related to a prolonged absence: reduction in retirement benefits, negative impacts on future promotions, difficulty in reentering the job market, gap in work experience, and deterioration of skills. There is also the issue of always having to start at the beginning when coming back to the workforce. This can result in losing the momentum and intensity related to pay, recognition, title, and promotion.

As significant as the practical issues are, the emotional impacts are also important. The effect on self-esteem, feelings of worthlessness, loss of daily structure and independence, and lack of recognition and status are some issues an individual may confront. Review Exercise 18 in Appendix B to help you focus on possible reasons you may have to work abroad and pursue your career.

There are several obstacles for the accompanying spouse to finding work in the host country. These can include:

- immigration regulations (i.e., work permits)
- language
- lack of transferable skills
- scarcity of volunteer opportunities
- high unemployment rate in the host country
- short and transient duration of assignment
- cultural barriers that do not allow women to work
- lack of professional network or contacts

Many of these factors are beyond one's control and can be an impediment to finding employment. Still, many spouses have successfully found work opportunities overseas and continued their careers.

As an accompanying spouse, if you are planning to work in the host country, you should begin your employment research *before* you leave. You must approach looking for work overseas as you would in a normal situation. There are several good books that can help you in your job search (i.e., Bolles, 1988). The first step in any job search is to determine your personal and career goals and to identify your skills and strengths. You can then develop a plan for your employment search and determine your needs to help you achieve your objectives.

Prepare a "functional" résumé — one that describes your skills and accomplishments, rather than a conventual chronological list of prior jobs. Ask for a personal recommendation from your present employer, on company stationery to enclose with your résumé.

Start a network for job support. Your current employer, colleagues in other companies who work in your field, friends, professional organizations, etc., are all avenues to help build this network. Write to prospective employers, enclosing your updated résumé and other pertinent details. Try to obtain assistance from your spouse's relocating company, as discussed above. Research the appropriate résumé, interview styles, and other employment customs that may be different from what you are used to. Find out information on labor laws and other constraints on the employment of dependents. This information can sometimes be obtained from the home-country or host-country embassy.

It is important to remember, though, that in almost all cases it is almost impossible to find a job before your departure. Employment information and building the appropriate networks and contacts can occur only in the host country. This can actually work to your advantage. You should wait a few weeks before focusing your efforts on work, to enable you and your family to get settled into your new environment.

Some countries have an expatriate network that can provide invaluable assistance to those seeking employment. For instance, in London, Brussels, and Geneva, there is an organization called **FOCUS Information Services Ltd.,** a nonprofit information and resource center for expatriates (see Resource 1, Appendix C). The center provides access to information on relocation issues and specific details on local employment conditions and how to get work permits. It also conducts seminars, workshops, and networking meetings. FOCUS has an excellent reference library and database of expatriate information and a telephone information hot line.

Other European cities have a professional women's association that can serve as a networking group for expatriates. Other sources of help include community networks, women's clubs, expatriate groups, religious organizations, and educational facilities. Other avenues to explore include friends and acquaintances, appropriate professional associations, employment agencies, and the classified sections of local newspapers.

An excellent source of information for U.S. citizens on overseas employment is the **International Employment Hotline** (see Resource 1, Appendix C). It is available by subscription, with each monthly listing including current openings abroad.

Several factors will affect what types of jobs are available in the host country and the ability to gain employment. Perhaps the biggest barrier to getting a job is the specific government regulations that limit employment. For instance, some countries will allow the spouse to work on the work permit of the relocating employee. Some, such as Great Britain, will allow this only if the accompanying spouse is a woman. Most countries, however, protect their resident labor force with strict regulations and tedious procedures for foreign employment. A separate work permit is required for each individual. This usually turns into a "Catch-22" for the spouse. You need a work permit to get a job, and you need a job to get a work permit!

Other factors that can affect hiring include lack of adequate language skills and personal employer bias. On the other hand, professionals often have excellent skills and specialized training that foreign countries highly regard.

If you have succeeded in getting through the government regulations, finding employment overseas poses much the same difficulties as any job search. Some key traits that are important when you are looking for a job include adaptability, self-confidence, perseverance, and flexibility (see Chapter 13). There are several professions that are more transportable and have significant opportunities for overseas employment (see Checklist 18, Appendix A). These include:

- social work
- counseling
- teaching
- private tutoring
- training
- research
- health care
- management consulting
- office management
- conference planning
- computer skills
- accounting
- banking
- sales
- public relations
- small-business ventures
- catering
- beauty-related services
- anthropology
- secretarial skills
- journalism
- writing and editing (e.g., technical, travel, and creative)
- graphic design
- various creative arts

If your career and skills are within these or related fields, you have better chances of finding a job than someone who is in a more technical career.

Some areas that you can target for employment opportunities include universities, international schools, institutions, nongovernmental organizations, and multinational companies. Your skills, along with the fact that an employer will not have to offer you any expatriate benefits, can be a strong plus. Contact employment agencies and executive recruiters. Do not have great hope for a job in your spouse's organization. Indeed, there are occasions when the accompanying spouse becomes a more valuable asset to the organization. Yet as a rule, your chances are slim.

If you are unsuccessful in your job search, do not give up. Be creative in your search and related skills. Inventory your skills and accomplishments (see Bolles [1988] for an excellent systematic approach to inventorying and evaluating your skills). Perhaps you will not find a job in your current profession, but most likely you have a multitude of skills that can turn into a new business enterprise or be applied to a related profession.

Another option for the spouse is to further the career in a different way or to begin an alternate career in the new location. This career break can be an opportunity to improve and learn new skills that will enhance marketability in the future. It can even be an opportunity to change your profession or add a new dimension to your existing one. This can be a good time to establish career priorities and undertake career planning. It can be an opportunity to complement your long-range career goals. You can take correspondence courses or even study via the Internet.

If paid work in your field is not available, consider volunteer work. You may find something in your own field or a related one that will provide satisfaction and meaningful activity. There is also a possibility that it will lead eventually to paid employment.

Try to find new ways of measuring and evaluating success that are appropriate to your overseas life and not just defining a career by status, salary, and promotions (Pascoe, 1992).

For spouses who choose not to or cannot have a job in the workforce, there are countless activities that can be fulfilling and rewarding.

There are many school-related options, such as classroom volunteer, Scout leader, and coach. Recreational clubs and gyms are a good way to meet people as well as keeping you physically fit. Learning new skills is always a rewarding and enjoyable activity. You can attend classes at a local university or school, either to learn a skill that will help your career or to learn a new talent such as gardening, painting, cooking, or language.

Many overseas communities have amateur theatrical groups, choirs, and orchestras. Your talents may be in great demand. Volunteer work is always needed and appreciated, and there are usually active volunteer organizations. Expatriate groups rely on the voluntary work of members to coordinate and organize activities. They are always looking for board and committee members.

You may need to acknowledge the fact that you do not have a conventional answer when someone asks you, "What do you do?" Sometimes this can bring back whatever feelings you have about not working (i.e, frustration, sadness, anger, or relief). The key is to be creative and active. There may be many opportunities available; it just takes effort and desire to seek them out. Remember, though, to take the time to appreciate and enjoy the culture. This may mean sitting in a café and watching people or going to the local street market and hunting for a bargain. Some expatriates find that once they are settled, their empty diaries become filled and they are actually too busy! Make sure yours is filled with things you really want to do that are meaningful, rather than just time fillers.

There are several specific challenges that affect the accompanying spouse, depending on gender.

Women's opportunities will vary considerably, depending on the host country, and men have the challenges inherent in playing a nontraditional role.

Women have a secondary and restricted status in many countries, which can make a Western woman's life more difficult. Some cultures are still very chauvinistic and exclude women in the working and social worlds. The Islamic cultures are an obvious example, but other cultures, such as Japan, also place women in a secondary role. It is important to recognize this and to be careful not to impose your values and beliefs on other cultures. Another problem Western women face in some cultures is that they are treated as sex objects, an image perpetuated by American cinema. This can be a very frustrating and angering experience for the expatriate woman.

Finally, because there are fewer expatriate women in the workforce, they may find less female support in the office, as compared with men. Many expatriate organizations have meetings for working expatriate women, which can be a good way to share difficulties and concerns and alleviate this lack of support in the office environment.

As more women pursue their own careers, an increasing number of them are asked to transfer overseas. This results in many more men being in the position of an accompanying spouse. Men face particular challenges in such a situation. Many social networks open to women (such as the American Women's Club) may not be as open to men, making it difficult for them to build their own support system. In addition, in some cultures it is socially unacceptable for the husband to be "financially dependent" on the wife, thus tending to further isolate the man.

The accompanying male spouse can have a hard time settling in and building a social network. As mentioned above, expatriate support groups are mainly oriented toward women, limiting a man's exposure to many of the networks. This lack of a sufficient network can make handling the day-to-day issues discussed earlier more difficult. Also, because most of the expatriate men are working, the male spouse can find it hard to meet other men. Finally, accompanying male spouses may be perceived as "odd," and thus some people may be uneasy in socializing with them. They may even have to deal with a negative attitude in some countries toward men who are not employed.

The accompanying male spouse must be more creative in discovering activities. Some of the same avenues for meeting people, such as a sports club or adult education classes, are open to men as easily as to women. In addition, if the spouse has children of school age, volunteer opportunities at international schools should be readily available. This is an excellent source for meeting people and creating a social network. It has a further benefit of providing a positive male role model for the children.

From the employer's perspective, the single employee is generally an excellent choice for an expatriate assignment.

The single employee is generally easier and less expensive to transfer, and perceived not to have emotional or physical ties to the home country. Such an employee also requires lower financial assistance and does not need the costly education fees.

Unfortunately, although from a practical standpoint the single employee seems ideal for an international transfer, there are several concerns that a married employee does not have. It is possible that this will be the first time the employee is truly alone and does not have the support system of family and friends (Coyle and Shortland, 1992).

A family that is transferring apportions to its members the domestic and personal tasks involved in leaving their home country and entering into the host country. For the single employee, the burdens of the whole moving process and winding up projects at work are on one set of shoulders. This overload can be very stressful and intimidating.

All the associated tasks of settling into the host country, such as opening a bank account, shopping, and building a social network, are completely the responsibility of the single employee. Of course, all these tasks must be accomplished while the employee is involved in new responsibilities at work. Often, shopping and household errands are more difficult because businesses in foreign countries generally do not cater to working people (i.e., shopping hours may be limited).

Another significant obstacle for the single employee involves the local community in the host country. It is always hard to meet people outside work and to form friendships, and this is equally hard overseas. Because most of the social networks are geared toward nonworking spouses and usually take place during working hours, the opportunities for extracurricular activities are even more limited for single employees.

Unless there is already a strong social group existing in the workplace (i.e., an established overseas office), the single expatriate should expect that it will take much longer and require more effort than might be expected. A single expatriate should expect at least six months or more to establish a good social network of friends.

The expatriate community is also predominantly oriented toward couples and families, which can make it hard for a single person to be included in social gatherings. Children can provide an excellent way to meet people and become involved in the local community. This option is, of course, not available to the single employee. Often, an international assignment involves travel, which will make it even more difficult to meet people.

Couples form a supportive and cooperative unit that helps them face the challenges of international life. The single employee has established such ties in the home country, with a partner, special friends, and relatives. After relocating, single employees will find themselves alone and will miss that support system. Dating host nationals can be difficult because of language and cultural differences or almost impossible in traditional societies.

Another challenge can be if the expatriate has a partner who did not accompany the assignment. Long-distance relationships are almost always hard. Frequent phone calls and lots of visits are essential to keep the spirits up.

Single women also face issues such as personal security, hesitation to travel alone, and concerns related to living and working in a male-dominated society. Not only can meeting people and establishing a social network be difficult, but some more traditional countries also have a negative attitude toward working women and discriminate against professional women. However, some avenues open to nonworking female expatriates may be useful to the working ones as well. Although expatriate women's groups usually meet during the day, most offer some evening and weekend activities. In addition, there may be professional women's associations which meet at lunch or in the evening for social and networking purposes. Names of these groups can be found through the American or British embassy or consulates.

To be successful, a single expatriate employee should have good interpersonal skills and should be outgoing. Joining clubs related to extracurricular interests, becoming active in church or in local professional organizations, seeking out other single colleagues, and finding (or even starting) a support group for singles are all ways to meet people with similar interests. In addition, the earlier suggestions of taking adult education courses, group language lessons, and getting out and exploring the area are all applicable to the single employee. Singles can enjoy the local scene and gain international experience as well.

It is a good idea to do things you might not feel like doing to make sure you get out and meet people. For example, always accept invitations initially, and become selective only later. It is worth following up contacts, however tentative, for instance, a name given by "a friend of a friend." Phone those people and at least introduce yourself. If they are unreceptive, then ask for their advice about something (e.g., where to shop, doctor's name, etc.). If they are friendly, arrange to meet them and hope to make new friends, but never seem desperate, because that can push people away.

One seasoned single expatriate's sage advice should always stay with you: *Hang in there, and persevere; it will get better!*

There are additional special concerns that relate to the single or divorced parent.

Single parents with children will need special assistance in locating suitable schools, day care, and medical options. Some single parents bring along a family member such as a grandparent to help and to provide companionship. Others find that more frequent visits home or visits from family members can be helpful. Live-in helpers such as a nanny or au pair may be another option to consider. Depending on the age of the child, attending boarding school or staying with a friend or relative back home may be other alternatives.

It is important to develop a social life in the host country despite the difficulty of being away from children in a foreign environment. Single parents need a break in a foreign country just as much as they do at home. Divorced parents, on the other hand, face the difficulty of prolonged separation from their children. The employer can help by providing additional paid home leave. Frequent letters, phone calls, and E-mail or fax communications between parent and children can be very helpful. Additionally, children, if old enough, can visit the expatriate parent, which provides the opportunity for the child to see the parent in a unique situation.

The trailing spouse or partner presents several concerns that are unique in an expatriate assignment.

You may face the loss of a career or at least a change in work or job. You are confronted with the brunt of the cultural adjustment and are often responsible for the emotional well-being of the family. Yet by approaching your assignment with an open mind and positive attitude, you will find your life richer because of the overseas experience. Your life may not turn out as you had envisioned, but it will be a wonderful and satisfying journey.

Chapter 15 (at a glance)

Travel

In this chapter you will discover ~

how to take advantage of international travel, a major benefit of being an expatriate.

suggestions to make your traveling more rewarding.

tips on how to travel with children.

how to make the most of your home leave.

Some key points ~

❶ Do not delay your travels and exploration, because time slips away quickly and corporate changes can often shorten the length of an assignment.

② Traveling with children overseas is much easier these days, and there are many places that accommodate them.

❸ Although a home leave can be stressful, it is important to return home and touch base with the people you care about and the culture that has shaped your lives.

Chapter 15

TRAVEL

It is interesting how everything depends on one's perception. I remember being at such a loss when I first came to Italy. Everything — currency, food, shopping — seemed so foreign. I never could imagine that it would seem natural.

Yet after a couple of years, it didn't seem so strange. It really seemed to all come into place when I took a holiday in surrounding countries. As was to be expected, everything was unfamiliar to me. Yet on my return, it felt very comforting. I understood the system, shopping was straightforward, the currency and exchange rates were not perplexing, and I could get around very easily. My command of the language was good enough that although it was obvious I was a foreigner, it was not clear where I was from. When we got back, a store attendant asked me if I was from Spain (i.e., similar language).

I knew then that I had made serious inroads into adapting to my new culture.

Traveling abroad in your host country and nearby countries is one of the greatest rewards of a foreign assignment.

Living in a foreign country is a chance to expand your individual and family's horizons (Roman, 1992). *Do not delay your travels and exploration, because time slips away quickly and corporate changes can often shorten the length of an assignment.* Some expatriates can then find that their assignment has concluded and they have seen very little.

As an expatriate, you may find that financially you are better off, and the temptation could be to save all your earned money.

Although this is important, do not let that rule your life and prevent you from experiencing travels that you would not ordinarily have.

The practical issues relating to traveling while living overseas are much easier than when planning a trip abroad from your home country. The most obvious is that it is a lot less expensive. Plane flights are not as significant, and often you can have holidays using your car for transportation. What a joy it is to find yourself in some exotic destination with *no jet lag!* Local expatriates and nationals can also ease the impact by advising you about less expensive options for accommodation and places to visit. You may even have the opportunity to stay at a friend's house.

Another benefit of traveling is that it enables you to explore the "B" sites, those off-the-beaten-track attractions. When planning a major holiday overseas from your host country, the tendency is to visit all the major attractions and sites (often accompanied by an asterisk in the guidebooks). By traveling from an overseas location, you have the opportunity to explore many out-of-the-way and lesser-known attractions. The excitement of discovery is truly wonderful.

Try to visit a new country for your vacations, learning about the history and culture. There are many options for children as well (see below), so do not let them deter you. Before you relocate, stock up on guidebooks of places you are interested in visiting, because versions in your own language may be hard to obtain in the host country. There are even "gourmet" travel guidebooks for those who like to travel with an appetite.

Make sure you plan holidays in the host country. Long weekends are a good opportunity to venture out and explore the countryside and little villages. This is probably the best way to learn and appreciate the culture and make some wonderful discoveries. You may have the joy of finding yourself to be the only foreigners. Being something of a novelty, you could come away with some very unusual adventures.

Talk to your expatriate friends about interesting and enjoyable places to visit. Even better, local nationals can be a wealth of information on interesting sites or festivals that you might not have even considered. Most people are always happy and willing to share their experiences, adventures, and advice. You should also try to find a good travel agent, particularly one who speaks English. A good travel agent is worth his weight in gold!

Be familiar with the security process at airports, and allow for delays. Identify all stopover countries and their regulations (e.g., transit visas, immunizations, etc.). Find out how and where to satisfy the requirements and how much lead time you need. In some countries (i.e., developing nations), you may need to confirm this information from more than one source. *Always confirm your reservations.*

Travel tip: Many foreign communities are empty for the summer season. Both nationals and expatriates depart during the summer months when schools let out and temperatures are unbearably hot (i.e., Northern Hemisphere). Often, stores and services even close. Friends of yours will be gone, and therefore, this is a good time to travel. Of course, the downside is that all the holiday resorts will be crowded and prices will be at high-season rates. It is important to make reservations early.

Do not delay, because the opportunities and rewards for you and your family are fantastic!

Holidays overseas will expose your children to sites and experiences they probably never could have in their home country.

Traveling with children overseas is much easier these days. There are many places that accommodate them, and some even offer child discounts. Many cultures welcome children openly, and their presence will more often bring smiles and pats on the head than disgruntled and unwelcome looks.

When traveling with children, you must orient and pace your holiday toward them. Almost all locations have sites that will appeal to your children, such as castles, archaeological ruins, zoos, parks, and interesting historical places. Many of these can be found in guidebooks. Some books have specific sections on traveling with children. Beach holiday resorts are always a good choice.

You must make sure that you travel at their pace. Plan to visit only one or two places in a day. You can mix the sites up with those that will appeal to adults and to children. Most children will probably balk at going to a museum, but do not let that deter you.

You can usually find something to interest them, and if you keep the visit short (i.e., one hour) it should be a successful outing.

Ice cream is always a special treat to follow the visit. Take frequent snack and rest breaks. Also plan for meals. Restaurants can have irregular hours, and a situation can quickly deteriorate when children are hungry and tired. Always keep provisions such as snacks and drinks on hand. Picnics are also great options, and there are many places to buy food. You must plan ahead, though, because food stores often will close for lunch!

Keep a scrapbook or photo album to record your travels, adventures, and events during your assignment.

It will be a great record that the whole family will enjoy and a good way to easily share your experiences with relatives and friends. Videos also can be a good way to capture memories, but be careful not to submit friends to hours of movies, because most are not interested.

It is also a good idea to encourage your children to have a scrapbook so they can remember their time overseas. Buying them postcards of your visits is easy and inexpensive. They can create a postcard portfolio using a photo album.

Home Leave

Surprisingly, home leave can be a very emotional issue (Pascoe, 1992).

Sometime during your assignment, you will face the decision of returning home for a visit. It may be sparked by loneliness and missing friends and family or by guilt for taking your family out of the country, away from aging parents. Perhaps when you started your assignment, you had grand designs of traveling to new and exotic places, with no intentions of returning home until the end of your assignment. Logically, you think it will be a wonderful opportunity to "see the world" and avoid the high cost of long-distance air travel. To your surprise, though, you will be drawn back to your home country like a magnet.

Costs

Many employers provide the cost of air travel back to your home base as an expatriate benefit, yet there are hidden costs. These can include:

- **Air travel.** Air-travel costs can be high. In the United States, for instance, if you must travel to many parts of the States to visit relatives (i.e., your two sets of parents live on opposite coasts or in cities far from major airports), costs can quickly add up. If you must travel by air to several destinations in the United States, you might reduce costs by using "air coupons." Essentially, these are like the European equivalent of a Eurail pass, except it is for air travel rather than train. These passes can be purchased only abroad. Your local travel agent can help you.

  Along with air travel, there are car-rental charges, hotels, meals out, and many other miscellaneous costs. Although some of your costs may be covered by your employer, do not be surprised if it does not completely cover all your expenses.

- **Consumer purchases.** You may have a strong urge to buy clothes, sundries, books, videos, CDs, etc. Either you cannot buy a product in your host country or it is excessively expensive there or you just "must" have it. In the United States in particular, shopping is so convenient and conducive to spending money. You can even go to shops at any hour of the night, perhaps even when you wake up early at 3:00 A.M. because of jet lag! It will be important to budget your purchase expenses. You will find, though, that as you spend more time as an expatriate, many items you thought you "never could live without" will lose their importance. Either you will find comparable substitutes in your host country, or you just do not miss them.

- **Vacation time.** Even if you have more holiday time because of your assignment overseas, home leave will use much of it.

- **Physical toll.** Jet lag, particularly with children, along with cramped quarters on arrival (i.e., spare sofa bed or floor), is difficult.
- **Emotional toll.** Visiting relatives may be stressful, and a long visit can exacerbate the demands.

Practicalities

Still, because the draw to return home will exist, there are some steps you can take to help ensure a successful home leave for everyone.

Where to stay

- **Family.** Staying with your parents or in-laws is fine *only* if you all get along. Otherwise, consider a hotel. If their house is small, maybe your children can stay with them and you can stay in a hotel. This gives your parents an opportunity to see their grandchildren and gives you some personal space.
- **Friends.** Staying with friends is also a good option, but only *good* friends who do not mind your spending time with other friends and family. If they expect you to be with them all the time, look for other accommodation. Remember to be a good guest (i.e., make your own bed, help with cooking and cleaning, respect your hosts' space, do not always be underfoot, and take them out to dinner or buy a gift to thank them for their hospitality).
- **Residence inn.** If you need to stay in a hotel, consider a furnished apartment or residence inn. This is a better option than a hotel, particularly if you have children. It will have a fitted kitchen, living area, and other amenities.

Finally, remember to rent a car rather than borrow one. It is best for everyone.

How long to stay

The length of your home leave is dependent on when you are going to visit and how many locations. You should try to reduce the time you stay with anyone to no more than seven to ten days if staying with family and four to seven days if staying with friends. Remember how you feel when guests descend on you! Rather than planning to see "everyone," keep it to a minimum (see below).

When to visit

If you have school-age children, the timing of your home leave will depend on their school vacation. This will most likely limit you to summer or December (unfortunately, this is peak season, and thus you will face high-priced airfares and crowded flights).

Summer is a good time to visit if your host country's temperatures soar and the expatriate and national communities empty out. December is a double-edged sword. On one hand, it is nice to share the holiday season with family, and you can be truly lonely if you are by yourself thousands of miles away. It is particularly difficult if you are in a country that does not celebrate the holidays. Yet the winter holiday season is always a stressful period, and you may not want to travel such a long distance for a potentially demanding time. In addition, the weather is usually bad.

Whom to visit

Certainly, family members and friends will be at the top of your list of whom to visit, but do *not* try to see everyone. Avoid the whirlwind tour of visiting people. Concentrate on family members and friends who are important to you rather than making a huge list and seeing people for only a few brief moments. No one enjoys such encounters. They are unsatisfying, and your stress and anxiety level is so high that you do not concentrate on them but rather on your next scheduled visit. You may find yourself running from one visit to the next, spending more time commuting than visiting. Everyone will want to see you, but unless your home leave is several weeks long, you simply will not have the time or energy.

Encourage your friends to come to you to visit. You have traveled thousands of miles and your time is limited; your friends can make the effort. Remember too that your children will not enjoy being dragged all over town visiting adults — boring! Avoid always meeting in a restaurant, because you may be going out a lot, and it can become unhealthy. For people you do not have time to visit, use the telephone. They may try to pressure you into making time for them by pushing your "guilt buttons," but try to resist. Enjoy catching up with them on the phone at lower rates!

What to do

Sometimes you plan and commence your home leave on automatic pilot, with little or no thought of the purpose of the visit. When you go on holiday, you are full of plans, yet somehow the home leave just happens. Try to avoid this trap. Remember that the home leave is also for you, not just an obligation.

Certainly, plan time to visit friends and relatives, but also schedule time for yourself and family. Use the opportunity to catch up on your culture, whether it is going to a movie or spending hours in a bookstore. The goal of your trip is really "to become acquainted with friends and family, and to remind yourself where you came from and your own culture's values and way of life" (Pascoe, 1992). Your home leave should be a fun and memorable trip, rather than something you must "get through."

Remember, too, this is a *holiday.* You have paid good money and time, and you deserve a break. Schedule time for fun activities, and do not forget the children. Do things that they will enjoy — go to amusement parks, movies, shopping, etc. Take them to a toy store and let them pick out something to buy for themselves. This might also be a good opportunity to expose your children to some historical and cultural highlights of their home country that they may be unfamiliar with. You may also want to take the opportunity to attend to practical matters — doctor and dentist appointments, consultation with financial and tax planners, etc. Meeting someone in person to discuss a technical issue is much preferable to long-distance phone calls.

Culture shock

Be aware that you may experience reverse culture shock (see Chapter 16). Returning home may seem strange and uncomfortable, particularly if you have successfully adapted to your new culture. Going back to the home country can also be difficult for some people. The return can be particularly unsettling for those who are still in the anxiety or reaction stages of culture shock.

Also be aware that some friends and relatives want to see you but are not interested in your life overseas beyond the polite inquiries. Many people, particularly those who have never been overseas or just have taken a holiday overseas, do not want to hear anything negative about your experience. They imagine that being an expatriate is like being on a holiday and is nothing but fabulous.

Returning to your assignment

Home leave can cause you to cycle back through some phases of adjustment that you experienced when you first arrived on your assignment. Fortunately, the effects are usually shorter and of less intensity. You may have even reached a point where "home" is "here" rather than "back there."

Although a home leave can be stressful, it is important to return home and touch base with the people you care about and the culture which has shaped your lives (Pascoe, 1992).

With proper planning and foresight, you can turn your home leave into a good experience for your family, friends, and relatives and also have time for fun and relaxation.

One of the benefits of an expatriate assignment is the increased opportunity for travel.

Your holidays may be more exotic and frequent than before and can make your assignment all the more special and rewarding. Returning home to visit family and friends is also important. A home leave can be stressful, although it is therapeutic to keep in contact with the people you care about and your home culture.

Chapter 16 (at a glance)
Repatriation

In this chapter you will discover ~

what to expect from the final stage of the relocation cycle, and the steps to take to make the adjustment.

"reverse culture shock" and why repatriation is challenging.

the impact of repatriation on the lives and careers of all the family members.

the financial issues you must be concerned about when returning home.

Some key points ~

❶ Returning to the home country results in challenges that confront the whole family and that are specific to each member.

② Children, particularly teenagers, are especially vulnerable when they return home, and they will require more than the usual attention.

❸ The culture-shock cycle resulting from repatriation is similar to that when you enter a new culture.

④ When you complete the relocation cycle with your return home, have the same open-minded, positive attitude as when you began your assignment.

❺ You must take charge of your career and aspirations.

⑥ The return home will mean a change in your financial situation.

❼ Continuing on the expatriate trail has adjustment issues associated with the transfer.

Chapter 16

REPATRIATION

After eight years and two assignments overseas, we were returning home. We had enjoyed our experiences, and had even "adapted." Yet we were ready to go back and settle down again. My company had given me an article about repatriation, but I didn't think it was a big deal. We were returning to the same city where we had friends, and I was going to slot right back into my company.

How wrong I was! We arrived home full of excitement and anticipation, and indeed, our expectations were met. The abundance and ease of life that America has to offer were ever evident. Our friends were happy to see us and even gave us a welcome-home party. My daughter was delighted to be back at school.

Yet slowly, we realized that things did not seem right. After the initial welcome, our friends retreated to their own lives, of which we were not a part. They seemed only mildly interested in our experiences, which we really wanted to share. We had changed profoundly and felt like international citizens. No one seemed to understand us.

The shine of America also seemed to wear off. What had seemed so natural to us years before actually felt foreign! We found ourselves longingly missing the excitement and differences of everyday life, and actually found America to be lacking in many aspects. It was all a dramatic shock, something none of us ever expected.

My job was an utter disappointment. Most of my former colleagues had moved on, and my current team seemed distant to me. I had learned a great deal overseas and was eager to apply my new knowledge, yet no one seemed interested. In fact, my current position has very little to do with what I had learned overseas. Considering the time *and money the company had invested in moving me overseas, it seemed like such a waste not to use what I learned. Finally, to further frustrate me, there had been several company reorganizations while I was away, and I had lost considerable ground. One of my managers had the audacity to tell me, "Now that you are back in the home office, we can get to know you and be able to judge your performance and capability."*

I certainly wish I had taken this repatriation issue more seriously. It has been a tough go. Dorothy may have been right in saying, "There's no place like home," but I think the expression "You can never really go back home" is more appropriate for a returning expatriate.

If you are like most expatriates, the idea of repatriation is the farthest thing from your mind when you begin your overseas assignment. You may reasonably wonder what all the big fuss is about. You know the language and culture, and you understand how to function daily in the environment. You will probably plan to return to your old social network of family and friends and to your old job. Right? Not exactly!

Both anecdotal and statistical evidence confirms that repatriation is a complicated and difficult experience. In one study of American returnees, 64% reported "significant shock" on repatriation (Black et al., 1992). Many expatriates say that readjusting after coming home is much harder than adjusting to living overseas (Storti, 1997). Expatriates usually expect difficulties when they transfer overseas and prepare themselves accordingly, but they often imagine that repatriating will be an easy and natural conclusion of their assignment. When it is not, they are surprised and confused. They neither expect nor prepare for the difficulties, and because they think there will be no problems, reentry is even harder!

"Home" can be a foreign country when you return from an assignment abroad. You think you are coming back to the old familiar life. Yet your work, friends, surroundings, and lifestyle have all changed.

Repatriation is essentially the completion of the expatriate cycle, yet going home does not necessarily mean you can pick up where you left off. Unfortunately, it is not just like returning home from a long vacation. It has many, if not more, of the concerns and issues you encountered at the beginning of your overseas assignment. The demands are made worse because the process often is not taken seriously and planned with the thoroughness of the move overseas. A common misconception held by the employer, employee, and family is that expatriates can return home and continue their lives at the point when they left.

The expatriates, however, have changed. Their lives and their perceptions of the world have altered. They have become used to a different lifestyle and standard of living which they have had to give up, along with newly made friendships. There will be less disposable income, and the budget will be much tighter. The extensive holidays and entertainment will also have to be significantly curtailed. All this can result in dissatisfaction and feelings of hurt and loss.

Returning to the home country results in challenges that confront the whole family and that are specific to each member of the family. You will be faced with almost all the issues presented in the past chapters — premove preparation, housing, education, taxation, medical concerns, culture shock, and a new job. Reviewing the manual will help you to consolidate and organize your thoughts.

There are facets of the repatriation cycle that deserve special discussion, with new adapting techniques to be mastered.

To understand why repatriation can be such an issue, it is important to appreciate the implication of "home."

Every expatriate is different and there are indeed many facets to repatriation, but the predominant underlying issue is the significance of "home" and your expectations (Storti, 1997). By looking at repatriation in the context of what we mean by "home," you will better appreciate why repatriation can be so challenging.

In *The Wizard of Oz*, Dorothy said, "There's no place like home." Home has a special meaning to all of us, beyond just the house or country we live in. Storti (1997) defines *home* as "the place where you are known and trusted and where you know and trust others; a place where you are accepted, understood, indulged, and forgiven; a place of rituals and routine interactions, of entirely predictable events and people and very few surprises; the place where you belong and feel safe and secure and where you can accordingly trust your instincts, relax and be yourself." In other words, *home* refers to a set of feelings and routines rather than just a physical place. Home represents security, understanding, trust, safety, and a sense of belonging.

From the above definition, we can see that there are essentially three elements to home — familiar places, familiar people, and familiar routines. A fundamental problem resulting from repatriation stems from situations in which these elements are no longer familiar. Buildings are new, friends have moved or changed, "home" is now different. Not only have things back home changed, but you have also changed as a result of your overseas experiences. Your perspectives on your home country will be markedly different.

Home now appears strange and different, and you will react in much the same way you did when you went overseas — confused, frustrated, and disoriented. You now begin to see the imperfections of your home country. For instance, some common negative reactions that returning expatriates have toward the United States include how materialistic the country appears, the abundance and waste, the pace of life, and Americans' attitudes and values (Storti, 1997).

Reverse Culture Shock

To your amazement, the adjustment you must make after taking care of practical matters related to returning home is, in essence, reverse culture shock (Munton et al., 1993).

If you have been away for only a few years, it may not be as dramatic, but nevertheless, everyone will feel some culture shock when repatriating. In some cases, particularly when a person has adjusted exceptionally well to the host country, reverse culture shock may cause greater distress than the original culture shock! Your response can almost be more acute because you do not expect any differences or problems. It is important to realize this and not to deny or dismiss your anxieties. Your emotions are all normal.

The culture-shock cycle resulting from repatriation follows a predictable pattern and is the same as that when entering a new culture, as presented in Chapter 9. Repatriation is a transitional period that unfolds over time. It is not just a matter of arriving at a certain place on a certain day.

The cycle begins with the honeymoon stage, as you appreciate being back in your home country. The service, convenience, and choice available to you, for example, will be very much appreciated and enjoyed by those returning to the United States. You will enjoy catching up with family and friends. Everyone is excited to see you, and you are a "minor celebrity." You do all the things you missed while overseas — shop, visit favorite places, and eat favorite foods. You may not be particularly objective about your home country during this stage, being inclined to see everything in a positive light.

Yet you will begin to notice that things are different, and the appropriate behavioral responses are not as you remember. The country and people's attitudes have changed and may seem confusing to you. You may even feel like an outsider in your own culture. You now are entering the reverse culture-shock stage (i.e., anxiety, rejection, and reaction, as described in Chapter 9). Refer to the section in Chapter 9 on the symptoms to expect in this stage.

The rose-colored glasses have been removed, and now things you do not like about home stand out with great clarity. You start to notice and criticize things and people, and you become judgmental and impatient. To make matters worse, you miss being abroad and selectively remember only the positive points. It is almost as if you are determined that your home country will not measure up to your host country!

By now, your novelty value with others has started to wear off. People are used to your being back, although you are far from used to it! Moreover, people expect you to have settled in and assume that you are fine (as you may have first thought, they too assume repatriation is "no big deal"). They probably do not ask how you are coping with being home, and instead, they leave you alone.

You are now confronted with daily living and attention to the practical details of life. Your lifestyle will have changed. You now have to deal with the realities of life and a reduced income (i.e., home ownership, tight finances, budgeting, housework, etc.). You may become anxious, frustrated, and even depressed with the reality of being back home. The lowest period is usually in the first few months after returning (Coyle and Shortland, 1992).

Whereas you had a role before leaving for your assignment and then developed one while overseas, you may find that at first you will not "fit in." You must rebuild your daily patterns and social network. Although you are coming back to a familiar environment, things will have changed. Old friends' lives will have moved on, and you are no longer an integral part of them. Perhaps most significantly, you and your family have changed as a result of the expatriate experience. Most likely, you will feel less familiar with your "old" environment as well. Often, you do not notice major changes to your surroundings on a daily basis, but on returning after several years, you will observe many differences.

You will also have altered your daily patterns, which you now need to adjust back to the old ways. The excitement of living abroad can further make the homecoming a disappointing experience. You may feel bored. After your international life, which was full of exotic adventures and experiences in a stimulating environment, your home country will feel one-dimensional. You may lose patience with friends. Their concerns may seem like trivial matters. It is common for returning expatriates not to have a complete sense of belonging; they have incorporated into themselves two different cultures, and they do not relate completely to either.

A common complaint of returning expatriates is how little interest people back home show in their experiences, including relatives and friends. You will find yourselves enthusiastic and wanting to share your experiences with friends. Beyond an initial and polite interest, many of your friends will not want to listen and may even show resentment and jealousy. This can leave you feeling disappointed and rejected. Do not feel that you are being treated in a unique way if others are indifferent to your stories and experiences; it is normal. You may have the tendency to appear snobbish and pretentious, given all your worldly experiences and travels, and that will turn people off. Your outlook will have become more international, which will contrast with many compatriots, who may seem provincial to you. So much has happened to you, and you may find it harder than you would expect to find common ground.

By having entered the adaptation stage of culture shock in the host country, you will now find some reverse nationalization. Your outlook on life and your perspective toward your own culture will have changed. You will miss some qualities that you preferred and became accustomed to in the foreign country. You may even partially reject your own culture, preferring the lifestyle and culture of the foreign country. You may constantly compare countries, and see your own and its people in an unfavorable light. Your home-country friends, without the benefit of your experience, will have difficulty relating to your feelings. In the end, you must accept that those who have not lived overseas can never really understand your experiences and how you have changed.

It takes roughly six months to become readjusted to your home country, and as long as two years to feel completely comfortable again. Some returning expatriates adapt within a few weeks, others after several weeks, and for others it takes a year or more (Storti, 1997). Some adjust rather quickly at work but more slowly in their personal lives; for others, it can be the reverse. Because we are dealing with individuals, personal circumstances will also greatly control the timing. For instance, variables of whether repatriation was voluntary or not, family circumstances, length of overseas assignment, amount of adaptation achieved in the host country, and the returning home-country environment all can affect the repatriation experience.

You move to the final adaptation stage after having reintegrated into your original culture, and your behavior more nearly matches the lifestyle in your home country. Yet your experiences overseas and living in alternate cultures will have touched you greatly, and you will never be as you were before. Your lives will be richer and more rewarding for your experience, and this will positively affect your daily life. Now you can focus on your life in your home country. You have a balanced view of your own country, and you are able to put both it and the overseas experience into perspective. You are able to see both home and host country objectively.

We had been expatriates for many years, stationed in several countries. At one point, we were in the U.K. and, after successfully adapting, felt it to be an absolutely wonderful place. We even considered making it our permanent home. Reluctantly, we were transferred to another location. At first, we found ourselves comparing our new host country very unfavorably to the U.K. (i.e., "home" country), just as we did when we first transferred overseas to the U.K. from America. Slowly, as we adapted, we began to look approvingly at our new host country, and to our surprise, we saw the U.K. in a not-so-perfect light. When we finally repatriated to America, we had the same experience, but it was much easier because we knew what to expect. We have incorporated the good points of each culture we have lived in, thus enriching our lives. We are now "home," and can appreciate the upsides and downsides of each culture, enjoying the former and laughing at the latter.

Adapting Techniques

Because it is important to understand that cycling through the culture-shock stages on repatriation is normal, you must also realize that you will reach the final adjustment stage.

Not only are you returning to your own culture, but you have also successfully developed adapting techniques to aid in reducing the impact of culture shock.

Some relocation experts suggest that you plan for your return home when you embark on your international assignment. That is hard because you are focusing so much of your energy on moving and settling into your new environment. What is important is that you understand that repatriating is indeed an issue and a complicated matter. Then gradually, when you are in your assignment, you can begin to plan and take steps to prepare for your return (see Checklist 22, Appendix A). Review the section in Chapter 9 on adapting techniques for culture shock. Probably the best thing you can do about readjustment is to expect it. You will not be caught off guard, and you will have more realistic expectations of yourself, your family, and your friends.

It is perfectly normal to find repatriation difficult. You may be depressed at times and long to go back overseas. Give yourself plenty of time to adjust. It may take several weeks or months, but you will adapt.

Communication is essential during repatriation. As with the commencement of your assignment, do not get caught up in all the details and practicalities of moving back. This is particularly important with children, because they will most likely feel apprehensive and scared. Realize that your children, especially if they were young when you left home, will view their home country as "foreign."

When you accepted your expatriate assignment, most likely you considered the impact on career, family, and lifetime goals. Returning home, though, can often be considered out of your control. On the contrary, it is a time to review your aspirations and fit repatriation into them. It is important to understand why you are going back home. The reasons why you are returning home can have a great influence on your adjustment. If you feel in control and are returning home because of personal reasons or your assignment has come to its logical end, then your adjustment will be easier.

It is also important to consider what you are returning home to after the assignment. Is your repatriation to be a relative continuation of your previous life or are you planning to take this opportunity to make a major life change (i.e., career, community, etc.)? In either case, you must take charge of your decisions. Examine your assumptions and expectations of yourself and others.

You must be emotionally and physically geared up to returning home. As with setting goals, it is also important to take control of the actual move. Preparation for repatriation is an important and often overlooked part of the relocation cycle. As you did at the beginning of the assignment, you will need to address all the tasks related to settling in, such as taking care of housing and finding appropriate schools. Look through the prepreparation list you used for starting your assignment (see Chapter 2), because many of the same things will apply. It may be helpful at first to consider yourself as a "foreigner" in your home country and to remember that many of the instincts you acquired abroad may not be of much use back home.

To successfully make your transition to your home country, you will need to let go of the past, which is known as "closure." You are not only packing up your house or apartment, but also closing your overseas life as well. Although they can be sad, good-byes are important. Make sure you say your farewells. People have their own ways of saying good-bye to friends, whether it is a grand party or individual engagements. The method is not important, but rather what works for you. Try to do the things you never got around to doing, such as visiting a town, tourist site, or museum you missed. On the other hand, do not get so preoccupied with this that you find yourself racing from one place to the next, running yourself ragged and unable to truly appreciate anything. Spend time appreciating the moments you truly enjoyed about your host country, such as sitting in an outdoor café and watching the world go by.

As the end of the school year approaches, we begin to think about all the endings and beginnings that are about to take place. Students finish one grade and get ready to go on to the next, others graduate, little ones get ready to start. Teachers say good-bye to students, while students think of changing teachers and sometimes leaving friends. In an international school, a much greater percentage of students leaves each year, and the school provides special activities to help them prepare. But the process of saying good-bye affects the entire community as parents, children, and staff anticipate leaving or saying good-bye to those who are moving on.

It is difficult to say good-bye, but I believe it is important to do so. Otherwise, you are left with a vaguely dissatisfied feeling, as if you neglected to read the last chap-

ter of an exciting novel. It is difficult to say good-bye because it is sad; we are really grieving a loss. People react to endings in different ways. Some become very busy and "don't have time to feel sad," but others may notice a sense of nostalgia and pay close attention to the "last time" for everything. Some people find the process too painful and withdraw or disappear without saying good-bye at all.

Hmmm . . . you're thinking, maybe we could just skip the whole thing and jump straight to September. But that last chapter is important, both for children and adults. To be ready for the next exciting adventure, we need to properly conclude this one. Whether you are leaving or staying, I think it is important to pay attention to your and your children's feelings during this time. Children and adults cope better with painful feelings if they are acknowledged rather than denied. Talk with your children about what is happening and how they are feeling. Discuss what they will miss and what they are looking forward to. Let them know it is normal to feel sad, anxious, excited, etc. You may want to make them "business cards" that they can give to friends with their name, address, E-mail address, and phone number.

Parents should also support each other and seek out friends and colleagues to talk issues over with when things get stressful. Take care of your health and avoid overscheduling (easier said than done, I know). Be kind to yourself and don't expect yourself to be "fine" all the time. Farewell parties and other gatherings can be a satisfying way to say good-bye to the community, but it is also important to find time to be with the friends and in the places that have been important to you. If you reach a point that you just don't want to say another good-bye, it may mean that you are now ready to move on or let go of those who are leaving.

I've lost count of how many times I've said good-bye. It doesn't really get any easier, but I do take comfort in the fact that I now have a worldwide network of friends. I may not see many of them on a daily basis, but I carry them with me in my heart wherever I go. As for my own

*good-bye, I will always treasure the years I spent overseas
and all of the people I've had the honor and pleasure of
knowing.*

To complete your leaving, if timing permits, take time on your
way home for a family vacation. It will give you the opportunity to
"decompress," feel refreshed to face the challenges ahead and, if
appropriate, reduce the effects of jet lag. This time will also give
you the opportunity as a family to reflect on your experiences and
share your feelings about repatriating.

One important factor of successfully entering the adjustment
stage is the rebuilding of your network, and this should be one of
your main priorities. If you still have some good friends in your
new community, they will be a good starting point in helping you
settle back in. Review previous chapters in the handbook for other
outlets to seek out people.

Keeping up with the political and social changes in your home
country, as well as current attitudes, perceptions, and trends, will
make it easier for you to reassimilate into the culture. Most likely
your cultural reference points are out of date. It is surprising how
the country and people change over time.

One challenge on returning home and dealing with culture
shock is that there is a lack of the typical support groups that were
available to you in expatriate communities. While overseas, you
had an outlet for your frustrations and an understanding from your
friends of the difficulties you confronted overseas. Back home,
your friends may not have awareness or concern about your problems. People may not be as willing and ready to help you settle
into your new community. Therefore, seek out other repatriated
expatriates. Talking to someone who understands what you are
going through and who can validate your experiences will be an
immense emotional relief.

As mentioned earlier, in reverse culture shock, you have the
added difficulty of scrutinizing and criticizing your own culture.
Perhaps it would help to view returning home as going to a "foreign country" and adopt the same open and accepting attitude you
did when going overseas. You will have changed, and things back
home will have too.

Although you need to adapt back into your new (old!) environment, you do not have to totally abandon your host-country culture. Cultural societies, universities, and art museums all can offer ways for you to keep in touch with your host country. Do not try to totally recreate your expatriate existence, however. Not only is it difficult and stressful, but it tends to put off other people.

Depending on the size of the community you live in, you may want to search out expatriate associations for foreigners from your former host country. Often, they will accept honorary members. This can be a good outlet to share your concerns and to channel your energies in a positive way by helping foreigners settle into their new environment. It is also a good way to share the positive feelings, experiences, and qualities of the previous host country. As when you were overseas, seek out people who have lived overseas, because they can relate to your experiences and provide support for you. When meeting new and old friends, share some of the feelings you have now and had while living overseas. Sharing feelings rather than experiences sounds less like boasting. You may want to consider hosting visitors from abroad or taking an exchange student into your home.

As with living overseas, the opportunities for travel are a benefit of returning home. Your home country is full of natural and cultural wonders that you most likely have missed. Furthermore, because your vacations and home leaves have consisted either of international travel or visiting relatives, your children have probably not experienced the opportunities your home country has to offer. For example, in the United States, the national parks are priceless jewels that few countries in the world can offer.

Most of all, realize that you are entering a new chapter in your lives and that there will be a period of unsettledness and transition. Temper your expectations and memories. Returning home will not live up to your idealized fantasies, just as going overseas was not an exotic holiday.

Impact on Life and Career

When a family accepts an expatriate assignment,
the employee usually expects to benefit from
career development or enhancement
(Coyle and Shortland, 1992).

In some ways, the professional side of repatriation is similar to the personal side. Just as home is no longer "home" in many ways, neither is your company the same when you return. The organization, people, and job have all changed, and so have you! As with culture, you should expect to experience some aspect of "job shock."

You should expect the international assignment to boost your career, but often, the transfer will seem at first to have had no positive influence on your upward career progression. Sometimes it can even have a negative effect. A common complaint of returning expatriates is that their organization does not value or make use of their international experiences (Storti, 1997). In a recent study, 80% of American expatriates felt their companies did not value their expatriate experiences, and only 39% reported using their experiences in their new jobs (Black et al., 1992).

As an expatriate, you have developed skills in dealing with international issues and interacting with people from other cultures. You have learned a great deal about the company's international operations, and you have a global perspective on issues. You expect to be able to apply all of your new skills on returning to the home office, and it can be very disappointing when the company does not use this experience and expertise.

Returning from an assignment can be "one step backward, two steps forward." The tendency will be to expect big things, but it may be best to temper the optimism initially. In another study, more than 75% of American managers reported having been placed in lower-level positions on their return (Black et al., 1992).

While overseas, you may have had a great deal of independence and authority, but your new job may involve diminished responsibilities. In the study cited above, nearly half the American managers reported less autonomy and control in their new positions (Black et al., 1992). Your job may seem boring after the prestige, excitement, diversity, and challenge of the international post. When overseas, you may have been in the habit of making major decisions without consulting the home office, but when you return, you find many layers of management that appear much more bureaucratic. Overseas, you were most likely very challenged and stimulated in your work, continually maturing professionally. To your dismay, you may find your new position back home much less demanding and challenging.

You may find that your employer has not planned for your return, and possibly you may not even have a job position. The "out of sight, out of mind" syndrome is very real, particularly if you have had a successful international assignment. Black et al. (1992) found that only 11% of Americans were promoted after having completed two-year expatriate assignments, and 77% were demoted after returning home.

You will probably find that your mentors have moved on, and you will need to reestablish your position and authority. In essence, you are beginning a new job and will need to "prove" yourself again. Your expatriate experience is sometimes not appreciated back home and can even be viewed with envy. Because you were overseas, you were probably overlooked when any opportunities became available. When you repatriate, there is a good chance that a good position is not available if it has not been planned.

As with home, the organization will be completely different. You will have to establish new relationships with new people and rebuild ties with others whom you have not seen in years. Policies and procedures have probably changed. The whole organizational culture, its focus, and goals may even have changed.

As with repatriation, you must take control of your career and your new position in the working world.

To help ease the transition, there are some things you can do besides leave the company. Try to map out your career development *before* the expatriate assignment, and certainly before returning home. Take the opportunity to assess your new skills and to incorporate them into your aspirations. Do not forget to update your résumé. You have enhanced and acquired many skills during your overseas assignment that will be invaluable in your future work.

During your overseas assignment, continually communicate with the home office, and keep abreast of organizational changes and opportunities. Also make sure that your accomplishments and skills do not go unnoticed by managers in the head office. Keep a high profile. Occasionally go back to the head office on your home leaves, meeting with managers who can help your career. Try to find a mentor who can assist you in securing a new position, keep you up-to-date with the corporate politics, and help your transition.

Six months before the end of your assignment, you should contact your manager to develop your new appointment. If possible, return to the head office at this time and initiate discussions on your new job and the direction of your career. Let your managers know what expectations and aspirations you have for your new position. Try to define a definite job that you are satisfied with before you return. It may not be the perfect position at first, but you want it to be both challenging and interesting and perhaps use your international skills. Use your new job as a base for getting the position you want.

As you settle into your new job, you and your employer will recognize the international experience and skills you have developed. This will make you more productive and successful and will most likely propel your career forward.

Even if your new position does not directly use your international experience, make a point of transferring your knowledge to others. Brief key managers on what you learned, giving insights not only to the specific country you were in and the work you did but also generally on doing business internationally. In addition, perhaps you can be a mentor for new expatriates.

If an appropriate position is not available to you in your company, it may be an opportunity for you to explore other options. According to one study, 40% of American expatriates left their companies after returning home (Black et al., 1992). By giving careful thought to your career and skills during your assignment, you will find it easier to move yourself into a new career. International skills are often in very high demand.

It is extremely difficult to find a job from long distance, given the complications of time changes and distance. Still, take the opportunity to rebuild your network, and use all the technological advances in communication to improve your search. If possible, take a reconnaissance trip back to your home country to make contacts and explore employment opportunities. You may not have a job when you return, but you will have built up a solid base to begin your search.

Review Chapter 13 for additional information on your career and repatriation.

One final note: On your return, remember that as with your personal life, you will also encounter reverse culture shock in the workplace, complete with frustrations and disappointments. As you are successfully able to readapt to your home culture, you will also do so in your career.

Spouse or Partner

The spouse must also take charge of career and aspirations.

As with the employee, the spouse must do the same planning and goal setting.

Consider what you have been doing while you have been overseas. Were you working in a paid position in your regular career or doing another kind of work? Did you work as a volunteer? Did you take a career break, study a foreign language, manage a family? Just like the employee, you should start planning for your return home at least six months ahead.

Assess your options. Depending on what you have been doing and what you want to do when you return, you may consider: (a) returning to your old company/position/career, (b) looking for a new job/career, or (c) not looking for a paid position.

Make a plan. If you intend to return to your old job, contact your employer and find out about available positions. If you are going to look for a new job or make a career change, begin by updating your résumé. There are several helpful books on the market, including *What Color Is Your Parachute* (Bolles, 1988).

Consider creating a functional résumé in which you emphasize your skills rather than positions held, if your experience is unusual. Explain your time away from the job market in a positive way, emphasizing the benefits. Parlay your international experience into an asset that can make you look more interesting to a prospective employer. Don't neglect to mention work you have done as a volunteer. You may also be able to take advantage of seminars on job hunting and résumé writing that local and expatriate groups offer.

The next step is networking and making contacts (see the chapter on networking overseas). Try professional organizations, people you know (talk to everybody), and the Internet (many companies now post job vacancies on-line). If you are not intending to look for a paid position when you return home, think about what you want to do.

Whether you join the workforce or not, it will be important to establish a new social and emotional network. Just as you did overseas, you will need a support system as well as meaningful activities for yourself. You now have a wealth of experience in settling in, which should help you to establish yourself in your new home or reestablish yourself in your old one.

> *Children are especially vulnerable when they return home and require more than the usual attention to settle into new schools and new routines (Pascoe, 1992).*

The repatriation experience for children will depend on many factors, including the age of the children and the length of the stay overseas. For very young children, repatriation is not a significant issue; for elementary and middle-school children, there are several adjustments; for teenagers, the adjustment can be significant.

Growing up outside their home country, children can develop positive and negative characteristics which will influence them throughout their lives (Drake, 1997). On the one hand, they will acquire many skills (e.g., learning a foreign language, living in multicultural environments, adapting to change) and will become more mature, worldly, and independent. Yet they can also experience a sense of rootlessness, insecurity, and sadness caused by breaking off friendships and never settling down. Remember that your children may not be "moving back" but rather moving to a new environment. Unlike yourself, they have radically changed, both physically and emotionally.

Easing reentry for younger children is a matter of making them feel secure and safe again, and that means trying to restore as much familiarity and routine to their world as possible. You are their greatest source of security, and your physical presence, on a regular and predictable basis, reassures them. For this reason, both parents should be home as much as possible during the first few months of repatriation.

Research shows that teenagers have the most difficult reentry of any age group (Storti, 1997). Adolescence is not easy under normal circumstances, and repatriation creates a new set of psychological and emotional adjustments. The most serious issue for teenagers is not fitting in with and being accepted by their peers back home. In the teen years, being accepted means being like your peers (i.e., conforming to the norm and not standing out). For the teenager who has lived overseas, this is not an easy matter. Expatriate children, with their unique experiences, may find it difficult to fit into groups where "sameness" is valued.

Teenagers will be more affected than you by out-of-date cultural reference points. They will have to deal with cultural ignorance, such as not knowing the current slang, current television shows and movies, pop and movie stars, sports personalities, fashions, and popular trends. They may not know the "in" phrases, and what's worse, they may be using talk that is now no longer "cool." This can be very embarrassing. If they are entering junior or senior high school, when peer pressure to conform is at its greatest, their feelings of alienation can bring about adjustment problems.

Expatriate communities and schools tend to be small and accepting of new people. Children are often included and accepted more rapidly than normal, precisely because the community is so transient. Back home, cliques are prevalent in teenage circles, and it may be hard for returning teenagers to become accepted. They may no longer feel unique or special, as they did overseas, but rather strange and undesirable. They may have to adjust to being in a larger school, having a lower profile and less individual attention than in an international school.

Your children, particularly those of school age, will have lived in a multicultural environment. They will have had experiences that have taken them to other countries, broadening their outlook on life. They are probably more mature and sophisticated than others their age. They should understand that they will have a different perspective on the world than most of their peers in the home country because they have lived abroad. As with adults, your repatriating children will find, to their disappointment, that many of their new friends will not be interested in their recent lifestyle and experiences. This can be especially disheartening for teenagers who need to share experiences with friends. What was normal and typical for your children will now feel awkward and possibly unwelcome. Your children, much like adults, may dislike many of the behaviors and values they see.

The major factor in adjustment of children to repatriation is a positive attitude.

Make sure you are positive about repatriation, and be aware of the common signs of culture shock in children, such as regressive behaviors, proneness to sickness or accidents, withdrawal, irritability, and change in habits (see Chapter 9). Continually reassure and support them. Although it may not completely register or seem important, remind them of how they have benefited and what they have learned from living overseas. They have made new friends and had exciting experiences, visited many wonderful places, perhaps learned a foreign language, are more confident and mature, and have gained valuable skills that they can use for the rest of their lives.

Children's two main concerns are friends and school. It is important to ensure continuity of education. If possible, try to arrange your repatriation to coincide with the school year. This may involve either the spouse going home early or the employee returning initially. If possible, try to visit the new school, and make the transition as seamless as possible.

Include your children in the decision-making process when possible. As you did overseas, help them find new activities and friends. If you know the neighborhood you are moving to, try to get to know families with children of the same age. Your children should notify any of their friends they have kept in contact with. Tell your children about reverse culture shock before it happens to them. Have them talk to similarly aged children who have gone through the repatriation process. They will be able to offer reassurance and support.

Create "closure" activities that include going-away parties, sleepovers, exchange of addresses, etc. It is important for your children to be able to say good-bye and to realize that they will still remain friends. Help your children remain in contact with their friends overseas. Remind them to keep in touch by letters or E-mail. Allow them occasional phone calls to their expatriate friends and perhaps even a trip to visit them.

Talk with their new teachers and principal, and brief them on your children's international life. Perhaps your children's unique experiences can be used as a teaching tool for their classmates. Help your children reenter their home country and understand the culture from *their* perspective. Have a similarly aged friend brief them on the current cultural highlights and fads (e.g., rock stars, pop idols, movies, TV shows, games, fads, and professional sports). Have tapes of the popular TV shows sent to them so they will be aware of what their friends in the home country are talking about. This will give your children more confidence and help them feel less isolated. Use your home leave to expose your teenager to the popular culture and attitudes.

Do not be surprised if your children regress, just as they did when you moved overseas. They may have shown strong adaptive qualities and coping skills during their time overseas, but you should not rely on those alone after the family returns. Older children and teenagers can become withdrawn or sullen. Younger children may have temper tantrums or display babyish behavior. Your children may be sad about leaving their friends, nervous about attending a new school, and angry with you for doing this to them. Allow them to cry and express their feelings, but remember that you do not have to feel guilty about causing them. Expect a period of adjustment of several months. They will feel better once they have made friends, have found activities that they enjoy, and have settled into their new home. Watch out for prolonged or severe reactions which may indicate a need for professional counseling.

Remind your children that it takes time to fit back in and be accepted, to feel as if they belong. Reassure them that although they may feel lonely and depressed at first, it will change. Not only will they adjust in due time, but when they do, they will treasure their overseas experience.

Finances

The return home will mean a drastic change in your financial situation (Piet-Pelon and Hornby, 1992).

No longer will you have the multitude of expatriate benefits, such as housing, private-school tuition, etc. Your lifestyle and standard of living will be reduced, and you will now find yourself struggling with your finances and a budget. In one study, 75% of Americans expatriates reported a reduced standard of living on repatriation (Black et al., 1992). Do not underestimate the financial impact and associated anxieties.

You will be faced with several major financial burdens all at once. A house, automobiles, clothes, furniture, appliances, and curtains are all essential costs you may incur. Excluding a house, these purchases can cost as much as $100,000. Usually these items are accumulated over a long period, yet now you must make them all at once.

If you have been away for a while, be prepared for higher prices and taxes. It is common to remember prices from five years ago (which you used in comparing how expensive things were overseas) and to lose sight of inflation and rising prices in your home country. Determining your monthly expenses and budgeting will be difficult at first.

The most important action you can take to lessen the impact is to plan. You may even want to consider consulting a financial planner. Prepare a budget of your anticipated expenses and liabilities. Calculate your expected take-home pay, and anticipate as many expenses as you can (both one-time and ongoing). Enlist the help of friends back home to find out the prices and tax rates. You can neither predict all your expenses nor calculate an accurate monthly budget, but you will at least get a sense of how much it will cost to live back home. Prepare in advance for financial purchases, and set aside some reserve funds.

When you return, be careful not to jump into major decisions hastily. For instance, purchases such as a home, car, or furniture, which you normally consider carefully (i.e., information gathering, price comparisons, consumer reports, shopping around, etc.), may be reached quickly and poorly because of your desire to immediately settle back into your home country.

You should prepare for these purchases in advance. For instance, six months before you repatriate, purchase a car magazine to find out what models are available, the recommended cars, and their prices. On a home leave, consider taking time to test-drive cars. If you have been away for a long time, most likely there will be new models that you have never heard of. If you have access to the Internet, you can do much of the research at your leisure and in the comfort of your foreign home.

The same sort of preplanning can be done with real estate and other major purchases. There are several consumer magazines that can aid you in your decisions.

Another aspect that returning U.S. expatriates can encounter concerns getting credit back in America. Although you have had a good position and salary and a large savings, you may find that your credit history in America is nonexistent. A good international credit history does not make much of an impression with U.S. lending institutions or credit-reporting firms that supply consumer-borrowing histories to lenders. Any positive credit history you had in the States before your assignment may have lapsed.

This lack of credit history, no matter what credentials you have — i.e., healthy income, secure employment, and substantial financial assets — can make obtaining a loan or even one of those ubiquitous credit cards almost impossible. Obtaining simple things such as checking-account overdraft protection and department-store credit cards can be difficult. In the worst case, you may be unable to qualify for auto loans or a home mortgage. This all comes at a time when you are trying to rebuild your life back home.

Most U.S. expatriates are not affected by these concerns

because their assignments are relatively short (i.e., less than five years). Furthermore, they tend to keep their credit history active while they are away by maintaining a home mortgage and using U.S. credit cards.

Expatriates who stay abroad for longer periods, though, find that they may have maintained little financial contact with the States. To compound matters, most credit-reporting agencies normally discard credit information after seven to ten years (Carey, 1993). Lack of a credit rating can also be a concern for younger expatriates who do not have much credit history to start with.

Most credit granted in America is based on reports generated by a few big credit bureaus that include credit histories for loans and credit cards and the payment patterns. The bureaus receive the information from their subscribers, such as banks, retail stores, mortgage lenders, and credit-card issuers. They then issue consumer-credit reports in response to authorized inquiries from lenders, employers, landlords, and other individuals requesting credit history. These credit reports do *not* include income, assets, or overseas credit activities. In essence, lenders are looking for a person's capacity to repay debt. Unfortunately, U.S. credit bureaus do not view foreign credit history as sufficient to predict future repayment patterns (Carey, 1993).

If you find yourself in a situation that could put your credit rating at risk, there are steps you can take to reduce the effect.

Some U.S. lending institutions rely so heavily on credit reports that you must try to maintain your previous credit history. If having a U.S. home mortgage is not practical, keep your U.S. credit cards in use. This will not be a guarantee of success in achieving a loan, but at least you will not be starting from scratch, as you did when you graduated from college.

On your return home, apply for other "low-key" credit cards such as department-store and gasoline charge cards. An American Express card can be transferred from a local-currency to a U.S.-dollar card without a credit check. Once a credit card is in use in the States, its activity will show up on the credit report.

Be prepared to have a bulk of documents relating to your expatriate financial status. Documents that are useful include letters from employers, letters of introduction from overseas bankers and other lenders, personal financial statements, tax returns, brokerage statements, and foreign credit-card billing documents. Also try to obtain letters of reference from your U.S. financial institutions and mortgage lenders *before* canceling your accounts. You may approach your company to help you secure a loan.

When you finally repatriate, write directly to the lending institution's bank manager to build a personal relationship with the lender. Try to avoid the customer-service clerks and associated bureaucracy, because they will show little sympathy for your extraordinary circumstances.

Many expatriates find themselves moving on to another international assignment after their previous overseas experience.

Often, families enjoy the enrichment and excitement of being expatriates and welcome the extension. The opportunity to live in more than one foreign country and to compare different cultures is a unique and exciting experience. They have gained a great deal of experience from their first assignment.

This is not without difficulties, however. You may feel like a seasoned veteran, but you should expect differences and surprises. Each member of the family will be at a different stage of life and will face new challenges. The culture you will be moving to is different, of course. You may have family and friends who thought your first assignment was a wonderful opportunity, but now they want you back home. Sometimes it can involve painful emotional adjustments.

If you are moving to another assignment, it is understood that you should review the sections in the handbook that will be appropriate to your transfer. There are few added issues that the "professional" expatriate has beyond the normal settling-in issues.

Uncertainty and change

The uncertainty and change related to being an expatriate are reinforced. You may have stronger feelings of being unsettled. Your life is still in transition.

Divided loyalties

Expect some sense of divided loyalties. Many techniques you learned to help you adapt in your "former" culture will not translate to the new one.

Culture shock

Culture shock will still be an issue. You may experience it more or less, largely depending on your own circumstances (i.e., children's ages, language ability, attitudes toward your new posting, parents' health back home, etc.).

Loneliness

You and your children may feel lonely and upset. You again have to say good-bye to friends, and then repeat the process of building new friendships and networks.

Lack of roots

You may feel rootless, at home everywhere but nowhere. It can be disconcerting not to have a "home." You may become adept at making friends or you may withdraw in anticipation of the next good-bye.

Children

Children may be closer to family and siblings but find it hard to form relationships outside the family. They may have formed many friendships throughout the years, but the friends are spread around the world. This is harder for children to handle than adults.

Much of this chapter has focused on the hardships of repatriation, yet it also has many joys and rewards.

Among all the challenges, frustrations, and difficulties are many wonderful experiences and moments of great satisfaction and happiness. They can range from very tangible moments, such as returning to your favorite restaurant, seeing wonderful sights you missed, or experiencing the ease of living back home, to the emotional, such as visiting your family and friends or finally having a sense of being "settled" (see the section on drawbacks of expatriate life in Chapter 9).

You have also grown from your experience, and there is a

tremendous satisfaction from incorporating the positives from your host culture into your home culture. In addition, there were undoubtedly many characteristics in the host country that you did not like. Perhaps they bothered you at first and you dismissed them when you adapted, but now that you are away, they have lost any luster.

When you return home, you must remember to live in the present. Value your experiences and the knowledge you have gained, and appreciate the cultural differences between overseas and home. This will make your life and your family's lives richer. Most likely, you will have changed, becoming more creative, self-confident, and flexible. You see the world more clearly and will appreciate your culture and others. Yet do not dwell on your experiences, particularly in social situations. People are interested, but only to a point.

When you complete the relocation cycle with your return home, have the same open-minded, positive attitude as when you began your assignment. Think of your home country almost as a foreign country, and take time to rediscover it. You have now started on another path of your life, bringing closure to your expatriate phase, and you have new experiences and adventures to encounter.

Conclusion

International relocation can and should be a chance to expand your horizons and learn more about different cultures. Living in a foreign country is completely unlike just being a visitor or tourist. You can absorb yourself in and become part of the new culture. You will gain an awareness and interest in the new culture, politics, and country that you never had before.

Our experiences and surrounding environment help shape who we are, and living overseas can be a very enriching and rewarding experience for the whole family. The changes you experience will occur at deep levels, leaving you more competent, self-assured, and vibrant. Perhaps even more so for your children, the experience of living overseas will form a lasting impression. The new social and academic skills they develop will be invaluable when they enter adulthood. As an expatriate, you will develop friendships with people all over the world. The bonds formed as you share your life experiences overseas will be very special.

Indeed, moving overseas is a challenge, and it can be difficult to adjust at times. You are playing a new game in which you do not understand the rules! Yet these challenges can also make you and the family unit much stronger and closer. The rewards of international living are tremendous. The entire family can acquire international skills and knowledge of other countries and peoples, and can gain self-confidence and become more well-rounded as individuals. You will understand different viewpoints and become more knowledgeable about others' perspectives and behaviors.

Moving, particularly to a completely new environment, is never easy and should not be taken lightly. Relocation requires forethought, planning, organization, and cooperation. Perhaps the most important ingredient in a successful move is communication. Talk and *listen* to one another.

If you feel a sense of control over the move and approach the relocation with a positive attitude, your move and related experiences will be rewarding. An understanding of the relocation process is the key to any successful move. Knowledge is indeed a powerful weapon. Unrealistic expectations or uncertainties can prove to be a big letdown when you are confronted with the reality of a situation. We hope this handbook has given you the knowledge, skills, and tools to prepare you for your international relocation, and that it will help you to achieve a successful and rewarding transfer.

Best of luck!

Appendix A

CHECKLISTS

Everyone approaches a challenge differently. Some people deal with issues in a more subjective manner, preferring to tackle them on a macro level. Others are more concerned with details, and they organize, organize, organize, preparing lists and "Things to Do" spreadsheets. And of course, most people probably fall somewhere in between. This section is aimed at the organizer and list maker. Still, anyone can benefit from briefly scanning the checklists and ideas that are an extension of the chapters in the manual.

Checklist 1
Sources for Information about the Host Country

Checklist 2
Information to Find out about the Host Country

Checklist 3
Moving Tips and Planning

Checklist 4
What to Take and What to Leave in Storage

Checklist 5
Survival Kit

Checklist 6
Items to Hand-carry

Checklist 7
Key Documents and Records

Checklist 8
Change of Address

Checklist 9
Companies to Notify for Final Bill Payment

Checklist 10
Wattage and Appliances

Checklist 11
House-hunting Factors

Checklist 12
House Ranking

Checklist 13
Questions to Ask When Looking at Schools

Checklist 14
U.S. Federal Tax Forms and Publications Relating to Overseas

Checklist 15
Medical Tips

Checklist 16
Adapting Techniques for Culture Shock

Checklist 17
Sources for Meeting People Overseas

Checklist 18
Potential Portable Careers for the Accompanying Spouse

Checklist 19
Traits for a Successful Executive in a Global Environment

Checklist 20
Key Factors an International Executive Must Understand

Checklist 21
Business Cultural Model

Checklist 22
Adapting Techniques for Repatriation

Checklist 1

SOURCES FOR INFORMATION ABOUT THE HOST COUNTRY

There are many sources to obtain information about the host country where you will be living. They include:

- embassy or consulate of the country. Some larger embassies have libraries you can access.

- local library

- bookstore

- briefing documents

- universities (seek out foreign student adviser, history or social science department, library)

- names of current or past expatriates from your assigned country

- tourist information

- local daily newspapers

- country and city maps

- public-transport maps

- guidebooks

- restaurant guides

Checklist 2

INFORMATION TO FIND OUT ABOUT THE HOST COUNTRY

- climate
- language
- culture
- geography
- society and history
- national symbols and customs
- political system
- demographic information
- economics and major industries
- educational approach and system
- religion
- national and religious holidays
- laws and customs
- living conditions
- foods
- public transportation
- standard of dress
- social life
- lifestyle
- local inhabitants
- fine arts and cultural achievements (past and present)
- communication networks (including newspaper, magazine, television, telephone, computer)
- recreation facilities and clubs
- sports
- entertainment
- cost of living
- medical practices and facilities
- inoculation requirements
- incidence and types of crime
- career and employment opportunities
- anything else that is of importance to you

Checklist 3

MOVING TIPS AND PLANNING

There are many tasks associated with the physical move and preparing to go overseas. The following checklist is intended to be a comprehensive list subdivided into the periods when you should do each item. Note that you may have additional things that apply to your own situation, or you may find things that are not applicable to you.

One Month Prior

- Meet with line managers and personnel coordinator.
- Call moving company to organize details.
- Arrange for moving agent to visit home to inspect items to be moved and provide an estimate.
- Check on moving insurance, and arrange for contents to be insured from the date of the move.
- Prepare valued inventory. Decide what to bring, store, and get rid of.
- Check regulations and organize shipping of pets (e.g., license, vaccinations, tags, etc.).
- Arrange for the home-country house to be taken care of (i.e., sell or rent house if applicable).
- Cancel all rental agreements.
- Arrange for living quarters in new location, both temporary and permanent. Go on an exploratory trip to host country if possible.
- Inquire about educational options.
- Make inquiries about the host country.
- Schedule cross-cultural orientation for self and family.
- Schedule language training for self and spouse.
- Organize valid passports.
- Organize visas, resident permits, import permits, work permits, etc.
- Take care of vaccination requirements.

- Arrange checkups (e.g., medical, dental, eye).
- Obtain medical, dental, and prescription histories, including referrals, prescriptions, eyeglasses, X rays, birth records, medical records, and vaccination and immunization records.
- Notify children's school and obtain necessary transcripts and records.
- Notify your lawyer, bank manager, insurance company, and any other official organization of your move. Get letters of reference when appropriate (e.g., insurance).
- Get professional referrals if possible.
- Check with your attorney about your will and its validity. If you do not already have one, write a will; if you already do, update it if needed. Arrange for someone to have power of attorney in case of emergency.
- Schedule meeting with tax adviser.
- Arrange for the sale or transportation, if moving, of any cars.
- Have any antiques or valuable items appraised separately.
- Register electronics, cameras, jewelry, and similar items with customs so there will be no problems during reentry.
- Schedule events and parties to say good-bye to family and friends.

- _____

- _____

- _____

- _____

Two Weeks Prior

- Notify and close the telephone, utilities, etc., accounts. Arrange for final reading of meters.
- Arrange for a telephone call-referral service.
- Make arrangements with your bank regarding how accounts are to be handled during your overseas assignment.
- Consolidate bank accounts (checking and savings). Open accounts in host country.
- Empty contents of safe-deposit box that you want to take with you, or cancel the box.
- Close unwanted local charge accounts, etc.
- If maintaining home-country bank accounts and credit cards, arrange for direct payment from bank account to avoid unwanted late charges and interest payments.
- Transfer/cancel insurance policies (e,g., auto, life, home). If renting your host-country house, convert homeowners' insurance policy. Obtain a letter of reference from your automobile insurance agent detailing your family's good driving record.
- Consolidate important documents, records, and papers. Make copies.
- Prepare travel itinerary; make necessary reservations.
- Make a list and organize items to be moved separately (i.e., air, ocean, storage). Get boxes, packing material, etc., to help in organization.
- Prepare a list and corresponding addresses for change-of-address forms (available at local post office). Complete forms, photocopy for future reference, and give to the post office.
- Prepare a list of important professionals (e.g., doctors, lawyers, etc.), including addresses and telephone numbers.
- Obtain local telephone numbers (rather than toll-free numbers) of any organizations you wish to telephone (e.g., investments, banks, credit cards, etc.). Using toll-free numbers is an expensive alternative because the calls

are not free from an international destination. You cannot always dial direct and thus may have to go through the international operator, adding a great deal to your cost.

- Transfer or cancel memberships of church, club, or civic organizations.
- Organize a special membership category for all mail-order clubs you wish to maintain, in which you will remain an active member without having to respond to monthly mailings. Put any other memberships (e.g., automobile club) on inactive status so as not to incur any joining fees when you return home.
- Arrange for children and pets to be looked after on moving days.
- Have a garage sale. Make donations to a charitable organization of what you do not sell (get receipts for tax purposes).
- Notify police of when house will be vacated.
- Cash in any coupons, offers, or refunds.
- Arrange for utility services to be connected at your new address.

- _____

- _____

- _____

- _____

One Week Prior

- Discontinue services and utilities (e.g., electricity, gas, water, telephone, milk delivery, lawn, garbage collection, pest control, newspaper, cable TV, unwanted subscriptions, etc.). Get appropriate refunds.
- Pay existing bills.
- Check on personal items that are on loan, being cleaned, processed, serviced, or repaired.
- Return all borrowed items and library books.
- Gather your valuables (e.g., jewelry, important papers and documents, deeds, currency, passports, work permits, keepsakes, souvenirs, etc.) to transport personally.
- Set aside all items to take personally.
- Tag items not to be moved or stored.
- Pack your survival box.
- Pack all items that have original packing cartons (e.g., stereo, computer, video).
- At the office, prepare to leave (hand over projects, pack, etc.).
- Make arrangements for house plants.
- Have your car serviced if it is being moved.
- Confirm travel plans, including the hotel, for moving day.
- Notify company in host country of your arrival date.
- Register with the county to receive absentee ballots for elections.

- _____

- _____

- _____

- _____

One Day Prior

- Wash dirty clothing.
- Water plants.
- Separate items to be packed by movers that you will need immediately in host country (e.g., bedding, towels).
- Label all rooms and items, based on your coding system.
- Designate and label storage and moving items.
- Complete packing items that you will carry with you.
- Remove curtains, yard items, smoke alarms, fire extinguishers, hoses, hooks, etc., that are not staying with the house.
- Put aside items that are not attached that are staying with the house (e.g., owner's manuals, directions, keys, etc.).
- Disconnect washing machine and dryer.
- Defrost refrigerator/freezer, and give away food contents. Leave the door open to dry.
- Dispose of all flammables and combustibles.
- Drain fuel from lawn mower, clean barbecue.
- If moving your car, reduce gas level to one-fourth tank.
- Discard all partially used containers.
- Arrange for cash to tip movers.
- Arrange with neighbors to leave sufficient space for parking of moving vehicles.
- Organize meals and drinks for moving day.
- Go to bed early!

- _____

- _____

- _____

- _____

Moving Day

- Strip bedding.
- Supervise moving crews. Explain any necessary arrangements and details to head packer/mover before moving process begins.
- Accompany the movers through the house as they inventory your belongings, and make sure that an accurate description of each item is recorded on the inventory.
- Check all rooms, garage, storage areas, basement, cabinets, shelves, closets, and drawers for overlooked items (e.g., telephone).
- Check the entire house, including garage — inside and out — with driver before movers depart to ensure that nothing is left behind.
- Check inventory and destination contract and driver's bill of lading, including estimated delivery date and contact numbers.
- Get driver's name and van number.
- Tip packers and movers.
- Make arrangements for your keys.
- Leave a forwarding address and telephone number with a neighbor.
- Turn down the heat (or turn up the air conditioner), check that all appliances are turned off, close all windows, turn off lights and faucets, and lock the doors.
- Remove trash and leave the house in clean condition.
- Go out to dinner; you deserve it!

- _____

- _____

- _____

- _____

In the Host Country*

- Record all travel and moving expenses.
- Arrange for medical services (e.g., doctor, pediatrician, dentist, optometrist).
- Schedule an appointment for your pet with a local veterinarian.
- Open bank account (e.g., checking and saving); transfer funds.
- Look into obtaining a local driver's license.
- Check on utilities for new home (e.g., gas, electricity, water, and telephone).
- Establish a list of local repair services.
- Register children in school.
- Register family with local authorities.
- Join appropriate civic organizations.
- Arrange for new insurance policies (e.g., homeowners').
- Contact moving company about your arrival; organize date of delivery.
- Decide on furniture placement, layout, etc., in your new home before delivery.
- Be present, preferably with another adult, to check items off inventory as they are unloaded and to direct movers of proper placement of boxes, etc., in residence.

- _____

- _____

- _____

- _____

- _____

*Note: Some of these tasks can and ideally should be done before leaving your home country.

Checklist 4

WHAT TO TAKE AND WHAT TO LEAVE IN STORAGE

It is difficult to compile a general list of what to bring with you. This varies considerably from individual to individual and is also dependent on what your situation will be overseas (for instance, are you renting a house or apartment; is the property furnished or unfurnished; does it have a garden?). The following list is intended to be a guideline of some things to consider. Whatever you do, you are bound not to get it perfect. You will bring things you wondered why on earth you did, and you will leave out things you wish you had brought with you. Do not worry too much about it. In the scheme of things, it is probably not that big a deal!

What to Pack

- Clothing. Try to do some research on climatic conditions in your new country (i.e., seasonal temperatures, humidity). If you are going from one extreme to another, consider leaving some of your clothing items behind. If you have any special needs (i.e., special shirts, sizing, etc.), purchase those items before you leave.
- Equipment for games, sports, and celebrations of your home country. Include sporting equipment and holiday decorations and ornaments.
- Eyeglasses, contact lenses, and related prescriptions.
- Kitchen goods — measuring cups and spoons, cake and pie pans, favorite (nonperishable) food items, cookbooks, and recipes.
- Linens and bedding, including towels, mattress covers, permanent-press sheets, blankets, and place mats.
- Medicines — special prescription and favorite cold medicines and vitamins, particularly children's.
- Household items. A limited supply of your favorite toiletries, such as shampoo and cosmetics, can be helpful to ease the transition.

- Phone book from your former city. This can be useful for tying up loose ends or for future correspondence.
- Materials for hobbies, arts, and crafts. Also include basic hand tools and gardening equipment.
- Children's things. Do not compromise on children's toys and clothes and baby items. Remember that children grow up quickly, and things you may not think they need, such as books and games, will soon be appreciated.
- Other items.

- _____

- _____

- _____

- _____

- _____

- _____

What Not to Take

- lightbulbs
- electrical appliances (unless accompanied by a transformer)
- home-country TV and VCR (unless using in tandem for videos only, or if they have a compatible format)
- abundance of furniture if moving into a furnished accommodation

Checklist 5

SURVIVAL KIT

It is a good idea to prepare a "survival kit" (so labeled for inclusion in the air shipment and immediate unpacking) that contains the essential items you will want immediately on your arrival. Some of these items could include:

- set of dishes
- glasses and mugs
- utensils
- frying pan
- cooking pot
- teakettle
- can opener
- knife
- linens (including sheets, blankets, and pillows)
- towels (cloth and paper)
- toilet paper, tissues
- soap, sponge
- first-aid kit
- toolbox
- tape measure
- flashlight
- cellophane and heavy-duty tape, scissors
- large plastic trash bags
- address book
- stationery (i.e., paper, pens, pencils, markers)
- stamps and envelopes
- other items

- _____

- _____

- _____

Checklist 6

ITEMS TO HAND-CARRY

You will need to set aside personal items to hand-carry with you on the airplane. These can include valuable items and documents, such as:

- valuable jewelry
- personal papers and documents (e.g., birth and marriage certificates, will, passports, work permit, etc.)
- insurance policies
- airline tickets
- extra passport photos and copies of your passports
- traveler's checks (keep receipts of numbers separately)
- valued inventory and household inventory
- address book
- map of new city
- guidebook and map of country
- hotel reservation details or key to new home
- any irreplaceable keepsakes
- other items

- _____

- _____

- _____

- _____

Checklist 7

KEY DOCUMENTS AND RECORDS

This is a comprehensive list of documents that are important to bring with you when you transfer overseas. Remember that you should always hand-carry these documents rather than packing them in the air/sea shipment. It is a good idea to make copies of all these documents and keep them separate from the originals.

- passports
- visa
- work permit
- residence permit
- offer letter or other related document from your company
- valued inventory
- immunization records
- will
- power of attorney
- insurance policies
- birth certificates
- marriage license
- traveler's checks and cash
- driver's license
- joint checking and savings bankbooks
- investment records
- safe-deposit keys
- tax forms, papers, and records (last three years)
- school records
- medical, dental, X-ray, and prescription records
- inoculation records
- Social Security numbers
- other items

- _____

- _____

Checklist 8

CHANGE OF ADDRESS

Some addresses to consider include:

- doctors
- attorney
- banks
- credit cards
- charge accounts
- magazine subscriptions
- relatives and friends
- professional associations
- national and alumni organizations
- charities
- mail-order clubs (e.g., books, CDs, videos)
- catalogs
- tax office (e.g., Internal Revenue Service in the United States)
- stockbroker and investment companies
- retirement and pension funds
- creditors
- insurance company
- driver's license
- motoring organization
- voter registration
- frequent-flier accounts
- other addresses

- _____

- _____

- _____

- _____

Checklist 9

COMPANIES TO NOTIFY FOR FINAL BILL PAYMENT

- local telephone
- long-distance telephone
- electricity
- natural gas
- water
- trash collection
- charge account (that you are closing)
- newspaper
- lawn and garden service
- diaper service
- delivery service
- TV cable
- other companies

- _____

- _____

- _____

- _____

Checklist 10

WATTAGE AND APPLIANCES

The following table will give you a rough guide to help you figure out the approximate size transformer you will need. Check the wattage on your appliance, though, to be sure. You can find it listed in the owner's manual and/or directly on the appliance.

Transformer Size	Appliance
100 watts	electric blanket, small radio, heating pad, handheld vacuum, answering machine, battery charger
250 watts	stereo, blender, sewing machine, small fan, television, VCR, coffee grinder
500 watts	refrigerator, power tools, computer
1,000 watts	coffee maker, vacuum cleaner, food processor, toaster, small space heater, waffle iron
2,000 watts	iron, electric frying pan, toaster oven, hair dryer
3,000 watts	electric kettle, dishwasher, washing machine, dryer, air conditioner

Note that some appliances are expressed in units of ampere; 240 watts = 1 ampere.

Checklist 11

HOUSE-HUNTING FACTORS

The following list is intended to help you evaluate each property that you view during your house/apartment hunting. Check each factor as you go through each room. This will help you evaluate each place's characteristic.

PROPERTY ADDRESS: _____

Entrance (hall)

- space
- coat closet
- well lighted
- outer porch protect
- other_____

Living room

- adequate size
- lighting
- electric sockets (#____)
- accessibility
- other_____

Dining room

- adequate size
- lighting
- electric sockets (#____)
- kitchen access
- other_____

Coatroom

- adequate space
- convenient location
- accessibility
- other_____

Kitchen

- adequate size
- accessibility
- lighting
- electric sockets (#____)
- counter/work space
- access to larder
- space for appliances
- cupboard space
- drawers/cabinets
- flooring
- gas or electric
- sink
- remodeled
- eating space
- other_____

Study

- adequate size
- space for furniture
- access
- shelving
- other_____

Second bathroom

- shower and/or bath
- access to bedrooms
- other_____

Master bedroom

- space for king/queen bed
- space for furniture
- adequate closet space
- "warm" feeling
- lighting
- en suite
- other_____

Master bath

- shower and/or bath
- layout
- remodeled
- other_____

Second bedroom

- adequate size
- location
- other_____

Third bedroom

- adequate size
- location
- other_____

Half bath

- functional
- convenient location

Fireplace

- adequate
- flue
- other_____

Utility room

- space for appliances
- space for laundry
- cabinet space
- other_____

Garden

- size
- sun
- condition
- maintenance
- garden shed
- other_____

Garage and driveway

- size
- access and approach
- storage space
- visitor parking
- other_____

Storage space

- linen closet
- attic
- storage closet
- other_____

Staircase

- easy to climb
- other_____

Electricity

- adequate outlets
- age of wiring
- other_____

Gas

- heating
- cooking
- other_____

Plumbing

- leaks
- faucet
- toilets
- shower/bath
- main shutoff
- other_____

Structure (inside)

- stains
- cracks
- paint
- quality
- condition
- doors and windows
- woodwork
- flooring
- other_____

Structure (outside)

- cracks
- paint
- foundation
- gutters
- quality
- condition

Neighborhood

- seclusion
- noise
- sidewalk
- neighbors
- traffic noise
- roads in front
- other_____

Distance from

- work
- bus stop/subway
- railway
- schools
- shopping
- "corner" store
- recreation center
- local entertainment
- churches
- other_____

Access to

- footpaths
- parks
- major roadways
- other_____

TV aerial

- connection points
- other_____

Miscellaneous

- insulation
- security
- other_____
- other_____

Checklist 12

HOUSE RANKING

This house-ranking sheet is designed to help you quickly rate the accommodation you are viewing and compare it with others you have seen. After you see several places, they will all tend to blur into one another. See the note below for instructions on how to use this checklist. To further help you remember each place, it can be helpful to sketch the floor plans. Use the back of this sheet for your drawing.

PROPERTY ADDRESS: _____

Rental Price: _____

Size (note: 1 sq. m. = 10.764 sq. ft.): _____

Overall general impression: _____(5 through 1)

Overall comments: _____

	Weighting (3 thru 1)	Rank (5 thru 1)	Total (5 thru 1)	Comments
LOCATION				
Quality location	3			
Quiet area	3			
Distance to work	3			
Distance to schools	3			
Proximity to neighbor	2			
Proximity to shopping	2			
Public-transport sites	1			
Access to major roads	1			
Proximity to airport	1			
Access to walking paths	1			
Health club	1			
Recreation facilities	1			
Other_____	1			
Subtotal	_____			

	Weighting	Rank	Total	Comments
	(3 thru 1)	(5 thru 1)	(5 thru 1)	

HOUSE

Overall ambience	3
Light	3
Character property	2
Three bedrooms	3
Four bedrooms	1
Large master bedroom	3
Study	3
Baths (2½ optimum)	3
Remodeled bath	1
Power shower	1
Large kitchen/eat-in	3
Remodeled kitchen	3
Family room	3
Living room	2
Dining room	2
Utility room	1
Coatroom	1
Larder	1
Back porch/patio	2
Storage space	3
Garage	2
Garden (quality)	2
Garden (size)	1
Front drive	2
Roadway	2
Ability to expand	1
Alarm, security lights	1
Other _____	1

Subtotal   _____

               TOTAL _____

Note: This system is designed so that each category is assigned a *weighting* (in this sheet, the weighting has been set; you can change it, based on your own priorities and needs). As you view each house, you can rate each category 5 through 1 (5 = excellent, 1 = poor) in the *rank* column. After you view the accommodation, rate your *overall general impression* (5 through 1).

Later, you can then multiply the *weighting* times the *rank*, and then divide by 5. The result is put in the *total* column. You can then add up all the *total* results to come up with a final result. To compare with your *overall general impression*, divide this result by the number of categories used. Because the location and the actual property are two critical, yet different, factors, you can compare these categories as well. To determine the sub-total for each section, add the totals within each section and then divide the subtotal by the number of categories in each section.

You can compare your detailed total with your overall general impression. You now have a subjective and objective method of rating the accommodation and then comparing it with other properties.

As mentioned above, do not forget to draw a floor plan.

Checklist 13

QUESTIONS TO ASK WHEN LOOKING AT SCHOOLS

You will undoubtedly have your own concerns and questions when evaluating a school, but some things you may want to consider include:

- accreditation
- academic standards
- academic test results
- mean SAT scores or equivalent
- percentage of students from high school applying to and being accepted by universities (and which ones)
- curricula, including language and math
- grouping of students
- availability of elective subjects
- diversity of programs, including music, art, drama, foreign language, and computer instruction
- honors program
- opportunities to pursue gifted programs and advanced study
- special-education availability
- standardized testing program
- counselor on staff
- student support services
- college preparation assistance
- provisions for new students
- sports programs and facilities
- extracurricular activities
- school history
- atmosphere of the school
- enthusiasm and attitude of teachers, staff, and students
- overall philosophy, values, and policies of the school
- dress code
- disciplinary procedures and current problem areas
- size of classes
- student-teacher ratio

- teacher credentials
- parental involvement
- building construction
- size and quality of library
- tuition
- transportation arrangements and fees
- other questions

- _____

- _____

Checklist 14

U.S. FEDERAL TAX FORMS AND PUBLICATIONS RELATING TO OVERSEAS

There are several tax forms and publications that pertain to U.S. citizens living overseas. You can contact your local IRS office or the central IRS service center in Philadelphia. There are many tax implications, and the issues are quite complicated. You are advised to contact a qualified tax consultant who specializes in international taxation.

- **Publication 54:** *A Guide for U.S. Citizens and Resident Aliens Abroad*
- **Form 8822:** "Change of Address"
- **Form 4868:** "Application for Automatic Extension of Time to File U.S. Individual Income Tax Return"
- **Publication 505:** *Tax Withholding and Estimated Tax*
- **Publication 909:** *Alternative Minimum Tax for Individuals*
- **Form 6251:** "Alternative Minimum Tax — Individuals"
- **Form 1116:** "Foreign Tax Credit"
- **Form 2555:** "Foreign Earned Income"
- **Form 3903-F:** "Foreign Moving Expenses"
- **Publication 523:** *Tax Information on Selling Your Home*
- **Form 2119:** "Sale of Your Home"
- Request for Earnings and Benefit Estimate Statement
- **Form TD F 90-22.1:** "Report of Foreign Bank and Financial Accounts"

Checklist 15

MEDICAL TIPS

Below are some tips for maintaining a healthy and secure life in an overseas posting:

- Become aware of the common health problems and diseases that exist in the host country.
- Make sure your routine immunizations and specifically recommended inoculations for the area are all up to date for the whole family.
- Get a routine medical examination for each family member.
- Confirm that you have sufficient medical insurance coverage.
- Seek out appropriate physicians and pediatricians as soon as possible after arriving in the host country, before you need them.
- Learn where the local hospital and emergency centers are and how to get to them.
- Become familiar with local medical procedures and the system.
- Prepare an adequate home medical kit.
- Have your prescriptions for medication, glasses, and contact lenses.
- Be sure to have each family member's blood type.
- Prepare an emergency travel kit that includes all the appropriate supplies and medicines.
- Purchase a good manual on health care that covers home diagnosis and suggested treatments.
- Make sure you maintain a healthy environment in your house, particularly when living in a developing country.
- Make sure you are familiar with common safety and accident-prevention methods.
- Be aware of the need for and appropriate practices used for maintaining healthy water and food supplies.

- Maintain a healthy body.
- If you have household helpers, take an active interest in their health and hygiene.

Checklist 16

ADAPTING TECHNIQUES FOR CULTURE SHOCK

Some suggestions to alleviate the symptoms of culture shock and to help you progress quickly to the final adaption stage include:

- Realize that all of your reactions are completely normal.
- Try to have realistic expectations about living overseas.
- Develop a positive attitude about your assignment.
- Take concrete measures to adapt.
- Learn more about the host country and culture.
- Be prepared.
- Take language training.
- Attend a cultural-awareness training seminar.
- Become in tune with the local rhythms of the host country.
- Appreciate the cultural differences.
- Set small, short-term goals or projects.
- Distract yourself.
- Create a home.
- Make time for your family.
- Try to establish a support group outside the family.
- Build your social network.
- Consider the reasons why you and your family are accepting the international posting.
- Establish goals.
- Travel (e.g., day trips, long weekends, and extended holidays).
- Remember to ask for help.
- Learn stress-resistant attitudes and behaviors.
- Keep in touch.
- If you or someone in your family feels miserable and cannot adapt, take action.
- Maintain a problem-solving attitude.

Checklist 17

SOURCES FOR MEETING PEOPLE OVERSEAS

Some areas for you to explore to meet people can include:

- areas of mutual interests (e.g., hobbies)
- similar stages of life (e.g., young children)
- work
- national organizations with local branches (e.g., Rotary Club)
- religious organizations or church
- through your children (e.g., schools, parents' organizations)
- evening classes
- language training or conversation classes
- university
- volunteer organizations
- sports and social clubs
- professional and business networks
- embassy or consulate (e.g., Community Liaison Office)
- in-country resource services (e.g., such as FOCUS Information Service, which provides a wide range of expatriate services in the U.K.)
- expatriate organizations or associations (e.g., American Women's Club)

Checklist 18

POTENTIAL PORTABLE CAREERS FOR THE ACCOMPANYING SPOUSE

There are several professions that are more transportable and have significant opportunities for overseas employment. These include:

- social work
- counseling
- teaching
- private tutoring
- training
- health care
- management consulting
- office management
- computer
- accounting
- public relations
- small-business ventures
- anthropology
- secretarial skills
- writing and editing (e.g., technical, travel, and creative)
- various creative arts

Checklist 19

TRAITS FOR A SUCCESSFUL EXECUTIVE IN A GLOBAL ENVIRONMENT

To be successful in the international marketplace, an executive must:

Global perspective

- have a global viewpoint
- understand international politics and economics
- have a deep understanding of cross-cultural issues and their impact
- be interested in foreign cultures
- have a sensitivity to different cultures and people
- be open to learning the language of the host country

Change orientation

- have an openness to change
- adapt easily
- be accepting of foreign cultures and realize that they are just as valid as your own
- be open-minded and able to consider issues from different perspectives
- have a tolerance of ambiguity
- be open to learning, and have a deep curiosity about people and the world
- be at ease with different types of people

People skills

- be innovative
- have excellent communication skills, including listening and observing
- be sensitive to the feelings and beliefs of others
- be self-confident and positive

- be self-motivated
- be outgoing and willing to seek contact with nationals and their culture
- be nonjudgmental and accepting of opposing views
- be patient
- be a problem solver

Last and most important, be flexible and have a positive attitude!

Checklist 20

KEY FACTORS AN INTERNATIONAL EXECUTIVE MUST UNDERSTAND

To be a successful executive overseas, there are several cultural factors, customs, and modes of behavior that need to be understand. These include:

- Are the people open- or closed-minded by nature?
- Are the people tolerant to change and open to taking risks, or is there a strong basis on following rules and established patterns?
- Do they base their actions on faith (i.e., religion), fact, or feelings?
- When people communicate, do they favor a direct approach or a more indirect style?
- Does the society favor an individualistic or a communal approach?
- What is more important, the project or building relationships among colleagues?
- What is the employees' attitude toward authority?
- Is the business environment formal or informal?
- How are decisions made: collectively, immediate/middle manager, or top level only?
- How important are social ranking and hierarchy to the workforce, and what is your position in the group?
- How do the people view others that are different (i.e., gender, race, religion, cultures)?
- What motivates people — personal achievements, money, titles, etc.?

Checklist 21

BUSINESS CULTURAL MODEL

A cultural model is developed to describe different attitudes and beliefs within a culture, breaking it down into a series of cultural components.

Personal Influence
- communication
- relationships
- interdependence

Outside Influence
- time
- hierarchy
- change

Checklist 22

ADAPTING TECHNIQUES FOR REPATRIATION

It is common for expatriates to expect challenges of adaptation when moving abroad but not to realize that challenges also arise with repatriating. Yet repatriation is a major issue.

Some suggestions to alleviate the symptoms of "reverse culture shock" include:

- See Checklist 16; many of the techniques also apply.
- Consider returning home as a new stage in your life.
- Review your goals and aspirations.
- Take control of your actual move.
- Build your network.
- Get involved with a local community group.
- Communicate with and listen to your family members.
- Do not wait for others to approach you; make the first move.
- Do not constantly talk about your stay abroad unless specifically asked.
- Do not make comparisons all the time.

Appendix B

EXERCISES

Throughout this manual, you have been exposed to the written word in helping you to understand the issues relating to international relocation. To help you understand how these matters relate to you, this section contains several exercises. They are not meant to be difficult or time-consuming. Rather, it is hoped that they will give you insight and will spur helpful discussion and thought. Also please review each exercise during your assignment if you find areas that are troubling.

Exercises 1 through 8
relate to culture shock and psychological adjustment issues.

Exercise 1
Moving to a New Culture and Associated Changes

Exercise 2
Effects of Change

Exercise 3
Managing Change

Exercise 4
Holmes-Rahe Social Readjustment Scale

Exercise 5
What Is Stress?

Exercise 6
Causes of Worry

Exercise 7
Strategies for Stress Control

Exercise 8
Cultural Self-awareness: Attitudes and Values

*Exercises 9 through 12 are designed to help you
settle into your new environment.*

Exercise 9
Decision Making and Goal Setting

Exercise 10
Day-to-day Living In . . .

Exercise 11
Creating a Life

Exercise 12
Culture and the Business Environment

Exercises 13 through 17 relate to finances.

Exercise 13
Financial Goals and Priorities

Exercise 14
Net Worth

Exercise 15
Net Cash Flow

Exercise 16
Financial Inventory

Exercise 17
Trailing Spouse/Partner: Possible Motives for Wanting to Work

Exercise 1

MOVING TO A NEW CULTURE
AND ASSOCIATED CHANGES

Below is a partial list of things that would typically change in your environment after you enter a new culture. Identify any of them that directly affect you and your family and mark each with a √.

__housing	__medical facilities
__attitudes toward the elderly	__friends
__educational system	__interpersonal relationships
__pace of life	__values
__religion	__roles
__family setup	__pets
__sense of space	__language
__children's customs	__priorities
__population density	__store hours
__own family dynamics	__own sense of identity
__status of women	__making friends
__social life	__mail system
__church activities	__cooking
__meal hours	__laws, taxes
__community activities	__books, newspapers
__radio, TV	__clothing/style
__finances	__child rearing
__telephoning	__continuing education
__foods	opportunity

How many have you marked with a √? Dealing with all these changes will require time, effort, and patience. Your first step in managing changes — becoming aware of and identifying them — is now complete.

Exercise 2

EFFECTS OF CHANGE

You have now identified the many changes you and your family are experiencing because of your international relocation. We all tend to be "creatures of habit," and change can often affect us negatively by creating stress and insecurity in our lives. The next step in managing change is to understand how these changes affect you.

Refer to Exercise 1, identify which changes most concern you, and indicate your responses.

RESPONSES

Event	Emotional	Behavioral	Physical
e.g., housing	irritable with children	smoking more	feel fatigued

1.

2.

3.

4.

5.

6.

Exercise 3

MANAGING CHANGE

Now that you have identified the changes (Exercise 1) and their effects on your life (Exercise 2), you need to learn how to manage change. Below are ideas to help you. Remember that you can also involve other family members in completing the tables.

1. Identify goals to help manage change, and break them down into discrete action plans. As you complete each goal, check it off.

> *For example, your goal may be to reduce the anxiety of living in a foreign country. Steps to help you reach this goal could be to take language lessons, learn about the culture, and explore your new environment with a friend.*

GOAL 1:   **Steps to reach goal** √

1.

2.

3.

GOAL 2:   **Steps to reach goal** √

1.

2.

3.

2. Develop positive thinking. You can accomplish this by identifying the recurring negative thought patterns. Second, remember the feelings and reactions associated with that thought. Finally, create an alternative positive thought to associate with the original event.

For example, you have difficulty in placing an overseas phone call. Your original feeling is one of incompetence and your thought is that you could never adapt. Rather, replace that thought with the idea that it is one temporary obstacle in living overseas that you can overcome. Remind yourself that you are a competent person.

Negative thought	Reactions & feelings	Positive new thought
1.		
2.		
3.		

Exercise 4

HOLMES-RAHE SOCIAL READJUSTMENT SCALE

Changes in our lives — whether good or bad — create stress. How many of the following things have happened to you in the past year? Circle the ones that apply to you. By adding up the corresponding numbers, you will have the score of your current stress potential.

Life Event Value

1. Death of spouse 100
2. Divorce 73
3. Marital separation. 65
4. Jail term 63
5. Death of a close family member 63
6. Personal injury or illness 53
7. Marriage. 50
8. Fired at work 47
9. Marital reconciliation .45
10. Retirement. 45
11. Change in the health of a family member 44
12. Pregnancy. 40
13. Sex difficulties 39
14. Addition of a new family member 39
15. Business readjustment 39
16. Change in financial state 38
17. Death of a close friend 37
18. Change to a different line of work 36
19. Change in number of arguments with spouse . .35
20. House mortgage 31
21. Foreclosure of mortgage or loan 30
22. Change in responsibilities at work 29
23. Son or daughter leaving home 29

24. Trouble with in-laws 29
25. Outstanding personal achievement 28
26. Spouse begins or stops work 26
27. Starting or finishing school 26
28. Change in living conditions 25
29. Revision of personal habits 24
30. Trouble with supervisor 23
31. Change in work hours or condition 20
32. Change in residence 20
33. Change in schools 20
34. Change in recreational habits 19
35. Change in church activities 19
36. Change in social activities 18
37. Mortgage or loan less than $10,000 17
38. Change in sleeping habits 16
39. Change in the number of family gatherings 15
40. Change in eating habits 15
41. Vacation 13
42. Christmas season 12
43. Minor violations of the law 11

  TOTAL . . . . ._____

Add up the total values of the life events you circled. You can interpret your score as follows:

Score	Stress potential
less than 150	mild
150–199	moderate
200–299	medium
300 or more	severe

(Reprinted from Holmes et al., 1967, "The social readjustment rating scale," *Journal of Psychosomatic Research*, vol. 2, pp. 213–218, with permission of Elsivier Science.)

Exercise 5

WHAT IS STRESS?

Stress is the individual's physical, mental, and emotional reactions to any condition that disturbs normal equilibrium. Stress becomes a problem when it exceeds the individual's ability to adapt.

Technically, stress is not what happens to you (the event or problem), but your response to that experience. The cause of your stress is called the "stressor." We are all subject to stressors; the amount of stress we have depends on how we react to them.

All of life's events, whether positive or negative, require us to deal with, adapt, or change to some degree. Stress cannot be avoided completely. We need a certain amount of stress to be alert and involved in life. Learning to manage stress can enhance the quality of life.

As the table below shows, responses to stress may be seen on a continuum from mild to severe:

	EMOTIONAL	BEHAVIORAL	PHYSIOLOGICAL
MILD	mild annoyance; amusement	improvement in performance	alertness
MODERATE	anger; joy	proneness to accidents	tears, headaches, indigestion
SEVERE	overpowering rage; ecstasy	changes in ability to get along with people	ulcers, heart disease

Individuals experiencing stress may develop symptoms of fear, anxiety, or depression. In other cases, they may feel angry, frustrated, or unwell. It is important to treat the symptoms and get at the underlying causes (stressors), because severe or prolonged unresolved stress can lead to emotional, psychological, or physical illness.

Here are several ideas for stress prevention and management:

- Keep fit. Eat healthy food, don't smoke, and get exercise and enough rest.
- Have a chosen form of recreation completely unlike your work.
- Leave the office at the office. Even if you work at home or your job is running the household, try to delegate and organize so that you don't have all the burdens.
- Consider your lifestyle and objectives in life. Outline what will provide you the deepest satisfaction in life, and make those things your priorities.

Exercise 6

CAUSES OF WORRY

An international relocation involves many issues, and any tendency to worry can increase dramatically. You may worry about a range of personal matters such as health, money, work, family, and relationships, to name a few.

List in the table below as many potential "worries" as you can envision facing in the next weeks.

For seven consecutive days, spend a few moments at the end of the day making check marks for each worry that came true that particular day.

Each morning, examine your list and try to identify a particular worry that you can make into a challenge, eliminating it before it becomes a reality. For instance, you can develop action plans to help solve the problem. Remember that worrying by itself does not accomplish anything but an upset stomach!

Worry Day:	1	2	3	4	5	6	7

Exercise 7

STRATEGIES FOR STRESS CONTROL

PHYSIOLOGICAL

Practice relaxation techniques • Get regular exercise • Spend time outdoors every day • Balance your diet • Breathe deeply each day • Avoid harmful substances • Drink six glasses of water every day • Practice cleanliness and hygiene • Change your pace frequently • Reduce noise • Dress comfortably • Seek professional help when sick

EMOTIONAL

Express cheerfulness (i.e., laugh, smile) • Develop self-respect • Eliminate undue fear by being realistic • Plan ahead to eliminate some worries • Reduce the amount of changes in your life • Reduce time pressures • Avoid irritations and arguments • Express gratitude • Develop positive attitudes and thinking • Regulate what you read and watch • Learn to make decisions • Develop appreciation of music and nature

PSYCHOLOGICAL

Develop good interpersonal relations • Go out of your way to help others • Compete with yourself, not with others • Set goals and priorities • Forgive and forget • Develop creative hobbies and interests • Join discussion and listening groups • Simplify your lifestyle • Avoid debt • Look for good in others • Do not give up if you fail • Do not take on more than you can handle; learn to say no!

SPIRITUAL

Meditation or prayer • Give your time and means to worthy causes • Learn self-control • Find meaningful activities • Learn to meditate • Live according to your values • Clarify your values and motives • Join a caring community • Participate in activities for the good of the community • Be content with doing your best • Be good to yourself • Put energy into those relationships that are important to you

Exercise 8

CULTURAL SELF-AWARENESS: ATTITUDES AND VALUES

It is difficult to be understanding of others without an aware-ness of yourself as a cultural being. Below are some questions to help you begin to think about how you view the world. Refer to Chapters 9 and 13 for insight into various cultural perspectives.

Your Ethnic Heritage

What ethnic background do you first identify with, e.g., nationali-ty, race, religion?

Where do your ancestors come from? Can you trace a family his-tory, perhaps with different ethnic, religious, and racial back-grounds?

List your heritage here. Remember to include the country where you live.

Review the list you developed and pick out the central cultural, ethnic, religious, or other groups involved in your development.

Your Cultural Values

Identify the values, behaviors, and expectations that people in your group(s) have come to emphasize.

List some key life messages given by your family or other cultural groups.

How do you fit with or differ from your heritage?

Dealing with Others

Which of your cultural values might make it hard for you to deal with people who are different from you?

Which cultural values in others might be difficult for you to accept?

Cultural Perspectives

What cultural perspectives (see business cultural model presented in Chapter 13) are most important to you and serve as strong forces that govern the way you think and act?

Exercise 9

DECISION MAKING AND GOAL SETTING

Now that you have settled in, are you beginning to feel "stuck" or unmotivated? Perhaps you have lost sight of what gives your life meaning. Below is a brief plan for decision making. It is important to take some time to think about what is really important to you and to set some priorities.

1. Establish your values. What is important to you and what isn't?

2. If there were no restrictions in your life, how would you live your life differently? What is holding you back?

3. Set goals: short-term, long-term, personal, professional.

4. Identify possible actions.

5. Collect information on all possibilities.

6. Look ahead to consequences of your actions and how they can be managed. (Eliminate "shoulds" such as "the house should be immaculate before I can go out and exercise"). Remember, family members can help.

7. Decide on a course of action and carry out your plans.

8. Review the action taken and evaluate the results. Go back to the beginning as needed or whenever you feel stuck.

Exercise 10

DAY-TO-DAY LIVING IN . . .

Below is a chart to fill in as you begin to locate local services. As you get settled, you may find it helpful to note where you found what. This is perhaps daunting at first, but there is satisfaction in discovering your way around a new city. Before long, you'll be telling people about your favorite places!

supermarkets: _____

food shops: _____

pharmacy: _____

restaurants:_____

books and videos: _____

hardware:_____

sundries:_____

speciality shops: _____

department stores:_____

hairdresser:_____

kids' stuff: _____

repair shops:_____

car: _____

electronics:_____

entertainment: _____

other:_____

Exercise 11

CREATING A LIFE

Back home, you had certain activities that provided the "anchors" to your life. Now that you have moved, you will need to reestablish your routine. Fill in the chart below. In the first column, list what you used to do. In the second column, write possible alternatives.

	What I did back home:	*What I might try here:*
Work		
Family		
Friends		
Special occasions/ holidays		
Hobbies/ interests		
Sports/ exercise		

Choose just one or two of the ideas from the second column to schedule into your diary every week until you have created your new life! Remember to be patient with yourself. Allow several months to get settled and to adjust to your new surroundings. Give yourself credit for each new accomplishment.

Exercise 12

CULTURE AND THE BUSINESS ENVIRONMENT
QUESTIONNAIRE

The following questionnaire is designed to help you gain an understanding of different cultures and how they impact the business environment.

The questions and answers relate to your observations of the local national culture, people, and attitudes where you work as an expatriate. Answer them as you believe your hosts think and act.

You can also use this questionnaire to evaluate your own cultural perspectives. Answer the questions as you think and act. Compare your results with those for the host country.

Host Country _____

Your Nationality _____

1. It is important to spend time building a strong personal relationship before working on a project or business venture with someone.
    (a) true
    (b) false

2. A great deal of responsibility lies with the individual.
    (a) true
    (b) false

3. The structure of the business organization is predominantly
    (a) flat
    (b) vertical/pyramidal

4. There are many nonverbal forms of communication, and they have a significant role.
    (a) true
    (b) false

5. Meetings begin and end on time and follow a set agenda.
    (a) usually
    (b) rarely

6. Which is more important?
    (a) taking risks
    (b) following rules and established patterns

7. You are working on a project with your colleague. You are both deeply engrossed in your work. Another host national comes into the office to ask a question. Does your colleague:
    (a) ask the person to come back later
    (b) interrupt work and briefly deal with the question
    (c) welcome the colleague and turn his attention to that person

8. An individual has control over his position, advancement, and life in general.
    (a) usually
    (b) rarely

9. Seniority and age are highly valued in the organization.
    (a) true
    (b) false

10. Communication tends to be
    (a) direct and open
    (b) indirect and subtle

11. Tasks are done
    (a) systematically
    (b) at the last minute

12. People are readily open to new ideas or new ways of doing something.
    (a) true
    (b) false

13. The strongest influence on the individual is
    (a) religion
    (b) family
    (c) facts and data

14. Loyalty tends to lie with the
    (a) individual
    (b) project group
    (c) company

15. Whom you know or your social status and rank are more important than what you know and have achieved.
    (a) basically true
    (b) basically false

16. People are very expressive and emotional in the business environment.
    (a) true
    (b) false

17. The approach to time is
    (a) past oriented (i.e., traditional)
    (b) present oriented (i.e., "live for today")
    (c) future oriented (i.e., task or goal oriented)

18. It is important to follow rules and established patterns.
    (a) true
    (b) false

19. The focus is on
    (a) the project or goal
    (b) people and building relationships

20. Employees tend to work
    (a) alone
    (b) in a group/team
    (c) independently but in a team environment

21. An individual would cancel a planned holiday or come into the office on weekends if the workload demands it.
    (a) rarely
    (b) readily

22. Employees are not bothered by disagreement or confrontation.
    (a) true
    (b) false

23. People appear to be
    (a) focused
    (b) disorganized

24. People tend to be
    (a) open-minded
    (b) closed-minded

25. Tasks usually are solved by the
    (a) individual
    (b) group/team

26. Business meetings or negotiations tend to proceed at
    (a) an orderly and rapid pace
    (b) a deliberate and slow pace

27. Employees expect lifetime employment with a company.
    (a) true
    (b) false

28. The reward structure tends to be based on
    (a) individual performance
    (b) success of the group/team as a whole

29. Equality and individualism are prominent beliefs.
    (a) true
    (b) false

30. The attitude toward time is that it is important and should not be wasted.
    (a) true
    (b) false

CULTURE AND THE BUSINESS ENVIRONMENT
QUESTIONNAIRE RESULTS

The following answers are used to score the culture and the business environment questionnaire, segmented by the six cultural components discussed in Chapter 13. For each question, circle the answer you gave. Then count the number of highs and lows you answered and total them in the space provided. The questions highlighted in **bold** are those that are most relevant to determining the cultural perspective; score twice for each of those answers.

After you have totaled your results, plot the corresponding number of high values on the spokes of the cultural wheel. You may wish to shade in each section to the appropriate level. A large number of high values corresponds to the relative importance of a particular cultural component, and a large number of low values corresponds to less orientation to a particular cultural component.

Communication

4.	(a) high	(b) low	
10.	**(a) low**	**(b) high**	
16.	**(a) high**	**(b) low**	
22.	(a) low	(b) high	
26.	(a) low	(b) high	

TOTAL: high____   low____   (7 maximum)

Relationships

1.	**(a) high**	**(b) low**	
7.	(a) low	(b) low	(c) high
13.	(a) high	(b) high	(c) low
19.	**(a) low**	**(b) high**	

TOTAL: high____   low____   (6 maximum)

Interdependence

2.	(a) low	(b) high	
8.	(a) low	(b) high	
14.	(a) low	(b) high	(c) high
20.	(a) low	(b) high	(c) low

| 25. | **(a) low** | **(b) high** |
| 28. | **(a) low** | **(b) high** |

TOTAL: high___   low___   (8 maximum)

Time

5.	(a) high	(b) low	
11.	**(a) high**	**(b) low**	
17.	(a) low	(b) low	(c) high
23.	(a) high	(b) low	
26.	(a) high	(b) low	
30.	**(a) high**	**(b) low**	

TOTAL: high___   low___   (8 maximum)

Hierarchy

3.	**(a) low**	**(b) high**	
9.	**(a) high**	**(b) low**	
13.	(a) high	(b) high	(c) Low
15.	(a) high	(b) low	
21.	(a) high	(b) low	
29.	(a) low	(b) high	

TOTAL: high___   low___   (8 maximum)

Change

6.	**(a) high**	**(b) low**
12.	**(a) high**	**(b) low**
18.	(a) low	(b) high
24.	(a) high	(b) low
27.	(a) low	(b) high

TOTAL: high___   low___   (7 maximum)

CULTURAL WHEEL
Culture and Business Environment Questionnaire

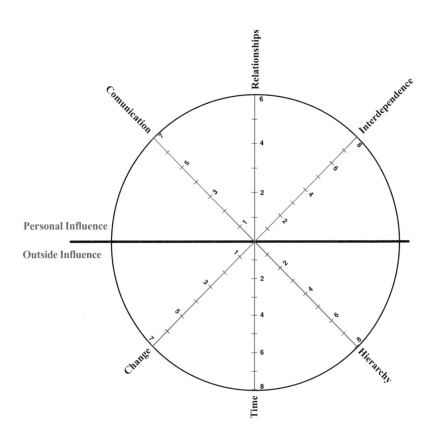

(Adapted from Seelye, 1996.)

Exercise 13

FINANCIAL GOALS AND PRIORITIES

Are you investing with a specific goal in mind or do you have several goals, ranging from the short to the long term? Short-term goals are those that fall within approximately two years. Accumulating the down payment for a car purchase is an example of a short-term goal. Midterm goals fall between two and ten years, and could include the financing of a child's college education. Finally, long-term goals are those that extend ten or more years in the future, such as planning for retirement.

Clearly, defining your investment objectives based on the time during which you wish to invest will help you devise an effective investment strategy. The greater time you have to invest, the greater amount of risk you are probably willing to tolerate. If an investment goal lies far in the future, you can ride out the periods of downward fluctuations in a stock that offers the potential for high growth. On the other hand, if your need for the money is sooner rather than later, you may be better off sticking with more stable investments that emphasize capital preservation.

1. To help determine your financial goals, please check the appropriate column for a particular goal and rank each goal (1 = high priority).

Financial goal	Rank	Short term (0–2 yrs)	Midterm (2–10 yrs)	Long term (10+ yrs)	Not relevant
Buy a house					
Home improvement					
Build cash reserves					
Reduce debt					
Retirement					
College expenses					
Expand insurance coverage					
Start or buy a business					
Wedding or honeymoon					
Vacation or travel					
Buy a car					
Other major purchase					
Buy a second home					
Other _____					

2. To help determine some of your financial priorities, check the appropriate column to indicate your priorities for the next few years and the appropriate rank.

Financial Priority	Immediate priority	Moderate priority	Not relevant
Review mortgage arrangements			
Increase savings			
Increase retirement contributions			
Maximize investment returns			
Maximize tax benefits			
Revise insurance (life, medical, accident)			
Increase standard of living			
Take an expensive vacation			
Raise cash for a particular purpose			
Reduce or eliminate personal debt			
Protect purchasing power against inflation			
Get married			
Have children			
Take an unpaid leave from work			
Start a business			
Take early retirement			
Other _____			

Exercise 14

NET WORTH

Whenever you evaluate your financial goals, it is important to understand what your current net worth is. This is one of the first steps to help you achieve your goals.

Fill out the work sheet below to figure your net worth or, in other words, your assets minus your liabilities. Do not forget to include any amounts you have in retirement accounts such as IRAs 401(k).

ASSETS
Property

Primary home . . . .$ _____

Secondary home . . . .$ _____

Furnishings . . . .$ _____

Jewelry . . . .$ _____

Collectibles, antiques, and art . . . .$ _____

Automobiles . . . .$ _____

Gold and silver . . . .$ _____

Other . . . .$ _____

Equity
Other real estate . . . .$ _____

Stocks . . . .$ _____

Mutual funds . . . .$ _____

Variable annuities . . . .$ _____

Business interests . . . .$ _____

Other . . . .$ _____

Other . . . .$ _____

Other . . . .$ _____

Subtotal . . . .$ _____

Fixed

Government bonds . . . .$ _____

Municipal bonds . . . .$ _____

Corporate bonds . . . .$ _____

Treasury securities . . . .$ _____

Fixed-dollar annuities . . . .$ _____

Cash loans to others . . . .$ _____

Other . . . .$ _____

Subtotal . . . .$ _____

Cash reserve

Checking accounts . . . .$ _____

Saving accounts . . . .$ _____

Credit unions . . . .$ _____

Certificates of deposit . . . .$ _____

Other . . . .$ _____

Other . . . .$ _____

Other . . . .$ _____

Subtotal . . . .$ _____

Total assets $_____

LIABILITIES

Unpaid bills . . . . _____

Taxes . . . .$ _____

Mortgage or rent . . . .$ _____

Insurance premiums . . . .$ _____

Utilities . . . .$ _____

Alimony . . . .$ _____

Child support . . . .$ _____

Other . . . .$ _____

Other . . . .$ _____

Subtotal . . . .$ _____

Mortgages and loans

Primary home . . . .$ _____

Secondary home . . . .$ _____

Home improvements . . . .$ _____

Automobiles . . . .$ _____

Education . . . .$ _____

Loans against life insurance . . . . . .$ _____

Charge-account balances . . . .$ _____

Margin accounts . . . .$ _____

Other bank loans . . . .$ _____

Other . . . .$ _____

Subtotal . . . .$ _____

Total liabilities $_____

TOTAL NET WORTH $_____
(Total assets less total liabilities)

Exercise 15

NET CASH FLOW

To help you achieve your financial goals as well as determine where your money is going, it is important to calculate your monthly cash flow. It can be difficult to accurately quantify your spending, particularly if your company provides you with expatriate benefits.

There will be some expenses listed below that you may normally incur in your home country but not overseas, and there will be other expenses that will be new. Nevertheless, the following work sheet can be a first start in establishing a realistic budget. You can also use this as a guide for your expected expenses when you repatriate.

Note that you have two types of expenses: fixed and variable. Variable expenses (e.g., food, long-distance telephone calls, vacations, entertainment, etc.) are more easy to control. There are options, though, to reduce your fixed expenses (i.e., mortgage, taxes, utilities, etc.), such as refinancing your house, but they are usually harder to realize. There are many ways to cut down on spending that will allow you to invest for the future, but you must be realistic and comfortable with any lifestyle changes. One of the best ways to increase your wealth is to save regularly; automatic monthly payments to a savings account are an excellent tool for increasing your wealth.

Fill out the work sheet below to figure your monthly net cash flow. The currency is listed in dollars for illustration, but if it is easier for you, you can keep track of your income and expenses in the local or home-country currency.

INCOME
Monthly

Salary (first income) . . . .$ _____

Salary (second income) . . . .$ _____

Dividends from stocks, etc. . . . . . .$ _____

Interest on savings, etc. . . . .$ _____

Capital gains . . . .$ _____

Annuities, pensions, etc. . . . .$ _____

Income from part-time work . . . . .$ _____
(e.g., consulting, tutoring, etc.)

Interest on loans . . . .$ _____

Child support, alimony . . . .$ _____

Other . . . .$ _____

Subtotal . . . .$ _____

EXPENSES
Monthly

Mortgage payment, rent . . . .$ _____

Second home mortgage . . . .$ _____

Automobile loan . . . .$ _____

Personal loans . . . .$ _____

Charge accounts . . . .$ _____

Telephone . . . .$ _____

Federal income tax . . . .$ _____

State and local income tax . . . . . .$ _____

Transportation (public) . . . .$ _____

Social Security tax . . . .$ _____

Real estate taxes . . . .$ _____

Homeowners' insurance ....$ _____

Car insurance ....$ _____

Life insurance ....$ _____

Health insurance ....$ _____

Savings and investments ....$ _____

Education expenses ....$ _____

Child care ....$ _____

Medical expenses ....$ _____

Furniture, decorating ....$ _____

Charitable contributions ....$ _____

Membership dues and fees ......$ _____

Personal care, haircuts ....$ _____

Pets ....$ _____

Computer ....$ _____

Cable television ....$ _____

Food ....$ _____

Clothing ....$ _____

Utilities (gas) ....$ _____

Utilities (electric) ....$ _____

Water ....$ _____

Gasoline ....$ _____

Dining out ....$ _____

Entertainment ....$ _____

Recreation ....$ _____

Vacations ....$ _____

Household maintenance ....$ _____

Household items ....$ _____

Car repairs . . . . :$ _____

Car registration, etc. . . . .$ _____

Home appliances . . . .$ _____

Books . . . .$ _____

Subscriptions . . . .$ _____

Gifts . . . .$ _____

Other   . . . .$ _____

Other   . . . .$ _____

Subtotal   . . . .$ _____

TOTAL MONTHLY CASH FLOW   **$** _____
(Total income less total expenses)

If the result is positive, this can represent additional funds for savings and investment. If the result is negative, you are spending more than you earn.

Exercise 16

FINANCIAL INVENTORY

It is a good idea to have an inventory of your financial instruments, including investments and credit cards. The following tables are to help you keep track of all your financial instruments.

CREDIT CARDS

Credit card _____

Account no.: _____

Telephone no.: _____

Credit card _____

Account no.: _____

Telephone no.: _____

Credit card _____

Account no.: _____

Telephone no.: _____

Credit card _____

Account no.: _____

Telephone no.: _____

Credit card _____

Account no.: _____

Telephone no.: _____

Credit card _____

Account no.: _____

Telephone no.: _____

SAVINGS

Bank (checking)   _____

    Account no.:   _____

    Telephone no.:   _____

Bank (checking)   _____

    Account no.:   _____

    Telephone no.:   _____

Bank (savings)   _____

    Account no.:   _____

    Telephone no.:   _____

Bank (savings)   _____

    Account no.:   _____

    Telephone no.:   _____

Bank (CD)   _____

    Account no.:   _____

    Telephone no.:   _____

    Maturity date: _____

Treasury   _____

    Account no.:   _____

    Telephone no.:   _____

    Maturity date: _____

INVESTMENTS

Stock/mutual fund   _____

    Account no.:   _____

    No. of shares: _____

    Purchase price: _____

    Date purchased: _____

Stock/mutual fund _____

    Account no.: _____

    No. of shares: _____

    Purchase price: _____

    Date purchased: _____

Stock/mutual fund _____

    Account no.: _____

    No. of shares: _____

    Purchase price: _____

    Date purchased: _____

Stock/mutual fund _____

    Account no.: _____

    No. of shares: _____

    Purchase price: _____

    Date purchased: _____

Stock/mutual fund _____

    Account no.: _____

    No. of shares: _____

    Purchase price: _____

    Date purchased: _____

Stock/mutual fund _____

    Account no.: _____

    No. of shares: _____

    Purchase price: _____

    Date purchased: _____

Stock/mutual fund _____

   Account no.: _____

   No. of shares: _____

   Purchase price: _____

   Date purchased: _____

Stock/mutual fund _____

   Account no.: _____

   No. of shares: _____

   Purchase price: _____

   Date purchased: _____

Stock/mutual fund _____

   Account no.: _____

   No. of shares: _____

   Purchase price: _____

   Date purchased: _____

Stock/mutual fund _____

   Account no.: _____

   No. of shares: _____

   Purchase price: _____

   Date purchased: _____

Stock/mutual fund _____

   Account no.: _____

   No. of shares: _____

   Purchase price: _____

   Date purchased: _____

IRAs

Where invested: _____

Account no.: _____

No. of shares: _____

Purchase price: _____

Date purchased: _____

Where invested: _____

Account no.: _____

No. of shares: _____

Purchase price: _____

Date purchased: _____

Where invested: _____

Account no.: _____

No. of shares: _____

Purchase price: _____

Date purchased: _____

Where invested: _____

Account no.: _____

No. of shares: _____

Purchase price: _____

Date purchased: _____

Where invested: _____

Account no.: _____

No. of shares: _____

Purchase price: _____

Date purchased: _____

FINANCIAL SUMMARY

WILL

Lawyer _____

        Address: _____

    Telephone no.: _____

Executor _____

        Address: _____

    Telephone no.: _____

Original copy kept where: _____

SAFE-DEPOSIT BOX

        Bank _____

      Location: _____

    Telephone no.: _____

      Contents: _____

_____

_____

        Bank _____

      Location: _____

    Telephone no.: _____

      Contents: _____

_____

_____

CHILDREN'S ACCOUNTS

        Bank _____

    Child's name: _____

    Account no.: _____

    Telephone no.: _____

Bank _____

Child's name: _____

Account no.: _____

Telephone no.: _____

LIFE INSURANCE

Husband's Insurer: _____

Policy no.: _____

Telephone no.: _____

Amount: _____

Beneficiary: _____

Wife's Insurer: _____

Policy no.: _____

Telephone no.: _____

Amount: _____

Beneficiary: _____

ACCIDENT, DISABILITY, AND ADDITIONAL LIFE INSURANCE

Insurer _____

Type: _____

Policy no.: _____

Telephone no.: _____

Amount: _____

Insurer _____

Type: _____

Policy no.: _____

Telephone no.: _____

Amount: _____

HOMEOWNERS' INSURANCE POLICY

Company: _____

Policy no.: _____

Telephone no.: _____

AUTOMOBILE INSURANCE POLICY

Company: _____

Policy no.: _____

Telephone no.: _____

LOANS

Lender: _____

Account no.: _____

Amount: _____

Terms: _____

Telephone no.: _____

Lender: _____

Account no.: _____

Amount: _____

Terms: _____

Telephone no.: _____

OTHER

_____

_____

_____

_____

_____

Exercise 17

TRAILING SPOUSE/PARTNER:
POSSIBLE MOTIVES FOR WANTING TO WORK

It is important to truly understand your motives for wanting to seek work abroad. You may use the chart below to outline some possible reasons and the realistic expectations you may have for achieving them.

Possible Motives	Ability to Achieve
Money	
Status	
Sense of purpose	
Having something to do	
Being with other people	
Intellectual stimulation	
Continuing current career path	
Learning new skills	
Recognition	
Respect	
Other	

Appendix C

RESOURCES

This section contains several resources that you may find helpful during your overseas assignment.

Resource 1
Resources and Contacts

Resource 2
Important Phone Numbers

Resource 3
International Telephone Country Codes and Time Differences

Resource 4
Conversion Charts and Tables

Resource 1

RESOURCES AND CONTACTS

GENERAL INFORMATION

Employee Relocation Council
1720 N Street, N.W.
Washington, D.C.   20036
telephone: (1)202-857-0857
Web site: www.erc.org
(provides information, reports, directories, seminars, referrals, etc.)

CBI Employee Relocation Council
Centre Point
103 New Oxford Street
London   WC1A 1DU
England
telephone: (44)171-379-7400
Web site: www.cbi.org.uk
(as in the United States)

Canadian Employee Relocation Council
20 Eglinton Avenue West
P.O. Box 2033
Suite 1202
Toronto
Ontario   M4R 1K8
Canada
telephone: (1)416-489-2555
(as in the United States)

Bureau of Consular Affairs
Room 4811 N.S.
U.S. Department of State
Washington, D.C.   20520
telephone: (1)202-647-5225
Web site: www.state.gov
(provides information on foreign countries and potential security
problems)

Family Liaison Office
U.S. Department of State
Washington, D.C.   20520
telephone: (1)202-647-1076
Web site: www.state.gov
(supports U.S. government employees and family members
assigned to diplomatic posts abroad)

American Citizens Abroad
16 Blvd. des Tranchées
P.O. Box 321
1211 Geneva 12
Switzerland
Web site: www.aca.ch
telephone: (41)223-476-847
(provides information for U.S. citizens overseas)

FOCUS Information Services Ltd.
22/23 Kensington Gardens Square
London   W2 4BE
England
telephone: (44)171-937-0050
(provides expatriate network and support, educational seminars,
professional workshops, and information on employment and
local resources in the U.K.)

FOCUS International Career Services
Rue Lesbroussart 23
1050 Brussels
Belgium
telephone: (32)2-646-6530
(as in England)

FOCUS International Career Services
17 Route de Collex
1293 Bellevue
Geneva
Switzerland
telephone: (41)22-774-1639
(as in England)

FOCUS International Career Services (WICE)
20, Boulevard de Montparnasse
15th arrondissement
Paris
France
(33)1-45-66-7550
(as in England)

Federation of American Women's Clubs Overseas (FAWCO)
Nassaulaan 1
3818 GM Amersfoort
The Netherlands
telephone: (31)33-4-618-211
Web site: www.fawco.org
(provides expatriate network and support)

General Federation of Women's Clubs
1734 N Street, N.W.
Washington, D.C.
telephone: (1)202-347-3168
Web site: www.gfwc.org
(provides expatriate network and support)

Culture Bank
Web site: www.culturebank.com
(provides information on cultural issues, with a special emphasis on the role of cultural differences in international business andmanagement; includes a special segment on international travel security)

Escape Artist
Web site: www.escapeartist.com
(on-line magazine, resources, and other Web site links for expatriates)

Intercultural Press, Inc.
P.O. Box 700
Yarmouth, ME   04096-0700
telephone: (1)207-846-5168
Web site: www.bookmasters.com/interclt/index.html
(provides extensive catalog of books and videos concerning international relocation and multicultural issues)

BR Anchor Publishing
P.O. Box 176
Hellertown, PA   18055-0176
telephone: (1)215-865-5331
(provides domestic and international relocation resources for
adults and children)

SPECIFIC INFORMATION

Country

Superintendent of Documents
U.S. Government Printing Office
Washington, D.C.   20402
attn. background notes, bibliographic surveys, and country studies
Web site: www.access.gpo.gov
(provides information about foreign countries)

Stanford Research Institute International
333 Ravenswood Avenue
Menlo Park, CA   94025
attn. business customs and protocol series
(provides information about foreign countries)

Overseas Briefing Center
National Foreign Affairs Training Center
4000 Arlington Blvd.
Arlington, VA   22204
attn. cross-cultural studies
(provides information about foreign countries)

The World Factbook
Web site: www.odci.gov/cia/publications/factbook/index.html
(provides general information on foreign countries, including
geograpy, people, government, economics, history,
communications and transportation; sponsored by the CIA)

Craighead Publications
International Executive Update Service
P.O. Box 1253
Darien, CT   06820
telephone: (1)203-655-1007
Web site: www.craighead.com
(provides information about foreign countries)

Schools

International Schools Services, Inc.
P.O. Box 5910
Princeton, NJ   08540
telephone: (1)609-452-0990
Web site: www.iss.edu
(provides a directory of overseas schools)

European Council of International Schools
21 Lavant Street
Petersfield, Hampshire
GU32 3EL
England
telephone: (44)1730-268-244
Web site: www.ecis.org
(provides a directory of international schools)

Association of Christian Schools International
731 Chapel Hill Drive
Colorado Springs, CO   80920
telephone: (1)719-528-6906
Web site: www.acsi.org
(provides details on Christian schools around the world)

International www Schools Registry
Web site: web66.coled.umn.edu/schools.html
(provides Internet home-page listing of international schools)

National Association of Independent Schools
1620 L Street, N.W.
Washington, D.C. 20036
(1)202-973-9700
Web site: www.nais-schools.org
(provides database on international independent schools)

International School
Web site: www.InternationalSchool.com
(provides a database of international schools that cater to children of expatriates)

Office of Overseas Schools
U.S. Department of State
Washington, D.C. 20522
telephone: (1)703-875-7800
Web site: www.state.gov/www/about_state/schools
(provides background information on worldwide American-sponsored elementary and secondary schools)

International Baccalaureate Organization
Route des Morillons, 15
1218 Grand-Saconnex
Geneva
Switzerland
telephone: (41)22-791-7740
Web site: www.ibo.org
(provides information on the nonprofit educational foundation which offers an international course of study)

Children

Global Nomads International
2001 O Street, N.W.
Washington, D.C. 20036
(1)202-466-2244
Web site: globalnomads.association.com
(provides information and support for young people who have lived overseas)

TCK World
Web site: www.tckworld.com
(provides information, support, and other Web site links for
children and parents of children who live or have spent a
significant part of their developmental years in a culture other than
that of their parents)

Medical

**International Traveler's Hotline at the Centers for Disease
Control**
1600 Clifton Road N.E.
Atlanta, GA   30333
telephone: (1)404-332-4559/(1)404-639-3311
Web site: www.cdc.gov
(provides information on required immunizations and disease and
epidemics in foreign countries)

International Association for Medical Assistance to Travelers
417 Center Street
Lewiston, NY   14092
telephone: (1)716-754-4883
Web site: www.cybermall.co.nz/NZ/IAMAT
(provides a listing of English-speaking physicians in foreign
countries)

World Health Organization
Avenue Appia 20
1211 Geneva 27
Switzerland
telephone: (41)22-791-21-11
Web site: www.who.org
(provides information on health issues around the world)

Financial

Internal Revenue Service Center
11601 Roosevelt Boulevard
Philadelphia, PA   19255-0002
telephone: (1)202-874-1460
Web site: www.irs.ustreas.gov
(provides U.S. tax information, publications, forms, etc.)

Social Security Administration
P.O. Box 17743
Baltimore, MD   21235
Web site: www.ssa.gov
(provides information on Social Security and rules regarding over-
seas employment)

International Association of Financial Planning
Two Concourse Parkway
Suite 800
Atlanta, GA   30328
telephone: (1)800-945-4237
Web site: www.iafp.org
(provides information on where to find professional financial-
planning advice)

Relocation Tax Services, LLC
1800 Grant Street
Denver, CO   80203
telephone: (1)303-894-3800
Web site: www.taxmove.com
(provides information on expatriate tax preparation)

Employment

International Employment Hotline
telephone: (1)703-620-1972
Web site: www.fvap.gov
(provides information on overseas employment opportunities)

Voting

Federal Voting Assistance Program
Office of Secretary of Defense
Room 1B457, The Pentagon
Washington, D.C.   20301-1155
telephone: (1)703-693-6500
Web site: www.fvap.gov
(provides information on U.S. elections and candidates)

Democratic National Committee
Web site: dnc@democrats.org

Republican National Committee
Web site: info@rnc.org

Final note: The Internet is a powerful tool. You can find a wealth of information on news, business, overseas information, and travel services.

Resource 2

IMPORTANT PHONE NUMBERS

GENERAL

Home	_____
Telephone:	_____
Fax:	_____
E-Mail:	_____
Address:	_____
	_____
	_____
	_____

Office	_____
Telephone:	_____
Company contact	
Name:	_____
Telephone:	_____

Office	_____
Telephone:	_____
Company contact	
Name:	_____
Telephone:	_____

Landlord	_____
Telephone:	_____

School	_____
Telephone:	_____

Neighbor _____

Telephone: _____

Neighbor _____

Telephone: _____

Other _____

Telephone: _____

Other _____

Telephone: _____

EMERGENCY

Fire _____

Police _____

Ambulance _____

Emergency hospital _____

Telephone _____

Address: _____

_____

Emergency hospital _____

Telephone: _____

Address: _____

_____

Doctor _____

Telephone: _____

Address _____

_____

Pediatrician _____

Telephone: _____

Address: _____

_____

Dentist _____

Telephone: _____

Address: _____

_____

Poison center _____

Red Cross _____

Gas _____

Electricity _____

Water _____

Telephone _____

Other _____

Other _____

SERVICES

Telephone operator

(local) _____

Telephone operator

(international) _____

Directory assistance

(local) _____

Directory assistance

(international) _____

Repair person _____

Plumber _____

Baby-sitter _____

Baby-sitter _____

Baby-sitter _____

Airline _____

Airline _____

Other _____

Other _____

Other _____

Resource 3

INTERNATIONAL TELEPHONE COUNTRY CODES
AND TIME DIFFERENCES

Country	Telephone Code*	Time Difference**
Afghanistan	operator assisted	9½ hours later
Albania	00-355	6 hours later
Algeria	00-213	6 hours later
Andorra	00-376	6 hours later
Angola	00-244	6 hours later
Anguilla	00-854	1 hour later
Antarctica	operator assisted	12 to 18 hours later
Antigua/Barbuda	00-854	1 hour later
Antilles	00-599	1 hour later
Argentina	00-54	2 hours later
Armenia	00-374	7 hours later
Aruba	00-297	1 hour later
Ascension Island	00-247	5 hours later
Australia	00-61	13 to 15 hours later
Austria	00-43	6 hours later
Azerbaijan	00-994	7 hours later
Azores	00-351	4 hours later
Bahamas	00-851	no time difference
Bahrain	00-973	8 hours later
Bangladesh	00-880	11 hours later
Barbados	00-854	1 hour later
Belarus	00-380	7 hours later
Belgium	00-32	6 hours later
Belize	00-501	1 hour earlier
Benin	00-229	6 hours later
Bermuda	00-851	1 hour later
Bhutan	00-975	10½ hours later
Bolivia	00-591	1 hour later
Bosnia	00-387	6 hours later
Botswana	00-267	7 hours later
Brazil	00-55	0 to 2 hours later
Brunei	00-673	13 hours later
Bulgaria	00-359	7 hours later

Country	Telephone Code*	Time Difference**
Burkina Faso	00-226	5 hours later
Burma	00-95	11½ hours later
Burundi	00-257	7 hours later
Cameroon	00-237	6 hours later
Cambodia	00-855	12 hours later
Canada	00-1	4 hours earlier to 1½ hours later
Canary Islands	00-34	5 hours later
Cape Verde Islands	00-236	4 hours later
Cayman Islands	00-854	no time difference
Central African Rep.	00-236	6 hours later
Chad	00-235	6 hours later
Chatham Island	operator assisted	17 hours later
Chile	00-56	1 hour later
China	00-86	13 hours later
Christmas Island	00-672-4	12 hours later
Cocos Islands	00-672-2	11 hours later
Colombia	00-57	no time difference
Comoros	00-269	8 hours later
Congo	00-242	6 hours later
Cook Islands	00-682	5½ hours earlier
Costa Rica	00-506	1 hour earlier
Côte d'Ivoire	00-225	5 hours later
Croatia	00-385	6 hours later
Cuba	00-53	no time difference
Cyprus	00-357	7 hours later
Czech Republic	00-420	6 hours later
Denmark	00-45	6 hours later
Djibouti	00-253	8 hours later
Dominica	00-854	1 hour later
Dominican Republic	00-851	1 hour later
Ecuador	00-593	no time difference
Egypt	00-20	7 hours later
El Salvador	00-503	1 hour earlier
Equatorial Guinea	00-240	6 hours later
Eritrea	00-291	8 hours later
Ethiopia	00-251	8 hours later
Estonia	00-372	7 hours later

Country	Telephone Code*	Time Difference**
Falkland Islands	00-500	2 hours later
Faroe Islands	00-298	5 hours later
Fiji	00-679	17 hours later
Finland	00-358	7 hours later
France	00-33	6 hours later
French Guiana	00-594	3 hours later
French Polynesia	00-689	5 hours earlier
Gabon	00-241	6 hours later
Gambia	00-220	5 hours later
Georgia	00-995	7 hours later
Germany	00-49	6 hours later
Ghana	00-233	5 hours later
Gibraltar	00-350	6 hours later
Greece	00-30	7 hours later
Greenland	00-299	1 to 3 hours later
Grenada	00-854	1 hour later
Grenadines	00-854	1 hour later
Guadeloupe	00-590	1 hour later
Guam	00-671	15 hours later
Guatemala	00-502	1 hour earlier
Guinea-Bissau	00-245	4 hours later
Guinea Conakry	00-224	5 hours later
Guyana	00-592	2 hours later
Haiti	00-509	no time difference
Honduras	00-504	1 hour earlier
Hong Kong	00-852	13 hours later
Hungary	00-36	6 hours later
Iceland	00-354	4 hours later
India	00-91	10½ hours later
Indonesia	00-62	12 to 14 hours later
Iran	00-98	8½ hours later
Iraq	00-964	8 hours later
Ireland	00-353	5 hours later
Israel	00-972	7 hours later
Italy	00-39	6 hours later
Jamaica	00-854	no time difference
Japan	00-81	14 hours later
Jordan	00-962	7 hours later

Country	Telephone Code*	Time Difference**
Kampuchea	00-855	12 hours later
Kazakhstan (CIS)	00-7	7 hours later
Kenya	00-254	8 hours later
Kiribati	00-686	17 hours later
Korea, North	00-850	14 hours later
Korea, South	00-82	14 hours later
Kuwait	00-965	8 hours later
Kyrgyzstan (CIS)	00-7	8 hours later
Laos	00-856	12 hours later
Latvia	00-371	7 hours later
Lebanon	00-961	7 hours later
Lesotho	00-266	7 hours later
Liberia	00-231	5 hours later
Libya	00-218	7 hours later
Liechtenstein	00-41	6 hours later
Lithuania	00-370	7 hours later
Luxembourg	00-352	6 hours later
Macao	00-853	13 hours later
Macedonia	00-389	6 hours later
Madagascar	00-261	8 hours later
Madeira	00-351-91	5 hours later
Malawi	00-265	7 hours later
Malaysia	00-60	13 hours later
Maldives	00-960	10 hours later
Mali	00-223	5 hours later
Malta	00-356	6 hours later
Marshall Islands	00-692	17 hours later
Martinique	00-596	1 hour later
Mauritania	00-222	5 hours later
Mauritius	00-230	9 hours later
Mexico	00-52	1 to 3 hours earlier
Micronesia	00-691	14 to 17 hours later
Midway Island	operator assisted	6 hours earlier
Moldova	00-373	7 hours later
Monaco	00-33-93	6 hours later
Mongolia	00-976	12 to 14 hours later
Montserrat	00-854	1 hour later
Morocco	00-212	5 hours later

Country	Telephone Code*	Time Difference**
Mozambique	00-258	7 hours later
Namibia	00-264	7 hours later
Nauru	00-674	17 hours later
Nepal	00-977	10½ hours later
Netherlands	00-31	6 hours later
Nevis	00-854	1 hour later
New Caledonia	00-687	16 hours later
New Zealand	00-64	17 hours later
Nicaragua	00-505	1 hour earlier
Niger	00-227	6 hours later
Nigeria	00-234	6 hours later
Niue Island	00-683	6 hours earlier
Norfolk Island	00-672	16½ hours later
North Mariana Islands	00-670	15 hours later
Norway	00-47	6 hours later
Oman	00-968	9 hours later
Pakistan	00-92	10 hours later
Palau	00-680	13 hours later
Panama	00-507	no time difference
Papua New Guinea	00-675	15 hours later
Paraguay	00-595	2 hours later
Peru	00-51	no time difference
Philippines	00-631	3 hours later
Pitcairn Island	operator assisted	3½ hours earlier
Poland	00-48	6 hours later
Portugal	00-351	5 hours later
Puerto Rico	00-1-809	1 hour later
Qatar	00-974	8 hours later
Réunion	00-262	9 hours later
Rodriguez Island	operator assisted	9 hours later
Romania	00-40	7 hours later
Russia	00-7	8 to 17 hours later
Rwanda	00-250	7 hours later
Saint Christopher	00-1-809-465	1 hour later
Saint Helena	00-290	5 hours later
Saint Kitts	00-854	1 hour later
Saint Lucia	00-854	1 hour later
Saint Pierre & Miquelon	00-508	1 hour later

Country	Telephone Code*	Time Difference**
Saint Vincent	00-854	1 hour later
Samoa	00-684	6 hours earlier
Samoa, Western	00-685	6 hours earlier
San Marino	00-39-549	6 hours later
São Tomé & Principe	00-239	5 hours later
Saudi Arabia	00-966	8 hours later
Senegal	00-221	5 hours later
Seychelles	00-248	9 hours later
Sierra Leone	00-232	5 hours later
Singapore	00-65	13 hours later
Slovakia	00-421	6 hours later
Slovenia	00-386	7 hours later
Solomon Islands	00-677	16 hours later
Somalia	00-252	8 hours later
South Africa	00-27	7 hours later
Spain	00-34	6 hours later
Sri Lanka	00-94	10½ hours later
Sudan	00-249	7 hours later
Surinam	00-597	2 hours later
Swaziland	00-268	7 hours later
Sweden	00-46	6 hours later
Switzerland	00-41	6 hours later
Syria	00-963	7 hours later
Tajikistan (CIS)	00-7	8 hours later
Taiwan	00-886	13 hours later
Tanzania	00-255	8 hours later
Thailand	00-66	12 hours later
Togo	00-228	5 hours later
Tonga	00-676	18 hours later
Trinidad & Tobago	00-854	1 hour later
Tristan da Cunha	operator assisted	5 hours later
Tunisia	00-216	6 hours later
Turkey	00-90	8 hours later
Turkmenistan (CIS)	00-993	7 hours later
Turks & Caicos Islands	00-854	no time difference
Tuvalu	00-688	17 hours later
Uganda	00-256	8 hours later
Ukraine	00-380	7 hours later

Country	Telephone Code*	Time Difference**
United Arab Emirates	00-971	9 hours later
Uruguay	00-598	2 hours later
United Kingdom	00-44	5 hours later
United States	00-1	0 to 6 hours earlier
New York City/Miami		no time difference
Chicago/Houston		1 hour earlier
Denver/Salt Lake City		2 hours earlier
San Francisco/Seattle		3 hours earlier
Anchorage		5 hours earlier
Honolulu		5 hours earlier
Uzbekistan (CIS)	00-7	8 hours later
Vanuatu	00-678	16 hours later
Vatican City	00-39-6	6 hours later
Venezuela	00-58	1 hour later
Vietnam	00-84	12 hours later
Virgin Islands (U.K.)	00-854	1 hour later
Virgin Islands (U.S.A.)	00-851	1 hour later
Wake Island	operator assisted	17 hours later
Yemen Arab Republic	00-967	8 hours later
Yemen (People's Dem.)	00-969	8 hours later
Yugoslavia	00-381	6 hours later
Zaire	00-243	6 hours later
Zambia	00-260	7 hours later
Zimbabwe	00-263	7 hours later

Note: For countries which cannot be dialed directly, consult your international operator.

Because technology and the world's political map are continually changing, you should consult your phone directory or international operator to confirm the code.

*To place a telephone call, follow the international code with the city code and then the customer number. Note that the international code is for calls originating from all foreign countries. Those originating from the United States and Canada would use 011 rather than 00.

**The time difference is referenced from New York City. To determine the appropriate time difference from another country, add or subtract the difference for that city. Do not forget to take into account daylight-saving time, which usually changes in April and October.

Resource 4

CONVERSION CHARTS AND TABLES

The following charts and tables will give you a handy reference to convert to/from metric and U.S. measurements. Included are both the approximate equivalents and the exact conversion relationship. Use them in the kitchen, on the road, and when out shopping!

Cooking dinner.....
    1. Liquid Measures for Cooking

Making bread.....
    2. Dry Measures for Cooking

Baking bread.....
    3. Oven Temperatures

What to wear.....
    4. Outdoor Temperatures

Not feeling well.....
    5. Body Temperatures

Filling up.....
    6. Liquid Measures at the Gas Station

On the road.....
    7. Speed Measures

How tall, how far, how long.....
    8. Linear Measures

Measuring floor space.....
    9. Area and Volume Measures

Keeping fit.....
    10. Weight Measures

(Formats adapted from Gelderman, 1990.)

I. LIQUID MEASURES FOR COOKING

cup	ounce	milliliters	
¼	2	60	
½	4	120	
¾	6	180	
1	8	240	= 1 cup (appx.)
2	16	480	= 1 pint (U.S.)
4	32	950	= 1 quart (U.S.)
16	128	3,800	= 1 gallon (U.S.)

Conversion Factors

1 gallon (U.S.) = 4 quarts (U.S.) = 3.785 liters
1 liter = 0.264 gallon (U.S.)

1 pint (U.S.) = 0.473 liter
1 liter = 2.11 pints (U.S.)

1 quart (U.S.) = 2 pints (U.S.) = 0.946 liter
1 liter = 1.057 quarts (U.S.)

1 gallon (U.S.) = 0.833 gallon (imperial)
1 pint (U.S.) = 0.833 pint (imperial)

2. DRY MEASURES FOR COOKING

ounce/ pound	grams	
1 oz.	30	
2 oz	60	
3 oz.	85	
4 oz.	115	= 1 cup (appx.) — flour
5 oz.	140	
6 oz.	170	
7 oz.	200	
8 oz.	225	= 1 cup (appx.) — sugar
16 oz.	450	= 1 pound
1½ lb.	680	
2 lb.	900	
2¼ lb.	1,000	= 1 kilogram

Conversion Factors

1 ounce = 28.35 grams

1 gram = 0.035 ounce

1 pound = 454 grams

1 pound = 0.454 kilogram

1 kilogram = 2.2 pounds

3. OVEN TEMPERATURES

°C	°F
110	225
120	250
140	280
150	300
160	320
180	350
190	375
200	400
220	425
230	450
240	470

Conversion Factors

$$°F = (°C \times \tfrac{9}{5}) + 32$$
$$°C = (°F - 32) \times \tfrac{5}{9}$$

4. OUTDOOR TEMPERATURES

°C	°F (appx.)	°F (absolute)	
-15	2	5	stay inside
-10	12	14	mountain gear
-5	22	23	ski gear
0	32	32	very heavy coat
5	42	41	heavy coat
10	52	50	coat
15	62	59	jacket
20	72	68	long sleeves
25	82	77	short sleeves
30	92	86	iced tea
35	102	95	shade
40	112	104	stay inside

Approximate Conversion Factors

$$°F = (°C \times 2) + 32$$
$$°C = (°F - 32) \times \tfrac{1}{2}$$

Note: The error accumulates as you move away (increase/decrease) from 0°C/32°F.

5. BODY TEMPERATURES

°C	°F	
37	98.6	normal body temperature
37.5	99.5	slight fever
38	100	fever
39	102	high fever
40	104	very high fever

6. LIQUID MEASURES AT THE GAS STATION

gallons (U.S.)	liters
2.5	10
5.5	20
8.0	30
10.5	40
13.0	50
16.0	60

Conversion Factors

1 gallon (U.S.) = 4 quarts (U.S.) = 3.785 liters

1 liter = 0.264 gallon (U.S.)

1 gallon (U.S.) = 0.833 gallon (imperial)

7. SPEED MEASURES

miles/hour	kilometers/hour	
20	30	residential
30	50	business
55	90	expressway/highway
70	110	freeway
80	130	freeway

Conversion Factors

1 mile/hour = 1.61 kilometers/hour

1 kilometer/hour = 0.62 mile/hour

8. LINEAR MEASURES

feet, inches	centimeters
4′ 10″	147
5′	152
5′ 2″	157
5′ 4″	163
5′ 6″	168
5′ 8″	173
5′ 10″	178
6′	183
6′ 2″	188

Conversion Factors

1 inch = 2.54 centimeters   1 yard = 0.9144 meter

1 centimeter = 0.394 inch   1 meter = 1.094 yards

1 foot = 0.3048 meter   1 mile = 1.61 kilometers

1 meter = 3.28 feet   1 kilometer = 0.62 mile

9. AREA AND VOLUME MEASURES

square feet	square meters
1,000	90
1,080	100
1,500	140
1,610	150
2,000	190
2,150	200
2,700	250
3,230	300

Conversion Factors

1 square inch = 6.452 square centimeters
1 square centimeter = 0.155 square inch

1 square foot = 0.093 square meter
1 square meter = 10.76 square feet

1 acre = 43,500 square feet = 4,047 square meters
1 square kilometer = 247 acres

1 cubic foot = 0.028 cubic meter
1 cubic meter = 35.3 cubic feet

1 cubic inch = 16.39 cubic centimeters
1 cubic centimeter = 0.061 cubic inch

10. WEIGHT MEASURES

pounds	kilograms
88	40
100	45
110	50
121	55
132	60
143	65
154	70
165	75
176	80
187	85
198	90
209	95
220	100

Conversion Factors

1 pound = 0.454 kilogram

1 kilogram = 2.2 pounds

1 stone (imperial) = 14 pounds

1 ton = 2,240 pounds = 1.016 metric tons

1 metric ton = 1,000 kilograms = 0.984 ton

Bibliography

Adler, N., 1991, *International Dimensions of Organizational Behavior*, PWS-Kent Publishing Company.

Adler, N., 1975, "The Transitional Experience: An Alternative View of Culture Shock," *Journal of Humanistic Psychology*, vol. 15, pp. 13–23.

Barker, M., editor, 1990, "Orientated for Success," *Australian International Development Assistance Bureau*.

Black, J., et al., 1992, *Global Assignments: Successfully Expatriating and Repatriating International Managers*, Jossey-Bass.

Black, J., and Stephens, G., 1989, "The Influence of the Spouse on American Expatriate Adjustment in Overseas Assignments," *Journal of Management*, vol. 15, pp. 529–544.

Bolles, R., 1988, *What Color Is Your Parachute*, Ten Speed Press.

Bond, M., 1985, *Stress and Stress Management: A Perspective* (unpublished).

Bond, R., 1997, "Creating a Life," *The Town Crier*, Benvenuto Club of Milan, March, p. 30.

Brake, T., et al., 1995, *Doing Business Internationally: The Guide to Cross-Cultural Success*, Irwin Professional Publishing.

Brett, J., 1980, "The Effect of Job Transfer on Employees and their Families," *Current Concerns in Occupational Stress*, John Wiley & Sons, Ltd.

Brocklehurst, A., 1996, "Feeling Blue? It's Because You're Back Home," "The Money Report," *International Herald Tribune*, May 11–12, p. 17.

Carey, S., 1993, "Expatriates Find Long Stints Abroad Can Close Doors to Credit at Home," *Wall Street Journal.*

Coles, M., 1997, "Flexibility Is Key to Success Abroad," *The Sunday Times,* June 8, section 7, p. 28.

Coyle, W., and Shortland, S., 1992, *International Relocation,* Butterworth-Heinemann Ltd.

Cushner, K., and Brislin, R., 1996, *Intercultural Interactions: A Practical Guide,* Sage Publications.

De Aenlle, C., 1996, "Taxing Time: Expatriates Figure out the Breaks," "The Money Report," *International Herald Tribune,* May 11–12, p. 15.

de Kieffer, D., 1993, *The International Business Traveller's Companion,* Intercultural Press, Inc.

De Leon, C., and McPartlin, D., 1995, "Adjustment of Expatriate Children," in *Expatriate Management: New Ideas for International Business,* Jan Selmer, editor, Quorum Books, pp. 198–214.

Drake, B., 1997, "Managing Children's Education and Development Overseas," www.tckworld.com.

Eakin, K., 1988, *The Foreign Service Teenager at Home in the U.S.: A Few Thoughts for Parents Returning with Teenagers,* Overseas Briefing Center, Foreign Service Institute, U.S. Department of State.

Employee Relocation Council, 1997, *Children and International Relocation,* Research Department, Employee Relocation Council, Washington, D.C.

Employee Relocation Council, 1997, *Selecting School Systems,* Research Department, Employee Relocation Council, Washington, D.C.

Employee Relocation Council, 1997, *Things to Do Before Leaving for an International Assignment,* Research Department, Employee Relocation Council, Washington, D.C.

Ervin, N., 1995, *Kids on the Move,* Conquest Corporation.

Fidelity Investments, 1992, "Check your Risk Tolerance," *Fidelity Focus.*

Fisher, G., 1997, *Mindsets: The Role of Culture and Perception in International Relations,* Intercultural Press, Inc.

Fisher, G., 1980, *International Negotiations: A Cross-Cultural Perspective,* Intercultural Press, Inc.

Flower, R., and Falassi, A., 1995, *Culture Shock! Italy,* Times Editions Pte Ltd.

Forster, N., 1990, "A Practical Guide to the Management of Job Changes and Relocation," *Personnel Review,* vol. 19, pp. 26–35.

Furnham, A., and Bochner, S., 1986, *Culture Shock: Psychological Reactions to Unfamiliar Environments,* Methuen.

Gelderman, C., 1990, *How to Survive in Style.*

Greenbury, L., 1988, "Relocating the Working Wife," *Relocation News,* vol. 5, pp. 3–5.

Grove, C., and Hallowell, W., 1996, "Does Diversity Travel Well? It Depends....," *Mosaics,* May and July.

Hall, E. T., 1976, *Beyond Culture,* Doubleday Anchor Books.

Hall, E. T., 1964, *The Silent Language,* Doubleday Anchor Books.

Hall, E.H., and Hall, M.R., 1990, *Understanding Cultural Differences,* Intercultural Press, Inc.

Harris, P., and Moran, R., 1987, *Managing Cultural Differences,* Gulf Publishing.

Hill, R., 1997, *We Europeans,* Europublications.

Hodge, S., 1997, "Culture Shock Bewilders Business Travelers," Research Department, Employee Relocation Council, Washington, D.C.

Hofstede, G., 1997, *Cultures and Organizations: Software of the Mind,* McGraw-Hill.

Hofstede, G., 1980, *Culture's Consequences: International Differences in Work-related Values,* Sage Publications.

Holmes, T., and Rahe, R., 1967, "The Social Readjustment Rating Scale," *Journal of Psychosomatic Research*, vol. 11, pp. 213–218.

Internal Revenue Service, 1991, *Tax Information on Selling Your Home*, Publication 523.

Internal Revenue Service, 1993, *Tax Guide for U.S. Citizens and Resident Aliens Abroad*, Publication 54.

International Schools Services, 1995, *The ISS Directory of Overseas Schools*.

Kaufman, J., 1996, "U.S. Engineer Counts the Rewards and Cost of Working Overseas," *Wall Street Journal*.

Kalb, R., and Welch, P., 1992, *Moving your Family Overseas*, Intercultural Press, Inc.

Kemper Financial Services, 1988, "What Type of Investor Are You?"

Kohls, R., 1996, *Survival Kit for Overseas Living*, Intercultural Press, Inc.

Kohls, R., and Knight, J., 1994, *Developing Intercultural Awareness: A Cross-Cultural Training Handbook*, Intercultural Press, Inc.

Larner, D., 1996, Getting Ready: Relocation Firms Show the Way," "The Money Report," *International Herald Tribune*, May 11–12, p. 17.

Mead, R., 1990, *Cross-Cultural Management Communication*, John Wiley & Sons.

Mitchell, S., 1990, "Ensuring Successful Expatriate Assignments," *Relocation News*, vol. 13, pp. 10–11.

Moran, R., 1988, "Culture Shock Can Be a Healthy Experience if You Roll with the Punches," *International Management*, July/August, p. 67.

Moran, R., and Stripp, W., 1991, *Dynamics of Successful International Business Negotiations*, Gulf Publishing.

Moran, R., and Harris, P., 1982, *Managing Cultural Synergy*, Gulf Publishing.

Morrison, T., et al., 1994, *Kiss, Bow, or Shake Hands: How to Do Business in Sixty Countries*, Bob Adams, Inc.

Munton, A., et al., 1993, *Job Relocation: Managing People on the Move*, John Wiley & Sons Ltd.

Ottaviano, D., 1994, "The International Child," *The Town Crier*, Benvenuto Club of Milan, November, p. 15.

Pascoe, R., 1992, *Culture Shock! A Wife's Guide*, Times Editions Pte Ltd.

Phatak, A., 1974, *Managing Multinational Corporations*, Praeger Publishers.

Piet-Pelon, N., and Hornby, B., 1992, *Women's Guide to Overseas Living*, Intercultural Press, Inc.

Post, K., 1990, "The Male Trailing Spouse: A Growing Minority," *Mobility*, March, pp. 32–34.

Rehak, J., 1996, "Overseas Fat Cats Face Tough Orders: Slim Down," "The Money Report," *International Herald Tribune*, May 11–12, p. 17.

Relocation Tax Services, 1998, *Taxation of U.S. Expatriates*.

Reynolds, C., and Bennett, R., 1991, "The Career Couple Challenge," *Personnel Journal*, March.

Ricklin, H., 1990, "When the Trailing Spouse Is the Husband," *Mobility*, May, pp. 90–92.

Ricks, D., 1993, *Blunders in International Business*, Blackwell Business Publishers.

Roman, B., 1992, *Moving Minus Mishaps*, BR Anchor Publishing.

Schell, M., and Dolins, I., 1992, "Dual Career Couples and International Assignments," *Journal of International Compensation & Benefits*, November/December.

Schell, M., and Solomon, C., 1997, *Capitalizing on the Global Marketplace: A Strategic Guide for Expatriate Management,* Irwin Professional Publishing.

Schell, M., and Stoltz-Loike, M., 1994, "Importance of Cultural Preparation to International Business Success," *Journal of International Compensation & Benefits,* no. 4, January/February, pp. 47–52.

Seelye, N., 1996, *Experiential Activities for Intercultural Learning,* vol. 1, Intercultural Press, Inc.

Seelye, H., and Seelye-James, A., 1996, *Culture Clash,* NTC Publishing Group.

Shannonhouse, R., 1996, "Overseas-Assignment Failures," "Living Overseas," *USA Today International,* November 8–10, p. 8A.

Shortland, S., 1990, *Relocation: A Practical Guide,* Institute of Personnel Management.

Solomon, C., 1996, "Expatriate Partners: Dual Career Issues," *Personnel Journal,* May.

Solomon, C., 1996, "CEO Mom: The Tie That Binds a Global Family," *Personnel Journal,* March, pp. 80–93.

Solomon, C., 1994, "Success Abroad Depends on More than Job Skills," *Personnel Journal,* April, pp. 51–60.

Stewart, E., and Bennett, M., 1991, *American Cultural Patterns: A Cross-Cultural Perspective,* Intercultural Press, Inc.

Stoltz-Loike, M., 1993, "Work and Family Considerations in International Relocations," *Journal of International Compensation & Benefits,* July/August, pp. 31–35.

Stoltz-Loike, M., 1992, *Dual Career Couples: New Perspectives in Counseling,* American Association for Counseling and Development.

Storti, C., 1999, *Figuring Foreigners Out: A Practical Guide,* Intercultural Press, Inc.

Storti, C., 1997, *The Art of Coming Home,* Intercultural Press, Inc.

Storti, C., 1994, *Cross-Cultural Dialogues: 74 Brief Encounters with Cultural Differences*, Intercultural Press, Inc.

Stuart, K., 1992, "Teens Play a Role in Moves Overseas," *Personnel Journal*, March.

Sullivan, A., 1996, "Home Away from Home? Call a Professional," "The Money Report," *International Herald Tribune*, May 11–12, p. 15.

Swaak, R., 1995, "Expatriate Failures: Too Many, Too Much Cost, Too Little Planning," *Compensation & Benefits Review*, November/December, pp. 47–55.

Swaak, R., 1995, "Today's Expatriate Family: Dual Career and Other Obstacles," *Compensation & Benefits Review*, January/February, pp. 21–26.

Tan Powers, E., 1996, "Expat Success Often Depends on Cultural Awareness," "Living Overseas," *USA Today International*, October 9, p. 7A.

Trompenaars, F., 1995, *Riding the Waves of Culture: Understanding Cultural Diversity in Global Business*, Nicholas Brealey Publishing.

Tung, R., 1988, "Career Issues in International Assignments," *Academy of Management Executive*, 2, no. 3, pp. 241–244.

Tung, R., 1987, "Expatriate Assignments: Enhancing Success and Minimizing Failure," *Academy of Management Executive*, 1, no. 2, pp. 117–126.

Wall, B., 1996, "Why Culture Shock Is Such an Expensive Business," "The Money Report," *International Herald Tribune*, May 11–12, p. 15.

Walmsley, J., 1986, *Brit-Think, Ameri-Think*, Harrap Books Ltd.

Wanning, E., 1995, *Culture Shock! USA*, Kuperard.

Which?, editors, 1994, *Which? Way to Buy, Sell and Move House*, Which? Consumer Guides.

Wraight, B., editor, 1996, "No Spouse Support from 54% of Employers," *International in Britain*, August, p. 4

NOTES